Globalisation for Sale

Money has been an important part of modernity ever since it was exchanged for goods centuries ago. The evolution of systematically standardised monetised exchanges, expedited trade between localities across space, standardised exchanges over time, and transformed work into wage labour. Money also generated the possibilities for specialisation which were not possible under a system of barter, and solidified the emergence and development of the modern epoch. The contemporary changes in monetised exchanges, such as the electrification and globalisation of monetary processes and financial markets, are unequivocal indicators of contemporary globalisation. They are also some of the most important, and far-reaching, social changes of out time. Understanding and managing global financial flows and their impact of social spaces and people, is one of the most complex and difficult tasks facing politicians and social theorists today. Helping to meet the challenges posed by these changes, this important volume focuses on three questions central to the interplay between globalisation, valorisation and marginalisation.

DR. COBUS DE SWARDT KRAUS has taught at the universities of Cape Town and Western Cape in South Africa, and the La Trobe University in Australia. He has also been a visiting scholar at the University of Nurnberg-Erlangen in Germany, as well as the Hiroshima City University, The Fukuoka City University, the Tokyo Keizai University, the Japanese Labour Research Institute and the Centre for Transnational Labour Studies in Japan.

www.keganpaul.com

GLOBALIZATION FOR SALE

An Analysis of the
Interdynamics of Globalization, Valorization
and Marginalization

Cobus de Swardt-Kraus

KEGAN PAUL INTERNATIONAL
London and New York

First Published in 2000 by
Kegan Paul International Limited
UK: P.O. Box 256, London WC1B 3SW, England
Tel: 020 7580 5511   Fax: 020 7436 0899
E-mail: books@keganpaul.com
Internet: http://www.keganpaul.com
USA: 61 West 62nd Street, New York, NY 10023
Tel: (212) 459 0600   Fax: (212) 259 3678
Internet: http://www.columbia.edu/cu/cup

Distributed by
John Wiley & Sons
Southern Cross Trading Estate
1 Oldlands Way, Bognor Regis
West Sussex, PO22 9SA, England
Tel: (01243) 779 777   Fax: (01243) 820 250
E-mail: cs-books@wiley.co.uk

Columbia University Press
61 West 62nd Street, New York, NY 10023
Tel: (212) 459 0600   Fax: (212) 259 3678
Internet: http://www.columbia.edu/cu/cup

© Kegan Paul International, 2000

Printed in Great Britain, IBT Global London

All Rights reserved. No part of this book may be reprinted or reproduced or utilised in any form or be any electric, mechanical or other means, now known or hereafter invented, including photocopying or recording, or in any information storage or retriev system, without permission in writing from the publishers.

ISBN: 0-7103-0666-0

British Library Cataloguing in Publication Data
A catalogue record for this book is available from the British Librar

Library of Congress Cataloging-in-Publication Data
Applied for.

Contents

Acknowledgements	7
Introduction	9
Observational path: Constructing a globalization story	12
A précis of the chapters	38
Chapter 1: Global Exchange Processes	42
Twentieth-century developments in global public cultural-material governance up to the 1970s	43
Post-1970s developments in global public cultural-material governance	50
Conclusion	74
Chapter 2: The Organization of Production Processes	77
Drastically reduced product development time and product life cycles	78
The ascendancy of automation technologies	81
The global repositioning of organizations	91
Conclusion	110

Chapter 3: The Recomposition of Production Relations   114

The redefinition of the social organization of labor processes by organizations   114

The recomposition of the global technical division of labor   130

Conclusion   140

Chapter 4: Social Identity Compositions and Narratives   145

State *vis-à-vis* private capital influences   147

Machine *vis-à-vis* virtual technological influences   160

Production *vis-à-vis* consumption influences   168

Conclusion   179

Conclusion

Globalization, valorization and marginalization: Some Zeitgeist reflections   183

Endnotes   201

References   250

Acknowledgements

A number of people have made a contribution, directly or indirectly, to this book. I am grateful towards all of them. They are: Johann Arnason (La Trobe University), Peter Beilharz (La Trobe University), John Benson (Melbourne University), Jeanne Daly (La Trobe University), Philip Debroux (City University of Hiroshima), Eva Fish (La Trobe University), Hitoshi Hirakawa (Tokyo Keizai University), Fred Hendricks (Rhodes University), Rowan Ireland (La Trobe University), Joel Kahn (Sussex University), Jeff Lever (University of the Western Cape), Yvonne Muthian (University of Natal), Marianne Roux (University of the Western Cape), Elaine Salo (University of the Western Cape), Gert Schmidt (University Nürnberg-Erlangen), Mary Simons (University of Cape Town), Yoshio Sugimoto (La Trobe University), Francois Theron (University of Stellenbosch), Malcolm Waters (University of Texas), Evan Willis (La Trobe University), and Masae Yuasa (City University of Hiroshima).

My thanks also go to the following institutions: La Trobe University, Melbourne, for its financial assistance towards my overseas fieldwork; the University of the Western Cape, Cape Town, where I was privileged to work and develop academically; as well as the Universities of Nürnberg-Erlangen and the City of Hiroshima, where I held visiting positions whilst working on this book. I would like to extend my appreciation to all the employees of Zem with whom I worked or who I interviewed for the purpose of this book.

On a personal note, I would like to thank my parents, Awie de Swardt, Gerda and Herbert Kraus, and especially Hannatjie van den Berg, as well as close friends Lee Norman, Mare Norval, Bernard Ross, Bernie Sheridan, Maria Sheridan and Leon Traut for their friendship, support, love and encouragement. To Kai de Swardt-Kraus, whose birth coincided with the writing of this book, my fondest appreciation for all the joy, challenges and compassion he has given me during this time. Finally, I would like to thank my dearest partner, Elke Kraus. This book would not have been possible, financially, emotionally or intellectually without the unconditional love, breadwinning work, support, inspiration and critical challenges from Elke.

Introduction

"... [W]e take this world of exchange value to be in some sense natural instead of for what it 'really' is, namely an artificial way of arranging our social lives based on the dominance of the commodity form. But because we have learned to take such an arrangement as natural we fail to see that such an arrangement is distinctly unnatural. It has the power to consume us and the bonds that unite us either as fellow humans or as members of cultures or communities"(Kahn, 1995:60).

Our ideas of the world are today saturated with globalization lingo. Globalization – as a conglomerate of social realities, ideas, myths, practices and identities – is indeed becoming a one-word *fait accompli* explanation of local and global social activities. The perception of globalization as a voluntaristic meta-social force, as articulated in the *it is all due to globalization* syndrome, permeates many current social debates.[1] Globalization is thus frequently blamed for many social problems, and often hailed as the force behind progressive and advanced developments. The narrative of meta-social globality is arguably one of the most overused and undersubstantiated social constructs of our time. The fine print on the back of insurance policies may as well add to *Act of God, Globalization* as a standard exclusionist clause.

At the end of the twentieth century social governance the world over is increasingly informed by the forces of global capitalism and rational monetarist ideas.[2] Consequently, governmental policies focus on reducing state intervention in the commodification cycle, privatizing state enterprises (e.g., electricity, public transport, etc.) which strategically subsidized certain users in the past, and progressively transforming state services (e.g., public education and health) into user-pays services. The *pari passu* expansion of global capitalism and market-mediated social governance renders people living in the advanced industrial world more vulnerable to the social vagaries of contemporary 'disorganized capitalism' (Lash and Urry, 1987, 1994a). This vulnerability arguably contributes to the present preoccupation with globalization within everyday, populist, media and academic discourses and the omnipresence of globalization lingo and rhetoric in our daily intellectual diet.[3] It is in this context that the narrative and ideology of globalization is evolving into a self-explanatory meta-social entity in itself – a supra-social force which seems to render social agency more and more obsolete. This book addresses the apparent desocialization of globalization in social narratives by focusing on the interdynamics of globalization, valorization and marginalization.

The current globalization epoch is defined as a macro social environment primarily constituted by the globally dispersed processes of European modernity which commenced and proceeded incrementally from the end of the 14th century onwards.[4] The geographical extension of European influences took place mainly through the controlled global spread of European technologies, the hegemonic reach of European empires, and the incremental enforcement of European monetization practices. The dispersion of European settlers the world over also created numerous diasporic European spaces (e.g., America, Australia and Canada), laid the foundations of the so-called Western world and solidified the Eurocentricness of the modernist epoch. Whilst some attention is given to historical developments, the main focus of this book is on the qualitatively different global processes and relations, the intensification of global connectedness, as well as the growing consciousness of this intensification since the 1970s.[5]

Generally speaking, valorization refers to the processes of value adding *and* monetization. In relation to European modernity these processes include the separation of use and exchange values, and the progressive extension of the

Introduction

monetization of goods to also include land, labor and aesthetic artifacts. As such, the social forces of valorization encompass the creation, realization and generation of monetary values. This notion of an encompassing monetization is used here to analyze developments in both the predominantly value adding (i.e., so-called production) and mainly monetizing (i.e., so-called exchange) spheres of activity. The third central concept, namely marginalization is used to refer to people or social spaces who are socially disempowered by, and/or dislocated from, the dominant social genres. Particular attention is given to the ways in which contemporary forms of marginalization are mediated by monetized valorization processes.

The specific evolution of monetized exchanges that occurred within the European network from the end of the 14th century is an inherent part of European modernity. Contemporary monetized exchanges are also intrinsically woven into the specific globalization and marginalization dynamics of the modern epoch. In general, monetized exchanges expedite trade between localities across space, standardize exchanges over time, transform work into wage labor and generate the possibilities for specialization not possible under a system of barter. Within the realms of the private appropriation of the means of production and private wealth accumulation, monetized exchanges facilitate the commodification, and consequently degeneration, of subsistence practices, reciprocal subsistence networks and feudal patronage relations. Monetization processes augment the possibilities for wide-spread post-subsistence wealth accumulation, storage and cultural-material growth.[6] They also contribute to the incremental weakening of imposed group bonds and the emergence of the self determining individual able to move with greater ease horizontally between social collectives, as well as vertically within them. At the same time, the potential for social deprivation, disempowerment and dislocation is increased for those people excluded from, by, or with limited access to, valorized activities (e.g., waged labor) and valorized spheres (e.g., state of the art technologies).[7]

Important changes to the present productive realm of the

dominant commodification genre (i.e., global capitalism), such as the emergence of electronic capital as a major source of monetary dispersion, also contribute to potential increases in private and social polarization. In this context, globalization, valorization and marginalization processes are of significant importance to contemporary social life, and an investigation into the associated impact of the interdynamics existing between them warrants sociological attention. However, sociologists have generally not addressed globalization, valorization and marginalization in this context, and there is little substantial conceptual or empirical investigation in this theoretical domain. It is into this apparent theoretical vacuum that this book enters.

Within the analytical boundaries of the 'globalization-valorization-marginalization conceptual triangle,' three sociological questions are addressed. Firstly, what is the nature of the contemporary techniques, patterns and practices of valorization?[8] Secondly, how do contemporary valorization processes influence the reorganization of global monetary flows, the restructuring of production processes, the recomposition of production relations, and the reconstruction of social identities? Thirdly, what implications do the contemporary forms of valorization have for the future of social collectives such as states, international organizations, trade unions, local communities and transnational corporations?

Observational path: Constructing a globalization story

"Theory is useful; it enables, it helps us better to understand what we already knew, intuitively, in the first place. But theory is always plural, theories, and multicentred. This makes theory in general difficult, so we turn to theories in particular – for communication, we see Habermas, for social movements, Touraine, modernity, Heller, and so on. This remains difficult, for each theorist has a different story to tell, and there are different interpretations of each theorist. But this is the way social theory works. It depends on enthusiasm, passion, suspicion, scepticism, tolerance, patience and judgement. The theoretical attitude is open-ended, for theory is culture and not an instrument" (Beilharz, 1991:1).

Introduction

It is often assumed that the inherently ideographical nature of intellectual discourses is the Achilles heel of the social sciences, undermining its social and scientific value to modern life. On the contrary, the massive dissemination of ideas via printed and other mediums, the systematic combination of related ideas in theories such as Modernization and Marxism, and the ways in which the modernist idea world forms part of a contested terrain of social forces, as seen during election campaigns for public office, have elevated ideas to be important precursors to, and even instigators of, social change. The dissemination, systematic combination and populist contesting of different ideas, or sets of ideas, is indeed a hallmark and arguably one of the most empowering and pervasive aspects of modernity. Thomas Carlyle used a historical anecdote to illustrate this point when he was once confronted after expressing some different ideas. "Ideas, Mr Carlyle, ideas, nothing but ideas!" Carlyle's response aptly articulated the social leverage of ideas, when he replied: "there was once a man called Rousseau who wrote a book containing nothing but ideas. The second edition was bound in the skins of those who laughed at the first" (Carlyle, cited in Bhagwati, 1989:17).

Similar to all intellectual discourses this book is a collection of ideas, informed by a number of guiding theorems. However, the social logic of the organization and narration of these ideas is embedded in the modernist cultural episteme and confined by the parameters of its macro-paradigms. The theoretical narrative used here draws from an analysis of modernist discourses, as well as from the author's participant observation and fieldwork as a researcher and an intellectual traveller. The structured part of the participant observation and fieldwork was mainly conducted within a particular transnational company where the author worked between 1995 and 1998.[9] For legal and ethical reasons, a pseudo name, namely Zem, is used for this corporation, which is one of the fifty largest transnational corporations in the world.

Transnational corporations are not the only possible unit of relevant analytical attention. Nevertheless, they are at the cutting edge of three primal forces in the transformation of contemporary global social life, namely global technological developments, production practices and consumption processes. As such, a focus on the operation of a transnational corporation renders potential insight into the body and soul of contemporary modernity in relation to the interdynamics between globalization, valorization and marginalization. The national spaces in which Zem and other relevant developments were studied consisted of Australia, America, Germany, Japan and South Africa. However, the overall analysis is not restricted to the national spaces within which the participant observations and fieldwork were physically conducted, nor does it focus on individual states as units of statistical comparison. Instead, the social organizational agency of the state and its impact on the global social dynamics of valorization and marginalization are addressed.

Over the last two centuries the nation-state became the highest authority within its own borders. During this time the nation-state consolidated its power in a centralized bureaucracy and most of the important social interplays took place within the realm of its practices, institutions and relations.[10] The expanding organizational capacities and social reach of the state facilitated what Habermas (1981) calls the 'colonization of the lifeworld' as the state nationalized social organization and intellectual narratives in general.[11] During this period a symbiotic relationship emerged between nationalism (i.e., the ideology of the nation as an 'imagined community' – Anderson, 1983) and the nation-state as its organized form and 'corporeal expression' (Axford, 1995).[12] During the colonial area the augmentation of the organizational reach of individual states coexisted with the hegemonic expansion of European empires and the global enlargement of the spatial boundaries of the European network of social spaces. These developments contributed substantially to the nineteenth and twentieth century perception in so-called Western discourses that (their) nation-states were 'economically' self-determining, and 'politically' independent.

Introduction

The increased institutionalization of transnational governance after the First and Second World Wars expanded the influence of governments, further strengthening the notions of the state as a self-determining, independent and endogenous social entity. As a consequence of both the real and perceived influences of the nation-state on social life, the geographical boundaries of the nation-state became conflated with the spatial boundaries of 'society.' This contributed to the conceptualization of the present globalization epoch in terms of the nation-state, 'national economies' and 'national cultural identities.' It is in this context that sociologists have tended to interpret the patterns of collective social life within the parameters of a nationalist framework.[13] As a consequence, sociological analyses frequently sought to explain social dynamics at a national level and often used the territorial nation-state boundaries as the given unit of social analysis, assuming that they constituted discrete social entities which could be used as units of social analysis.[14]

In contrast to the encapsulation of sociological analysis by nationalism, sociological theories are mostly based on various generalized and universalistic paradigms, such as Modernization and Marxism. The continued co-existence of these two incommensurable trends constitutes a major paradox in sociology. In practice, the contradiction between 'nationalistic' sociological analysis and 'universalistic' sociological theory was often resolved by the domestication of concepts.[15] For example, concepts such as 'class' were frequently treated as appropriate to a national level, whilst the global dynamics which underpin them became rather inconsequential analytical anecdotes. This transnational approach is dependent on a view that negates global interdependencies and relies on a notion which could be labeled 'modernity-in-one-country.'

Late twentieth century developments in the global landscape have undermined the notions, practices and theoretical feasibility of rigidly bounded and endogenously determined state-defined social entities, whilst also underlining the complexity of the organizational agency of the contemporary state in the realm of global social dynamics.[16] In contrast to the view of the state as a discrete, globally independent and endogenously determined social and analytical entity, this book seeks to focus on the interrelationships of global social processes, and aims to articulate the socially constructed relationships between individuals and social collectives that exist within, across and beyond the organizational reach of the state.

Theoretical abstraction - guiding theorems

The theoretical domain of sociological studies, the construction of intellectual postulates and coherent observation, is not primarily a methodological question. It is foremost a question about the theoretical assumptions that are made about the social totality in question. In this regard Albrow (1996) argues that we cannot arrive at the specific characteristics of any epoch without generalization and abstraction, nor without an analysis of the dominant social institutions and the lives of ordinary people. For this reason, Albrow asserts that "if we explore the Modern Age we have to identify the abstract factors of modernity, but also try to specify the ways in which they are embedded in national traditions, promote dominant personality types, and carry forward the inheritance of Greek philosophy and Judaeo-Christian religion. As well as congruences they include contradictions, such as the promotion of rights and the exclusion of people from those rights" (Albrow, 1996:24). Both these elements, namely theoretical abstraction and contradiction, are here woven into the construction of an introductory scheme used to outline the phenomena pertinent to the three central sociological questions of this book. These phenomena are classified into general modernist features or tendencies.[17]

The four central features particularly relevant to this book are the interdynamics that exist in relation to: the modernist cultural epistémé *vis-à-vis* the modernist cultural praxis; dominant *vis-à-vis* marginal developments, spaces and people;

Introduction

systematic standardization *vis-à-vis risk*; and existentialist liberty *vis-à-vis* valorized subjugation. The complementary, yet contradictory constituting elements and processes which characterize these features are highlighted in the introductory scheme.[18] This methodological practice is employed to highlight both contradiction and ambivalence as central motifs of the modern epoch. In addition, the constituent elements of these features provide a brief overview of some aspects of the historical construction of the globalization-valorization-marginalization triangle. They also form an analytical point of departure and a heuristic guide (i.e., a simplified, generalized and lineal scheme of a complex, idiosyncratic and labyrinth social universe) used to network ideas related to the main sociological questions. The cultural epistémé *vis-à-vis* the cultural praxis and the dominant *vis-à-vis* marginal features underpin, and strongly inform, the methodological genre used. The systematic standardization *vis-à-vis risk* and existentialist liberty *vis-à-vis* valorized subjugation features are similarly central to the theoretical genre used.

The modernist cultural epistémé vis-à-vis *the modernist cultural praxis*

(i) Formulation: Since the social world cannot be transmitted and represented as it is, all social representations and narrations tend to be interpretative translations. The events, processes, institutions, practices and relationships which actively constitute globalization – i.e., globalization as a social condition – is referred to as the modernist cultural praxis. However, social life is also composed through the interpretation and narration of it in everyday, populist, media and academic discourses. This realm of ideas about globalization – i.e., globalization as a social narrative, a shared social imagination – is referred to as the modernist cultural epistémé. Despite the theoretical distinctiveness of the modernist cultural praxis and epistémé spheres, neither of them can be explained exhaustively in terms of the other, nor can they be understood in isolation from each other. In order to grasp the central social dynamics of the globalization-valorization-globalization triangle, it is important to problematize the constituent elements of both the cultural praxis and cultural epistémé spheres.

(ii) Introductory snapshot: The distinction between the cultural epistémé and the cultural praxis is based on work by Albrow (1996). Albrow argues that modernist exploration, power, and wealth occurred in tandem with an expansion of human experience, informing a permanent reflexive reassessment of the human condition altogether. For Albrow, the 'Modern Project' effectively sought to unite the world through the particular practices of individual rationality. On the one hand, these practices 'imposed' practical rationality upon the rest of the world. This took place through the social reach of new technologies, the agency of the state and the mechanism of the market. On the other hand, individual rationality was also central to the generation of universal ideas and values which tended to encompass the diversity of the world.[19] For the purpose of this book, Albrow's technology, state and market domain is extended to include material exchange and production processes, as well as social identity composition practices – i.e., the modernist cultural praxis sphere. Albrow's idea domain is similarly enlarged to include the various aspects of the modernist cultural epistémé, such as its discourses, its general social imagination and its social identity narratives.[20]

The cultural praxis of the modernist globalization epoch is predominantly rooted in the changes that occurred in the social organization of life and production within Europe from the fourteenth century onwards. The new and distinctive system of commodity production and exchange accelerated the scope and speed of cultural-material growth in Europe. It also spawned dramatic increases in inter-European commercial and other cultural flows.[21] The rapidly increasing output of commodity production quickly outgrew local markets. This led to the geographical exploration of large parts of the world, which were later infused into the commercial and cultural orbits of the European network. At first this resulted in new and more directly integrated systems of trade. In the merchant phase of capital, sophisticated long-distance trade and commerce focused on natural resources and agriculture. This trade was mainly organized by European mercantile companies (e.g., the Dutch VOC), dependent on profitable interconnections and trade between existing productive social systems which produced goods or owned resources with commercial value.[22] For this reason, the merchant capital phase of European expansionism focused on the extraction, creation and accumulation of surplus without overtly transforming local productive systems outside of Europe *en masse*.[23] However, over time European mercantile companies such as the Dutch VOC in Southern Africa and India started to combine virtual trade diasporas with active colonization.[24]

Despite some active colonization, the participation of colonial spaces and people in the European network was intermittent and limited during the merchant phase of capitalism. This changed with the advent of industrial capitalism and new forms of power, such as steam power. No longer were European commercial interests principally geared towards the raw materials and goods of spaces and people outside of Europe or in marginal European areas. Instead, as the transition from an agrarian to an industrial environment in Europe accelerated, a large industrial labor force became an important requirement for cultural-material growth. In combination, industrial capitalism and European expansion spawned a system of differentiated global labor divisions and labor migrations, reorganizing both the social, technical and spatial processes and relations of production.

From the late seventeenth century onwards, European social expansion dislodged indigenous and traditional production systems. As raw materials, goods and labor were increasingly drawn in substantial quantities from remote locales outside of Europe the importance of indigenous raw materials and labor for European production processes diminished.[25] Under a new regime of export orientated production, resource extraction and the increased commodification of the entire social environment, including human beings as private property (i.e.,

19

slaves), colonial people became colonial subjects laboring in plantations, mines and settler farms.[26] At the same time colonial spaces were fundamentally transformed by the progressive replacement and destruction of the traditional realms of agriculture and craft through, for example, tax induced cash cropping, as well as by the loss of resources, the colonial division of labor and involuntary movement of people.[27]

Over time the European modernity package became pivotal to the reconstruction of indigenous cultural organization and the transmutation of cultural and physical spaces the world over into reconstructed, peripheral and diasporic European spaces. Local ways of life tended to whither away under the impact of European cultural practices, commercial influences and military invasions.[28] In general, European geographical expansion undermined the relative local autonomy over physical and social spaces, cultural practices, the local management of social meaning, and local social identity compositions. Around the world few spaces, cultural codes or identities remained untouched by the global spread and military enforcement of European modernity. For example, at the beginning of the twentieth century, the geographical parameters of the European network included about 85 percent of the world in the form of colonies, commonwealths, dependencies, dominions and protectorates.[29] This social geography was characterized by distinct core and peripheral spheres, separated by large physical and intellectual distances, as well as by substantial discrepancies in wealth, power and cultural primacy.[30]

European geographical exploration and social expansion expedited not only the extraction of goods, resources and labor, but also the appropriation of cultural ideas, practices and artifacts from a spatially dispersed social universe (e.g., Chinese bureaucracy, Indian and African astronomy, Islamic mathematics and astronomy, American Indian democracy, etc.).[31] Long distance sea voyages were central to the appropriation of cultural ideas, practices and artifacts from a spatially dispersed social universe. The most important early

Introduction

long distance sea voyages of the modernist epoch included the so-called discovery of the New World in 1492 by Columbus, the first recorded sea journey from Europe to India in 1499 by Da Gama, the circumnavigation of the earth in 1522 by Magellan, and the three Pacific journeys of Cook between 1768 and 1779 which included a landing in Australia.

The impact of European expansion was not restricted to cultural-material activities, or to the colonial invasion of physical spaces, but also included a sophisticated invasion of, and appropriation from, intellectual spaces outside of Europe.[32] From early on, European expansion had a significant impact on the modernist imagination and the philosophical genres of European modernity. This was articulated by various early modernist philosophers, such Bacon (1906), Descartes (1912) and Spinoza (1910). Bacon's book 'The New Atlantis' (1906), for example, deals with the voyage of discovery to a lost continent. Bacon's own voyage of discovery included going to Morocco to learn mathematics.[33] 'The New Atlantis' is an important early modernist text, encapsulating the emerging modernist cultural epistémé. It is also one of the earliest known modernist texts that systematically articulated the advent of instrumental reason and individual rationality. In 'The New Atlantis' Bacon addresses the related extension of human knowledge, social intervention and social order through the mediation and imposition of instrumental reason, and the existentialist development of the self-conscious individual.

The articulation of the existentialist development of the self-conscious individual is also present in the work of the prominent early sociologists, such as Comte, Spencer, Saint-Simon, and Marx, who attempted to provide a science of humanity based on timeless principles and verified laws. Ideas generally associated with the Enlightenment period, such as 'humanity, reflexivity and universalism,' were reflected in the sociological writing of this time, and informed the ways in which classical sociology engaged with notions of globalization. Post-Enlightenment early sociological writing was, however, also influenced by the expansionist and subjugation practices characteristic of European modernity. This meant that the world outside of the dominant European core became the object of scholarly attention within an eurocentric intellectual milieu. Sociological narratives during this time most often reflected this eurocentrism in their articulation of the notion of otherness.

In modernist writing the articulation of anteriority and other (than Europeaness) culminated in the scientific organization of the cultural hierarchies of the modernist social universe as articulated, for example, through the 'civilizations, races and cultures' dialogues. The first academic publications on hierarchical human racial classification appeared during the latter part of the eighteenth century. The author Blumenbach (1865), a professor at Göttingen university during the 1770s, focused on the racial superiority of whites. Blumenbach's work was complemented by a shift in scholarly focus from individuals to social groups and social institutions, which surfaced in Göttingen and other European universities. These social groups were often defined along racial lines and were saturated with notions of Caucasianism or whiteness.[34] Generally speaking, the early and colonial phases of European spatial expansion established the interplay between the modernist cultural praxis and the modernist cultural epistémé, and solidified the dependency of the European package on globalization.

Dominant vis-à-vis *marginal developments, spaces and people*

(i) Formulation: Historically, the dominant developments in the core spaces of the European network (i.e., the so-called Western world) tended to have a major influence on the social arrangements in peripheral and colonial spaces. Generally speaking the daily social lives of the majority of the world's population have little in common with the everyday lives of people within the dominant modernist spaces. Nevertheless, social life in dominant, intermediate and marginal social spaces around the world is often related to developments in the axial forms of European modernity.[35] It is difficult for marginalized

Introduction

social and intellectual spaces and peoples to escape from the dominant forms of modernity, particularly with regard to one of its central ingredients, namely global capitalism. For example, whilst most of the world's population is not directly connected to the global market place, local social relations across the world are nevertheless influenced by the practices and logic of global markets.[36] Even the social dynamics of so-called isolated African villages are today by and large products of the developments within the dominant spheres of global capitalism – which may be 10,000 km away. For this reason, many African scholars, for example, argue that they cannot study marginalization in Africa without a global perspective as such studies would merely illustrate the symptoms of social disempowerment and dislocation.[37] As such, a focus on dominant modernist developments constitutes a relevant methodological practice for comprehending marginality.

In order to address the context and manifestation of the central marginalization dynamics of contemporary modernity, this book consequently does not focus on marginalized spaces – e.g., small marginalized African villages – as such. Instead, the focus is on the developments in the dominant forms and spheres of modernity and global capital, with reference to the impact of these developments on marginal spaces.

(ii) Introductory snapshot: The extent of the global polarization mediated mainly by valorization processes and practices, and manifested in income and wealth discrepancies, has advanced dramatically since the 1960s. Data from around the world indicate that a bimodal pattern of income and wealth distribution occurs on a truly global scale in all possible units of analysis (e.g., global, regional, and transnational spaces, cities; the so-called developed, developing and under-developed world; corporations, individuals, etc.).[38] For example, the richest 20 percent of the world's population had incomes 30 times greater than the poorest 20 percent of the world's population in 1960. By 1990 this ratio had increased sixty fold.[39] In 1996 it was estimated that the wealthiest one-sixth of the world's population possessed a disproportionate five-sixths of the world's wealth, whilst the wealthiest 358 people in the world owned assets with a combined net worth of US$760 billion. This amount was equal to the total net worth of assets of the bottom 47 percent (2.5 billion) of the world's population.[40] Two years later (1998) the same data sources and research methods were used to regauge this division. Whilst the position of the poorest 2.5 billion people remained unchanged, the concentration of wealth at the top had increased further. The wealthiest 225 people in the world now owned assets with a combined net worth of US$1 trillion.[41]

In the early 1990s the 22.9 percent of the world population living in the advanced industrial world accounted for 84.2 percent of global GNP.[42] In comparison, the rest of the world (77.1 percent) accounted for only 15.8 percent of global GNP.[43] By the late 1990s the fifth of the world's population living in the advanced industrial world accounted for 86 percent of global GNP and the bottom fifth for only 1 percent.[44]

In regard to specific national spaces Hutton (1995) argues that Thatcherite labor market reforms have transformed Britain into a '30/30/40 society.' According to Hutton, 40 percent of the British were better off in 1995 than before the Thatcher era, and were holding tenured jobs. The middle 30 percent of the workforce were structurally insecure in terms of employment (e.g., holding jobs as temporary, part-time, self-employed, or casual contract workers), whilst the bottom 30 percent are either unemployed or 'economically' inactive, forming a marginalized disadvantaged group.[45] According to research by Lee and Townsend (1993) the wages in the lowest decile of income earners in London declined by 14 percent between 1979 and 1991. During the same time, the ratio of real income between the richest and the poorest deciles almost doubled, from 5.6 to 10.2. percent.[46]

Similar patterns can be observed in America. For example, between 1973 and 1994, American per capita GNP increased by a third in real terms. However, only the income of the top 25 percent of households increased, whilst the income of the bottom 75 percent dropped by 19 percent in real terms.[47] In

Introduction

the mid-1990s, the upper 20 percent of American households earned 48.2 percent of the total income, while the lower 20 percent earned 3.6 percent.[48] Despite its immense wealth, America has the largest percentage of people living in poverty of any industrialized country today. The wealthiest 1 percent of its population presently owns 40 percent of all assets.[49] This is twice the amount of the mid-1970s, and once again at the level of the late 1920s, before progressive taxation.[50] From 1979 to 1999 the inflation ajusted incomes of the richest 20 percent of Americans increased by 38,2 percent (from US$234,700 to US$515,600 without correcting for inflation), whilst the income of the bottom 20 percent decreased by 12 percent (without correcting for inflation an increase from US$10,000 to US$18,400, but after adjusting for inflation a reduction to US$8,800).[51]

A Los Angeles survey mapped this pattern in detail within a smaller unit of analysis. It established that the number of people with incomes over US$50,000 per annum tripled during the 1980-1990 period, soaring from 9 to 27 percent of the city's population.[52] During the same period, the number of people with low incomes (i.e., under US$15,000), increased from 30 to 40 percent. Within only one decade, the middle income group had shrunk from 61 percent to only 32 percent of the city's population.[53]

The current polarization of income and wealth in advanced industrialized spaces follows a similar pattern in the rest of the world. For instance, in Mexico during the 1980s the top 2 income deciles accounted for 72 percent of wealth and the number of billionaires increased from 2 to 24, whilst the measurable income and living standards of 60 percent of the population declined.[54] Similarly, the wealthiest 20 percent of the Indian population controlled 30 percent of the total national monetary assets in 1960. By 1990, the wealthiest 20 percent controlled 60 percent of the total assets, whilst the poorest 20 percent controlled only 1 percent thereof.[55]

Similar to urban and wealthy spaces the world over, there are strong indications that poor rural communities, such as the extremely poor African village of Spoegrivier, have also seen a major divergence between the richest and poorest sections of their populations over the last decades.[56] Based on elementary data, the gap between the richest and poorest 20 percent of Spoegrivier's population has, for example, increased from about 2:1 in the mid-1960s, to about 6:1 in 1988, and to 9:1 in 1993 – an increase of 300 percent over 30 years.[57] Overall, research from around the world indicate that the Hutton '30/30/40 society' model today permeates many social spaces as monetary polarization accelerates across and within national spaces. The gap between the rich and the poor is indeed soaring around the globe.

In regard to regional spaces the African continent is today in a precarious position as arguably the world's most marginalized region. According to the World Bank (1990) and the United Nations Human Development Report (1998), the number of people classified as poor in Asia, Latin America and the Caribbean has dropped substantially between 1985 and 1998, with Asia's portion estimated to decline by 19 percent during the last 15 years of the twentieth century.[58] However, the estimated number of poor people in Sub-Saharan Africa is set to rise by 85 million (i.e., to 265 million people) during the same period, doubling its portion of the world's poor from 16 to 32 percent.[59]

The extent of productive output and wealth disparities in relation to the African continent is indeed staggering. For example, while Belgium's GNP was similar to that of the total Sub-Saharan Africa during the 1990s,[60] Belgium has a population of about ten million, compared to the Sub-Saharan population of approximately 450 million people. Viewed from a different angle, during the 1990s the yearly sales of General Motors (e.g., US$133 billion in 1992) were about equal to the aggregate GNP of Tanzania, Ethiopia, Nepal, Bangladesh, Uganda, Nigeria, Kenya and Pakistan together. About 500 million people, nearly a tenth of the world's population, live in these countries. These productive output discrepancies between the so-called First and Third Worlds furthermore take place in the context of real monetary flows out of the 'Third World.' Since the 1960s the net transfer from the 'Third' to the 'First

Introduction

World' was between US$20-30 billion per annum, with a large percentage of this amount coming from the poorest continent, namely Africa.⁶¹ In order to highlight the interdynamics between dominant *vis-à-vis* marginal spaces and people, developments in the advanced industrial world are thus contrasted throughout with related African developments in particular.

Systematic standardization vis-à-vis *risk*

(i) Formulation: Systematic standardization and risk – as analytical constructs – constitute a specific Janus-faced modernist mixture. The systematic standardization of social relations, institutions and practices is an essential aspect of modernity. Whilst the phenomenon of risk is not unique to modernity, specific risk practices are nevertheless integral to it.⁶² One of the key historical attributes of the modernist cultural habitat (i.e., the modernist cultural epistémé and the modernist cultural praxis spheres) is the management of risk through the processes of systematic standardization.

(ii) Introductory snapshot: Systematic standardization can be understood through a focus on accumulative historic events, as well as through the construction of related analytical constructs. Generally speaking, the systematical standardization of social processes and relations was facilitated by the development and implementation of new technologies, the ascendancy of mass industrial production and monetized exchange processes *vis-à-vis* subsistence processes, the emergence of new cultural-political practices, such as the development of civil bureaucracies, and the increased mechanical control of nature, time and space. Over time social processes and relations became embedded in an evolving social epoch with a technological nexus as new machine technologies not only transformed nature *en masse*, but also rapidly restructured and standardized social life. The social world was increasingly mediated more directly by new technologies.

In no other known era did technology transform the social

and natural worlds as rapidly and dramatically. Various authors, such as Bentley (1993), argue that the evolving military and production technologies were the dominant force that fueled early European expansion. The transformation of colonial spaces and the colonial cultural environment was mainly a result of the competitive advantages in production and warfare technologies held by European social conglomerates (e.g., mercantile companies and national empires), and their ability to control the diffusion of new technologies from the core to the colonial periphery. These developments contributed to the centralization of surpluses, goods, natural resources and cultural assets in the core during the colonial period. Self-sufficient and subsistence systems of European and other spaces tended to whither away under the impact of the monetization of social life which accompanied the structural – and sometimes violent – introduction and enforcement of the cultural practices (e.g., industrial production), cultural values (e.g., individualism), cultural logic (e.g., the increased monetization of social exchanges), and cultural institutions (e.g., private property and civil bureaucracies) of European modernity.

The increased technological control of nature, the ascendancy of production processes and the systematic standardization of social practices initiated a number of important developments. These included: unprecedented cultural-material growth; a shift from agricultural to industrial production as the core sector of productive activity; the concentration of productive activities in cities; technological innovations which embraced all spheres of social life; the development of competitive labor markets and unemployment; the concentration of labor in large industrial enterprises; the increased and perpetual commodification of more and more aspects of social life; and the replacement of human and animal power by inanimate sources of energy.

The use of inanimate sources of energy increased rapidly from the mid-nineteenth century onwards when electricity was effectively harnessed as a source of power for the first time. This led to a new proliferation of valorized opportunities as oil and coal could now be used to run motors for transport and production. In combination, electric power machinery and the industrial division of labor dramatically augmented the productive capacity of enterprises, ushering in the era of large-scale mass manufacturing industries. The systematically standardized and commodified production cycle became pivotal to the organization and development of social life.[63]

The general shift from subsistence processes to commodified production processes impacted on social relations and social identities in a number of ways. Two of these are particularly relevant to this study. Firstly, the shift to commodity production was instrumental to the increased historical polarization of wealth within national populations, as well as between the national populations of the core and the colonial periphery. The global polarization of wealth and poverty is a relatively recent phenomenon in historical terms.[64] As recent as 200 years ago, social production was characterized by subsistence systems with comparatively small differences in quantifiable global living standards. These differences soared only with the advent of industrial capitalism and European expansion. For example, the ratio between 'the rich' and 'the poor' was about 2:1 in 1800, by 1945 it had risen to 20:1, by 1975 to 40:1, and by 1999 it has mounted to 72:1.[65] Secondly, the shift towards commodity production fundamentally reorganized social relations and social identities, which became increasingly embedded within the relations of production. As a consequence, class emerged as an important acquired social identity and cultural constituency, and class based social relations and social organization became one of the central motifs of the twentieth century.

The processes of systematic standardization were not only central to the transformation of the production sphere, but also to the creation *and* management of mundane, potentially advantageous and hazardous risk and uncertainties. The social management of time/space compression, the practices in the food industry and the restructuring of cultural-political governance are three examples of the interdynamics in the systematic standardization/risk phenomenon.

Firstly, time/space compression was a direct result of the systematic standardization of knowledge and production processes. The resulting technological innovations culminated in, for example, the development of steam trains and ships during the nineteenth century. In turn, steam trains and ships were integral to the increased compression of time and space by providing dramatically faster methods of travel, thereby contributing to the creation of new uncertainties and social risks (e.g., accidents, and incompatible timetables and timezones). In 1884, the International Meridian Conference in Washington, D.C. dealt with some of these uncertainties and risks by systematically standardizing time across space. A global system was established which divided the world into 24 one-hour time zones with the 180th meridian as the international date line. Standardized time, in combination with a proliferation of other systematically standardized processes – such as quality controls in manufacturing processes, passports, air regulation, etc. – reduced existing risks with regard to, for example, international travel. These risk management developments inadvertently created new risks. For example, mass air travel advanced in part by reducing existing risks simultaneously facilitated the emergence of new risks, such as the rapid spread of diseases due to rapid mass movements. In this regard, the systematic standardization *vis-à-vis* risk phenomenon tends to form part of a self-perpetuating dialectic.

Secondly, developments in the food industry also illustrate the systematic standardization/risk phenomenon. As the preparation of food shifts from the personal to the public terrain, new uncertainties and risks (i.e., preparation methods, taste, cost, etc.) emerge. Ritzer (1993) argues that in order to remove the unpredictable circumstances from both the production and consumption of food, the practices of McDonaldization [systematically] standardizes all processes as much as possible, thereby eliminating surprises, removing uncertainties and minimizing risks.

Thirdly, the systematic standardization of information about the social world, as well as the abilities of governments

Introduction

and other managerial entities, such as international organizations and transnational corporations, to technically intervene in everyday social life contribute to the technocratization of social organization. Social problems and risks are consequently often articulated in technical terms. For Habermas (1963) the augmentation of a technocratic consciousness means that technology is evolving into a partly autonomous social phenomenon as there is a progressive rationalization of technical control. Habermas (1970) argues that the technocratic consciousness which permeates the forms of instrumental reason contributes to the orientation of 'political' governance towards the avoidance of risks by technical means. This phenomenon is of particular relevance at present. In this book attention is given to the historical interface between systematic standardization and risk, as well as to contemporary changes to systematic standardization and risks practices.

Existentialist liberty vis-à-vis *valorized subjugation*

(i) Formulation: European modernity is characterized by a complementary, yet contradictory tension between various elements of individualism particularly in relation to the monetization of social exchanges. On the one hand, the incremental but perpetual monetization of more and more social exchanges contributes to the notions of existentialist liberty – the reason and practices of individual freedom, often mediated by indirect (i.e., labor and wages) and direct (i.e., goods and payments) monetary processes. On the other hand, the monetization of social exchanges have also spawned the dynamic processes of valorized subjugation – the reason and practices of individual subjugation, often mediated by indirect and direct monetary processes.

(ii) Introductory snapshot: The modernist cultural account emphasizes the possibility of complementary, and *pari passu* individual and social progress. The individual is generally seen as the ontological center of the social universe and everyday, populist, media and academic narratives often emphasize existentialist notions of liberty – or formulated differently, the reason and practices of individual freedom. Existentialist notions of human liberty are frequently complemented by modernist practices, such as perpetual commodification, and cultural-material growth outcomes (e.g., cultural practices, such as individual wealth accumulation, and certain social technologies, such as private telecommunications) which partially dissociates the individual from social collectives. These developments augment the ability of the individual – *vis-à-vis* social collectives, such as the state – to influence and control his/her own social universe.

The ability of the individual to dissociate him/herself from social collectives not only reduces the obligations of the individual to social collectives, but also provides the individual with the opportunity to refer to their own beliefs and values in the construction of their daily social lives and the composition of their social identities. In addition, the democratization of certain consumption and lifestyle choices (e.g., private cars, leisure travel) have augmented the experience of individual choice and freedom for large numbers of people. Overall, the modernist notions and practices of existentialist liberty – often mediated by monetary processes – are related to *individual freedom* from the *constraints* of extended social collectives.

Existentialist notions and practices of liberty are, however, also part of a modernist praxis characterized by the increased valorization of goods, resources, labor, as well as social processes and relations in general.[66] Increased valorization was central to the mostly incremental replacement of the old, and the evolution of a new cultural environment in Europe over the last 400 hundred years. Both in and outside of Europe social transformation was, in the final instance, frequently achieved through the subjugation of the natural and cultural environment. During the early and colonial phases of European expansion this subjugation took place through a combination of monetization practices and bureaucratic processes (e.g., hut and poll taxes that coerced colonized people into wage labor), alien cultural and religious customs

Introduction

(e.g. private property and Christianity), and was often enforced through military intervention. In the colonial periphery, in particular, increased valorization and subjugation tended to accompany each other.[67]

On the one hand, *pari passu* valorization and subjugation enlarged the abilities of the modernist project to deliver social benefits to core spaces and peoples *vis-à-vis* peripheral and colonial spaces and peoples. On the other hand, the coalescence of core centralization (e.g., of cultural-material wealth) and the valorized subjugation of colonialized people (e.g., as cheap wage laborers and as slaves) coexisted with the social externalization of social difference. The general social vagaries which accompanied the rapid growth of industrial capitalism in and outside of Europe,[68] and the specific social construction of the other (than European) as an inferior specimen within the cultural hierarchies of the modernist social universe, were central aspects of the historical context in which the moral construction of disempowered colonialized people as the other (than European) took place. It is in this context that the specific narrative of race (other than European) and the practices of racism (towards other than Europeans) unfolded to became pivotal aspects of modernist marginalization.[69]

A similar process of social externalization, fueled by the increased monetization of the social universe and the emergence of class as a social force and a social classification system, occurred within Europe. The social narration of valorized otherness (e.g., modernist race and class catogories) now became both a form of social marginalization and a context into which social polarizations could be woven and morally justified.[70] Generally speaking, the modernist notions and practices of valorized subjugation – often mediated by monetary processes – are related to *individual isolation* from the *reprocipical care* of extended social collectives.

This book attempts to address the inter-dependencies between existentialist liberty and valorized subjugation with particular reference to the impact of contemporary valorization processes on both elements, as well as on the changing technical processes, social dynamics and spatial patterns of marginalization.[71] The emphasis on valorization warrants a more detailed discussion of its theoretical roots and its relation to labor and other more directly monetized processes. Generally speaking, modernist academic narratives about the world often focus on one or the other of the existentialist liberty or valorized subjugation spheres.[72] Those theorists who focus on existentialist liberty tend to emphasize the progressive cultural elements, ideas and practices of modernity. Despite their seminal insights into the general cultural features of European modernity (i.e., differentiation, specialization, commodification, pluralization, individualization, etc.), these discourses tend to maintain a relative intellectual detachment in regard to, and from, the destabilizing imperatives and social marginalizing dynamics of modernism.[73] On the other hand, those theorists – such as the dependency theorists – who address the marginalization tendencies of modernism, generally fail to integrate the cultural logic of modernism into their mostly material deterministic analyses.

The most important historical analysis of the wider theoretical and cultural relevance of monetization processes to modernity have arguably been Marx's work on commodity fetishism and the labor theory of value, and Simmel's 'The Philosophy of Money' which was first published in 1900. Marx (1970, 1972, 1973, 1977) makes a general distinction between producing for one's own use and producing a commodity – an object created solely to be exchanged. Commodities mostly have both use-value and/or exchange-value. However, in systems of production where commodity production prevails, objects are produced mainly for their exchange value. These exchange values *attach* themselves to the objects in question. As a result, the commodified objects *represent* the social relations of production. People then tend to view the exchange value of a given commodity not as the consequence of people's labor, but as a naturally fixed property of the commodity itself. Marx argued that through the exchange process, and its subsequent fetishization, unlike phenomena are equated, resulting in social theorists becoming oblivious to the social dynamics which underpin their social analysis.

For Marx this process of commodity fetishism occurs in two related ways. On the one hand, social phenomena are reified whilst, on the other hand inanimate things are treated as if they had the qualities of social phenomena. For Marx this commodity fetishization means that the social relations which evolve in relation to exchange relations are perceived as a natural given state of affairs. Marx's schematic theoretical construction of commodity fetishism problematized the interdynamics of monetized exchanges and social relations – in other words of money as a social relation – of a specific commodification genre, namely nineteenth century European capitalism.

The labor theory of value is another aspect of Marx's work relevant to the theoretical domain of this book. For Marx capital increases its value through the creation of surplus value. In the 'Capital' volume 3 (1972) Marx referred to this augmentation of the value of capital, or the valorization process as the 'self-expansion of capital' ('Verwertung'). Marx argued that the creation of surplus value occurs as a result of two distinct processes, namely the labor process through which labor power produces use-values, and the valorization process through which labor power produces additional (i.e., surplus) value over and above its own value. The labor theory of value is based on the premise that ultimately it is the labor time expanded in production processes that determines exchange value. Whilst surplus value is *created* during the labor process, it is only *realized* through the sale of commodities. For Marx it is only at this point that the value of capital is increased.

During the last century the separation between the processes which creates surplus-value and the processes which realized it has been eroded substantially. This development occurred mainly as a result of the increased technolization of production and exchange processes. Even within a Marxist framework, the dependency of surplus-value creation on labor power is diminishing as surplus-value is today more and more created, realized and even generated through scientific and technological innovations. These innovations progressively reduce the active labor component required for the commercial reproduction of a specific product. For example, whilst the development of a specific computer software program might require intensive research and especially intellectual labor, the commercial reproduction of the final product on cd-rom discs is today performed with a relatively small number of workers and with relatively minimal labor time in comparison to the production processes of Industrial capitalism until to the 1970s. This development generally characterizes the state-of-the-art forms of capital augmentation, and also informs our understanding of valorization processes. Marxist analysis of monetization processes have generally focused on the valorized subjugation aspects and little attention was given to the existentialist liberty aspects of modernist monetization as articulated in this book.[74]

The most important historical alternative to the Marxist construction of the wider social implications of commodification processes *per se*, has arguably been Simmel's 'The Philosophy of Money.' There is today a renewed interest in Simmel's work on the interrelationship between monetization and modernity.[75] This is in part the result of the fundamental changes that have occurred in global financial markets and their management since the 1970s, such as the partial demonetization of gold *vis-à-vis* the increased monetization of the total social universe, and the increased monetization that occurred through and within electronic processes (such as the augmentation of electronic capital in global financial markets).[76]

In relation to this book, three aspects of Simmel's work are of particular relevance. Firstly, Simmel extends valorization beyond the Marxist focus on labor commodification, including all aspects of cultural life (e.g., art, religion, 'economics,' 'politics,' etc.). Secondly, Simmel regards monetization to be intrinsically woven into the modernist motif. As such, money embodies, and instigates, the complementary, yet contradictory elements and processes of modernity. For Simmel the

Introduction

evolution of 'economic' exchanges from barter to paper money to credit not only represents the quantification of social exchanges, but also a rationalization of everyday social life and the general standardization of social exchanges.

Simmel argues that the increased monetization of social exchanges also facilitates freedom from traditional ties, from feudal patronage and from social groups in general. This often leads to greater individualization and the possible experience of a personal and personalized destiny as the relationship between the individual and the market over time replaces age, gender, religious allegiance and other traditional factors as the main determinant of social status and destiny. "Certainly the worker is tied to his job almost as the peasant to his lot, but the frequency with which employers change in a money economy and the frequent possibility of choosing and changing them that is made possible by the form of money wages provide an altogether new freedom within the framework of his dependency. The slave could not change his master even if he had been willing to risk much worse living conditions, whereas the industrial worker can do that at any time. By thus eliminating the pressure of irrevocable dependency upon a particular individual master, the worker is already on the way to personal freedom despite his objective bondage. That this emergent freedom has little continuous influence upon the material situation of the worker should not prevent us from appreciating it" (Simmel, 1990:300). For Simmel the freedom imparted through modernist monetization, whilst liberating in many ways, is primarily a 'negative freedom' (Simmel 1990) – freedom from something rather than freedom to do something.[77]

Thirdly, Simmel argues that the specific modernist processes of monetization establishes money as the 'representative of abstract value' (Simmel, 1990). For Simmel money – as a form of social exchange – links individuals together, and that money – as a tangible substance – embodies the general 'cultural and economic' values of modernity. In addition, money – as a visible symbol – also expresses the value relationships between several other objects, as well as

37

their exchangeability relative to the aggregate of all other commodities and values. According to Simmel, money only begins to develop "when a single object is exchanged not against another single object but against several others" (Simmel, 1990:127).

Generally speaking, money is an instrument capable of representing value, as well as a mechanism for value transfer. As such, money is a concrete symbol for abstract and infinitely relative social value of, for example, a specific article, experience, idea, etc. *vis-á-vis* all other commodities. In contrast to other units of measurement such as kilogram money is not a constant unit of measurement. On the contrary, the value of money is inherently and permanently unstable, reflecting the ever-changing social coherence of exchangeables.[78] The fact that money has no intrinsic value adds to its instability and volatility. This is one of the reasons why money was historically supported by giving it an equivalence in gold namely the Gold Standard, and why its capacity to value continues to depend on its social legitimacy and a stable social environment.

Overall, the *creation, realization* and *generation* of monetary values in twentieth century valorization processes encompass both the predominantly value adding (i.e., so-called production) *and* mainly monetizing (i.e., so-called exchange) spheres of activity. This notion of an encompassing monetization will be used to analyze developments (e.g., in relation to electrification and computerization) in the production processes of the dominant commodification genre (i.e., global capitalism), the changes in the industrial techniques of valorization, the refiguration of the interdynamics of value adding and monetization processes, as well as the interplay between valorization, globalization and marginalization in the realm of the global reorganization of valorization processes.

A précis of the chapters

Chapter 1 *(Global Exchange Processes)* focuses on the

Introduction

most important developments in monetary exchanges, with a particular focus on the interaction of private interests and public governance. The first part of the chapter deals with the developments in global public institutions and forms of global public cultural-material governance during the twentieth century up to the 1970s. The second part of the chapter addresses post-1970s developments, such as the deregulation of world trade, the so-called 'de-monopolization of capital markets,' and changes that occurred in the constitution of global financial exchange spaces. Particular attention is given to the deregulation of off-shore money markets; the 1980s monetary crises (including, the new debt politics and the Uruguay Round of GATT); and the emergence of a New Global Financial Environment (including, the composition of the NGFE, and the *pari passu* globalization of money and the valorization of speculation).

Chapter 2 *(The Organization of Production Processes)* deals with the organization of the dominant contemporary production processes. At the beginning of the twentieth century, the principles and practices of the scientific management movement, generally referred to as Taylorism and Fordism, dramatically restructured the organization of production in European and American workplaces. Under the Fordist production regime work and production were organized around the semi-automatic assembly line, costly fixed-purpose machinery, and producer networks clustered around heavy industries with large concentrations of semi-skilled workers. The world-wide diffusion of machine technologies, accelerated technological advances (e.g., computer electronics), the information revolution, and changes in consumption patterns are some of the important developments which contributed to the reordering of the internal and global dynamics of production processes in the post 1970s. This reordering of the Fordist labor and technology regimes is discussed in the light of the changes in global production and exchange processes. Particular attention is given to the following aspects: drastically reduced product development time and product life cycles; the ascendancy of automation technologies; and the proliferation of corporate strategies and new management theories in relation to the global repositioning of corporations.

In Chapter 3 *(The Recomposition of Production Relations)* the impact of the reorganization, fragmentation, deterritorialization, the selective transfer of technologies, and the computerized electrification of exchange and production processes affecting the recomposition of the social and technical division of labor, are highlighted. The discussion addresses some of the important developments in the general social and technical division of labor, particularly in regard to the spatial reordering of marginalization. Specific attention is given to the redefinition of the social organization of production and labor processes by organizations, and to the recomposition of global technical divisions of labor.

Chapter 4 *(Social Identity Compositions and Narratives)* focuses on some of the central aspects of contemporary identity compositions and narratives. Particular attention is given to the recomposition of modernist marginality in reference to the dominant globalization and valorization dynamics. Within the modernist network, classical identity compositions and narratives were primarily mediated by the state (as manifested in nationalist narratives), by production relations (as manifested in class narratives), and by industrial technologies (as manifested in the reorganization of social relations via numerous technological interventions which resulted in the social compression of time and space). Towards the end of the twentieth century, the interdynamics of the globalization-valorization-marginalization triangle are changing significantly. The general contradictory and complementary tensions existing between the influences of the globalization-valorization-marginalization triangle and the resulting impact on social identity compositions and narratives, are discussed in reference to three particular social intersections. They are: the state *vis-à-vis* private capital; machine technologies *vis-à-vis* virtual technologies; and production *vis-à-vis* consumption.

The final conclusion briefly reflects on some of the most

Introduction

important aspects of the modernist Zeitgeist in relation to the globalization-valorization-marginalization triangle.

Chapter 1
Global Exchange Processes

"We wanted democracy, but we ended up with the bond market" (Polish graffiti, cited in Martin and Schumann, 1997:40).

This chapter focuses on some of the central monetary exchange processes of the twentieth century. Particular attention is given to the interaction of private interests and public governance. The twentieth century public governance of global monetized exchanges (e.g., goods and money) can be classified into four distinctly different periods. These are: the period from the mid-nineteenth century to the First World War; the period between the two world wars; the period between the end of the Second World War and the 1970s; and the period from the 1970s to the present. The first part of the chapter deals with some of the most important developments in the relevant global public institutions and forms of global public governance during the pre-1970 periods.

The second part of the chapter addresses the post-1970s developments in global public cultural-material governance. During this period the deregulation of world trade accelerated and the so-called 'de-monopolization of capital markets' occurred. In addition, the constitution of global financial exchange spaces changed from a conglomerate of national financial spaces (i.e., the so-called 'international finance economy') to a hybrid of national and private financial spaces (i.e., the so-called 'transnational finance economy'). Particular attention is given to the deregulation of off-shore money markets; the 1980s monetary crises (including, the new debt politics and the Uruguay Round of GATT); and the emergence of a New Global Financial Environment (including, the composition of the NGFE, and the *pari passu* globalization of money and the valorization of speculation).

Twentieth century developments in global public cultural-material governance up to the 1970s

"If the goods cross the frontiers, the armies won't" (Cry of the free traders of Victorian times).

During the global expansion of capitalism from the mid-nineteenth century to the First World War, the social management of global monetized exchanges was by and large organized by *laissez faire* market forces. There were few formal restrictions or governmental constraints on the cross-border flow of money or on the transfer of profits. In addition, protectionist taxation and tariff barriers were generally absent. During this time of *laissez faire* market governance there were dramatic increases in international trade. Between 1870 and 1913 the proportion of international trade relative to world production increased threefold, and there were high levels of cross-national ownership of securities and government bonds.[1]

The minimal governmental regulation of monetary flows and production activities in general, however, coexisted with an interventionist labor regime which complemented *laissez faire* market forces. An important aspect of this labor regime was the colonial relationship which existed between core and marginal spaces. With about 85 percent of the world under some form of European colonial rule or control by 1914,[2] the inevitable asymmetrical relationships between the core and periphery ensured institutionalized labor flexibility within the spatial boundaries of the European network. Colonization provided labor-on-demand, whilst the intercontinental migration from Europe to the colonies (i.e., settler colonialism) provided more control, and increased the manageability and flexibility of the core's reserve army of labor.³

In the period between the two world wars major shifts occurred in the relations between and within nationally defined spaces (i.e., in regard to the so-called 'international economy' and 'national economies' respectively). During this time, world trade failed to recover to its pre-war level due to persisting wartime controls after 1918. In addition, the international financial environment was marked by increased instability since many parts of the world suffered a major recession after the war. Together with a public backlash against pre-war *laissez faire* governance, this recession added public pressure for state intervention in cultural-material affairs.

The challenges to *laissez faire* market forces included the Bolshevik revolution of 1917 in Russia, the development of the New Deal policies in America, and later the emergence of National-Sozialismus in Germany.⁴ Whilst the Bolshevik revolution totally rejected capitalism, American New Deal protagonists favored state intervention and regulation within a capitalist framework. Under Roosevelt's New Deal policies, the state increased its active participation in, and management of, cultural-material activities. State intervention particularly focused on the creation of jobs and assistance to the unemployed. In general, the post-1920s were characterized by a strong focus on nationally defined public recovery strategies, the regulation of trade (e.g., through tariffs) and state cultural-material management which enhanced public control and also solidified the national-capital project.

After the Second World War, politicians and economists attempted to deal with the two major issues which affected social life during the first half of the twentieth century. These issues were the lack of national control and regulation of *laissez faire* private market forces in the period before the First World War, and the deficiencies in the international control and regulation of the nationalist agenda in the period before the Second World War. Together, these two issues informed the development of a new international paradigm of general public governance. National control and regulation of *laissez faire* private market forces were increased by institutionalizing greater state control over cultural-material affairs. For example, the banking and finance sectors were now regulated by governments in order to serve national objectives. At the same time, the sovereignty of individual states *vis-à-vis* other states was partially externalized in order to deal with the lack of pre-war international control over particularistic national agendas. As a result, national sovereignty became a more contested issue within the institutions of the international state system.

The new international paradigm of public governance facilitated the emergence, and extended the scope, of international institutions such as the United Nations, the International Court, the General Agreement on Tariffs and Trade, etc. Within this international paradigm there was a proliferation of international organizations, agencies and policies over time. For example, in 1909 there were 37 intergovernmental and 176 international non-governmental organizations. By the 1990s, these increased to 286 and 4,696 respectively, whilst their influence and scope had expanded considerably, and their organizational identities now incorporated more and more transnational aspects.[5] Presently there are more than 26,000 NGOs.[6]

The foundation of the post-Second World War system of international cultural-material institutions was laid at an international meeting by representatives of forty-four countries in Bretton Woods, New Hampshire in 1944. John Maynard Keynes, on behalf of the British government, proposed new forms of international co-operation aimed at ensuring full employment and currency stability. These proposals included new international institutions, such as an International Trade Organization, a Development Fund and an International Bank with its own world reserve currency, backed by gold or national currencies. To some extent Keynes' proposals were juxtaposed against those put forward by American delegates, particularly Dexter White.

The 'liberal American' and 'social Keynesian' positions represented the two dominant interpretations of the roots of the 1930s 'economic' and military crises. For liberals, restricted trade was a central cause of both the depression and the war. They argued that in a free trade regime, competition for scarce resources is generally settled by monetary and not military means. Keynesians argued that trade was a secondary problem to the 1930s crises. For them the crises in domestic demands was a causal, and not a symptomatic aspect of the 1920s' depression and the war. For Keynes future international stability was dependent on the 'political' management of sustained 'economic' growth. Keynes thus wanted to create an international system in which governments would not be forced to limit domestic growth in order to sustain a balance of trade, and avoid 'beggar-thy neighbor' competition.[7]

Keynes' proposals were selectively accepted, amended or rejected by American negotiators at Bretton Woods. In the aftermath of the war, America assumed the position as the new global hegemon and used its position to negotiate a trade system that suited its interests.[8] Whilst much of the rest of the industrialized world had been exhausted or devastated by war, America was particularly well placed, both in terms of a largely intact infrastructure and its global superpower position, to take advantage of a liberalized trade regime. After the war about half of the world's commercial trade goods was produced in America.[9] The new international financial and trade system that evolved from the Bretton Woods negotiations, was characterized by a managed monetary system which had fixed exchange rates and an International Monetary Fund that would assist countries with balance-of-payments problems. At the same time, liberal principles, such as moving to a negotiated free trade regime through the General Agreement on Tariffs and Trade, was embedded in the institutional framework of this new international financial and trade environment.

In general, the Bretton Woods system was ultimately premised on the notion that international trade would become the stimulant of enduring growth. This assumption was based on a philosophy that international trade needed to be underpinned by a unitary and stable framework for trade and financial relations between countries. This was essential in order to prevent a return to the fragmented and competing monetary blocs which exacerbated the Great Depression of the early 1930s, and contributed to the social instability which formed part of the backdrop to the First World War.[10] In practice, this premise was translated into a monetary system of stable fixed exchange rates and currency convertibility which facilitated trade between countries. It also prevented the kind of unilateral and competitive currency devaluations which had punctuated and underpinned the Great Depression. The international institutions that developed in the period between the end of the Second World War and the 1970s attempted to manage the orderly international flow of money, goods and technology.[11] In the final analysis, the Bretton Woods Agreement was thus designed to create a new 'international political-economy' which enhanced the control of nation-states over domestic affairs, whilst at the same time facilitating the liberalization of international trade.[12]

Certain areas of the Bretton Woods regime warrant more attention. Under American pressure, Keynes's proposed International Bank became the International Monetary Fund (IMF). In effect, The IMF was an extension of the American Treasury and treated the American dollar, initially backed by gold, as the world's reserve currency.[13] The proposed International Trade Organization was replaced by the General Agreement on Tariffs and Trade (GATT) which had a purely free trade remit. The International Bank for Reconstruction and Development (World Bank), was another key institution of the Bretton Woods system. The other major tools of 'liberal Keynesian' management were taxation, interest and exchange rates. International monetary flows were also strongly regulated in order to deal with balance-of-payments problems and to control longer term cross-border financial transactions. The controls were also used to prevent tax evasion, the cross-border flight of financial capital and currency speculation. In essence, the state, as the main investor and controlling agent of national spaces, used its budget controls as an internal interventionist device to stimulate or deflate cultural-material activities. All of these 'liberal Keynesian' mechanisms were dependent on a stable international financial environment.

The required international financial stability was partially provided by fixed exchange rates pegged to the American dollar. Another important stabilizing factor was linking the value of the dollar to a specific gold price (US$35 an ounce). At that time it was possible to covert the dollar into gold since America then held 67 percent of the world gold stock.[14] Each country's central bank was obliged to defend its own currency's par value to the dollar within a margin of 1 percent above or below parity. In order to maintain stable currency exchange rates and to overcome periodic balance-of-payment deficits the International Monetary Fund (IMF) provided temporary loans to states. In practice this often meant that the IMF returned American balance-of-payments surplus to countries in deficit. Fixed currency exchange rates provided a stable monetary framework which resulted in fixed domestic interest rates. It also enhanced the ability of national governments to implement medium- to long-term policies.

The main post-war international institution organizing the international flow of goods and trade, was the General Agreement on Tariffs and Trade. GATT was established in 1947 by 23 countries and grew to include over 100 member countries at the Uruguay Round of GATT in 1986. Under GATT, the regulation and promotion of trade were guided by the principles of multilateral reciprocity between member countries. GATT members were encouraged to initially restrict protection to tariff duties only, as opposed to quotas and subsidies, and then to seek mutual consensus on the reduction of tariffs. The fundamental aim of the GATT regime was to liberalize international trade based on four basic principles, namely reciprocity, transparency, nondiscrimination, and the organization of periodic negotiations between participating parties in order to further liberalize trade.[15] For example, under the GATT regime American tariffs on industrial goods were reduced from an average of 60 percent in the early 1930s to 4.3 percent in late 1980s.[16] Between 1947 and 1980, GATT agreements reduced tariff rates on trade in manufactured goods by more than 75 percent.[17]

In addition to the four basic GATT principles, the GATT

regime was also premised on two assumptions, namely that a so-called open trading system is more efficient and beneficial than a protectionist one, and that 'national economies' prosper if they concentrate on areas where they have a comparative advantage. However, this form of product and labor specialization is problematic for so-called less developed countries. For example, it means that countries and areas whose comparative advantage comes from cheap labor will concentrate on labor-intensive rather than on high value-added industries. This inevitably locks them into low value-added activities, resulting in a poverty trap since their comparative advantage is dependent on the continuation of relative mass poverty in order to maintain a cheap labor force and stay competitive within the GATT framework. Once conditions and wages improve too much, these areas lose their specific and even sole comparative advantage, resulting in capital flight to cheaper labor destinations. On the other hand, countries and areas with higher labor costs, but capital and technological advantages, are given the opportunity to specialize in more lucrative high value-added and high-tech industries. These anomalies in GATT constructed competition favored asymmetrical core-periphery production and accumulation processes and relations.[18]

Despite the inherent asymmetrical dependency which characterized the 1945-1970s institutions of international trade, these public governance institutions did manage to regulate and control international trade.[19] Generally speaking, the Keynesian model of growth, in combination with the Bretton Woods system of governance, brought unprecedented prosperity and social stability to advanced industrialized countries from 1945 to the early 1970s. However, even in the late 1950s, the major industrialized countries initiated a long-term trend of financial liberalization. This process was incrementally institutionalized from 1961 onwards when the Organization for Economic Cooperation and Development (OECD) adopted the codes of 'Liberalization of Capital Movements' and the 'Liberalization of Invisible Operations.'[20]

By the 1970s the Bretton Woods system came under

increasing pressure as various factors undermined its financial and social stability. This development was a consequence, as well as a symptom of a number of factors which included the following: the formation of a seller's cartel by the Organization of Petroleum Exporting Countries (OPEC), leading to oil price increases from 1973 to 1979; the rise of regional trading blocs that wanted to take advantage of regional 'economies of scale;' the emergence of the European Community (EC) and the Newly Industrialized Countries (NICs) as major players in global production and trade relations; the decline of the comparative advantage of American manufacturing industries and trade relative to those of Japan; and the increased influence of private enterprises, especially transnationals, on social life.[21] The oil price increases in particular threatened to spiral inflation out of control.

During the 1970s America's role in the international financial system changed from a creditor to a debtor. The American federal reserve began to finance American debts by pumping dollars into the market. During this time, the OPEC countries were also dumping their dollar-denominated surplus on international financial markets. These developments contributed substantially to an oversupply in liquid funds which were then channeled to poor and so-called less developed countries, where uncontrollable debt levels were accumulated.[22] All in all, the central aspects of the Bretton Woods system (e.g., strong market regulation by the IMF, a relatively strong American 'economy,' low inflation, and a hegemonic international system dominated by America) diminished during the 1960s until the system collapsed in the 1970s.

Post-1970s developments in global public cultural-material governance

"We are now in production twenty four hours a day around the globe. But this is not only a time phenomenon, it is much more than that. Very often these [dispersed] production sites are very dependent on

Global Exchange Processes

developments in other production sites, and on financial markets, half way around the world. We are thinking more and more of the world as a single production site, today more integrated than our different production sites within this country were ten to fifteen years ago. National boundaries are becoming more and more irrelevant. Today they are only lines on a map. ... As a result, business is no longer business. Fifteen years ago we developed new products, produced them and sold them. When we wanted to enter foreign markets or invest abroad, the politicians negotiated on our behalf. Today we negotiate most of our so-called 'foreign' business without assistance, and without hindrance, from our own and foreign governments. We are now our own politicians, representing our shareholders, and negotiating the best deals for Zem" (Zem manager).

The post-1970s period of the public governance of global cultural-material affairs is characterized by three major interrelated developments and events, namely the deregulation of off-shore money markets; the 1980s monetary crises (including, the new debt politics and the Uruguay Round of GATT); and the emergence of a New Global Financial Environment (including, the composition of the NGFE, and the *pari passu* globalization of money and the valorization of speculation).

The deregulation of off-shore money markets

During the 1950s and 1960s, the international money markets were highly regulated. Monetary markets were dominated by IMF loans, foreign aid and foreign direct investment (FDI), all in the form of American dollars. Over time, the use of the American dollar as the international reserve currency spawned an off-shore market for American dollars, also known as the Eurodollar or Eurocurrency market. Fueled by the Soviet Union's desire to hold dollar deposits outside of America (thus avoiding the possibility that the American government might freeze them) and by the dollars earned in relation to the rising oil prices during the 1970s,[23] this globalized 'stateless' money (i.e., offshore capital) increased in volume from US$7 billion in 1963, to US$50 billion in 1973, to US$475 billion in 1979, to US$2 trillion in 1987, and to more than US$6 trillion in the early 1990s.[24] The American government contributed to the growth of the Eurodollar with the expansion of American military (e.g., during the Vietnam War) and other foreign spending.

The Eurodollar market was partially beyond the control of national governments, including the American government. By converting and depositing their earnings in the Eurodollar market, transnational corporations, for example, evaded the established central bank controls associated with the fixed exchanges of the Bretton Woods system. The growth of Eurodollars relative to American gold reserves eventually became a liability to the American government. In addition, the American Federal Reserve's stock of gold had fallen rapidly as it attempted to support the falling dollar. The scale of central bank intervention required to maintain the fixed exchange rate parity grid proved too large. In combination with the relatively declining competitiveness of American goods and trade, these developments were in the end instrumental to the suspension of the American dollar-gold convertibility in August 1971 by the Nixon Government. This act brought an end to the gold-dollar standard which fixed all currencies to a specific gold value through the American dollar.

The floating of the American dollar against other currencies increased the potential for global monetary instability, as national currencies fluctuated relative to changes in their own and American domestic and foreign affairs.[25] Currencies floating in value relative to each other also contributed to the emergence of overtly speculative money markets. Financial markets and currency speculation, in addition to trade, production and national governments, began to codetermine currency values.[26] The shift from fixed to floating currency exchanges and increased capital mobility resulted in highly volatile money markets during the 1980s. The dramatic growth in the size and the importance of these money markets is most often explained as a result of new risk management strategies by transnational corporations and banks in particular.[27] In contrast to the Bretton Woods system of fixed exchange rates, the stability of the financial assets, profits and borrowings of corporations were now relative to potentially volatile money markets and changes in currency values.

For corporations, such as Zem, floating exchange rates meant that sudden changes in once stable exchange rates could "overnight totally overturn long-term planning as our products became too expensive in export markets, or our labor costs too high, ... or new ventures were no longer viable due to interest rate increases related to exchange rate changes between the [German] mark and the [American] dollar .... This was a forced incentive to companies to diversify their production locations [on a global scale] and to dramatically increase their focus on the management of their money in global financial markets. ... For a century the business acumen of this company was based on technological innovation. Suddenly this was no longer enough. We now had to complement our products with a complex money management strategy that went way beyond the old price-minus-cost-equals-profit or mere interest calculations" (Zem manager). In addition to increased speculative behavior, the deregulation of financial markets also facilitated, contributed to, and coexisted with the growth of global debt, the restructuring of public/private debt relations, and the debt crisis of the 1980s.

The 1980s monetary crises (the growth of debt and the restructuring of public/private debt relations)

The debt crisis of the 1980s was partly due to the surplus of petrodollars which had to be recycled in the 1970s global financial markets. Historically, these surpluses were usually injected into productive activities in advanced industrialized countries. However, at this time many of these countries experienced their worst recession since the 1930s. To some extent, this recession was the result of inflation caused by the higher oil price which led to higher energy prices and, consequently, to increased food and production costs. Consequently, relatively low interest rates yielded negative returns in real terms. At the same time, OPEC states deposited most of their petrodollar surpluses in off-shore banks, thereby significantly expanding off-shore money markets.[28]

New debt politics

Two major shifts in the global financial environment occurred in the post 1970s period in direct response to the above events. Firstly, large surpluses were now controlled by private interests, particularly by private banks who increasingly operated on a global scale.[29] Secondly, with the advanced industrial world in recession, the historic markets for surplus money were no longer viable. At the same time, advanced industrial spaces were less and less dependent on the primary commodities of less industrialized spaces.[30] Under pressure from international institutions and local communities, many so-called Third World governments responded to this situation by embarking on a process of rapid industrialization in the manufacturing sector, and by commercializing their agricultural sectors.[31] In doing so, many so-called developing countries adopted the trappings of industrial development without having the basis (e.g., in terms of skills, infrastructure, markets, etc.) needed to sustain rapid industrial and commercial development. Nevertheless, once 'Third World' governments embarked on this restructuring path, they became dependent on financial support from the public and private financial institutions of the advanced industrial world. Consequently, the 'Third World' became prime markets for commercial banks. This created new dependency relations and increased the control of private capital over African and South American affairs in particular.

During the colonial period African people were unable to exert any real influence over 'their own' or global cultural-material affairs, since they were effectively European protectorates. However, from the 1970s onwards the locus of control shifted more and more from public institutions, which were under the auspices of the governments of the advanced industrialized countries, to private institutions. Official, bilateral and multilateral lending to the 'Third World' was effectively displaced by unregulated, often undersecured and overextended private bank lending. In the early 1970s bank loans accounted for 13 percent, multilateral loans for 33 percent, and effect and export credits for 25 percent of 'Third World' debt. Within a decade, this pattern was reversed with banks holding 60 percent of 'Third World' debt by the end of the 1970s. In the case of Africa, official/public loans fell from 40 percent in 1970 to 12 percent in 1978. All in all, foreign bank and bond financing rose from 7 percent in the early 1960s to 65 percent of all foreign financing in the late 1970s.[32] In real terms, private bank lending to the 'Third World' increased from $US2 billion in 1972, to $90 billion in 1981.[33]

By the early 1980s, the stage was set for a monetary crisis, dominated by two interrelated issues, namely the 'debt crisis' and 'structural adjustment programs.' The unregulated, often undersecured and overextended post-1970s lending to the 'Third World' was the direct cause of the 1980s debt crisis. However, a number of occurrences contributed to the 1980s debt problems. For example, from the late 1970s the American Federal Reserve adopted a monetarist policy of reducing money supply, restricting credit, raising interest rates, and reducing social spending in order to counter the fall of the American dollar against other major currencies. For 'Third World' countries, this meant higher repayments due to increased interest rates, as well as decreased local currency values relative to the American dollar in the absence of fixed exchange rates. Real and potential recession and social instability also made it particularly difficult for 'Third World' governments to reduce social spending. Whilst many of the 'Third World' loans were incurred in order to expand the local public sector, the maintenance of these expanded sectors became very expensive during the 1980s.[34] In addition, higher oil prices accounted for more than 25 percent of the total 'Third World' debt.[35]

The official debt crisis erupted in 1982, when first Mexico, and then a number of other countries, could no longer serve or reschedule their debts. Many 'Third World' countries were caught in a debt trap. Borrowing was no longer a strategy for growth via public sector expansion and export diversification, but a governmental attempt to prevent the collapse of the state and its bureaucracy. Many 'Third World' governments were in a position where they had to incur new loans in order to serve old ones, even devoting new loans entirely for this purpose.[36] For example, during the 1980s Mozambique owed US$929.9 million to the advanced industrialized world. Presently it owes around US$2 billion. This increase is not the result of new debt as Mozambique has effectively been prohibited from establishing new loans, but the result of the accumulated intrest it owes on original loans.[37] During the late 1980s 19 African countries had debt-service ratios of more than 300 percent, with 3 having debt-service ratios of more than 1,000 percent. This meant that these countries had to increase their exports tenfold solely to meet their debt obligations.[38]

As a result of the 1980s debt crisis, it became possible to quantify the money flow between core and periphery spaces more accurately. According to OECD estimates (1990, 1991), the total resource flows to developing countries amounted to $927 billion in the period between 1982 and 1990. This figure includes official bilateral and multilateral aid, grants by private charities, trade credits, direct private investments and bank loans. A substantial proportion of this inflow was not in the form of grants, but consisted of new debt and interest on old debt. For example, during this period, the 'developing' countries remitted a total of US$1,345 billion to their creditors in the advanced industrialized countries in debt service alone. George (1997) argues that even the US$418 billion difference in favor of the rich is understated since it excludes many other macro 'poor-to-rich' outflows, such as royalties, dividends, repatriated profits, and underpaid raw materials.

In order to highlight the extent of these money flows from the 'developing' countries to their creditors, George reasons that by comparison, the US Marshall Plan transferred $14 billion 1948 dollars to war-ravaged Europe, or about $70 billion in 1991 dollars. "Thus in the eight years from 1982 to 1990 the poor have financed six Marshall Plans for the rich through debt service alone" (George, 1997:210). Articulated differently, in the 108 months from 1982 to 1990 debtor countries remitted an average US$6.5 billion in interest payments to their creditors. This amount in interest alone, equals US$1,000 for each person living in North America and Europe.[39] Despite these substantial outflows, the absolute size of the debt burden increased by 61 percent in the period from 1982 to 1990, whilst Sub-Saharan Africa's debt rose by 113 percent during the same period.[40] It is estimated that in 1998 the 'Third World' repaid US$250 billion to advanced industrialized countries, whilst receiving about US$30 billion in public development aid.[41] The general pattern of debt-peonage continues despite some attempts to address it, such as the June 1999 G7 decision to cancel some 'Third World' debt.

The debt crisis, and the development of debt-peonage within an emerging new global financial environment formed the basis for the second major 1980s monetary issue, namely so-called structural adjustment programs, and the general rearticulation of core-periphery dependency relations. Four important aims and practices of 'structural adjustment' measures in general, and the restructuring of the 'Third World' in particular, can be identified. Firstly, there was an emphasis on the control of inflation, especially through increased fiscal austerity, stricter credit control measures and the active intervention of governments to control real wages. Secondly, governments were encouraged and/or forced to reduce governmental and social spending, particularly in regard to reductions in social welfare expenditure. Thirdly, the large scale privatization of the public sector through the selling of state-owned firms, state property and the downsizing of the state was initiated. Fourthly, there was an emphasis on the reduction of restrictions on cross-border financial transactions.[42] These measures have essentially succeeded – so far – in globalizing local production, comsumption and exchange activities.

On a macro level debt and exponential debt profits currently constitute a large percentage of the profits of capital in general and finance capital in particular.[43] The repayment of debt to private institutions places severe restrictions on

'Third World' governments. Nevertheless, most governments today spend substantial amounts on debt repayments. For example, during the 1990s, the American national debt interest payments amounted to more than 20 percent of government spending. During this period, the American federal government borrowed one dollar for every four it spent.[44] In 1980 the debt of American state and local governments totaled US$360 billion, by 1988 this increased to US$759 billion and by 1995 in reached US$1,301 billion.[45] Private, corporate and household debt is presently more than US$31 trillion worldwide, and growing at a compound rate of more than 9 percent per annum.[46] This is three times more than that of the global GDP and global trade.[47] In America, as in many industrialized countries, federal and state goverments and consumers continue to spend more than what they are receiving/earning.[48] For this reason the American Treasury continues to issue securities in order to finance its operations.

The Uruguay Round of GATT (1986-1993)

The Uruguay Round of GATT (1986-1993) was an important monetary and trade event. Whereas previous GATT rounds focused mainly on the free trade in manufactured goods, the Uruguay Round addressed a wider range of trade categories. These included trade in services; banking, tourism, telecommunications; trade related investment measures; trade related intellectual property rights; trademarks, patents; and the trade in agricultural produce.[49] After the conclusion of the Uruguay round of GATT in 1993, the general liberalization of trade functions performed by GATT negotiations, was absorbed into the new World Trade Organization (WTO) which was established in 1995. The Uruguay Round negotiations had a number of important implications for 'Third World' countries, and for the extended global growth of private influences.

In accordance with the GATT principle that 'national economies' prosper when they concentrate on areas in which they have a comparative advantage, American negotiators

Global Exchange Processes

proposed that this should also apply to agricultural produce. In 1986, the American Agriculture Secretary, John Block, argued that "developing countries should feed themselves is an anachronism from a bygone era. They could better ensure their food security by relying on US agricultural products, which are available in most cases at lower cost" (Block, quoted in Atkinson, 1994:7). However, the continued subsidization by the American government of its agriculture produce highlights the anomalies in the free markets of the 1980s. For example, in 1986 America sold subsidized wheat surpluses to West African countries like Mali and Burkina Faso at prices as low as US$60 per ton, which was far below the production costs of local cereals.

Whereas the Uruguay round of GATT addressed some of these anomalies it also created new problems for the estimated 3.1 billion people in the world who live from the land. Goldsmith (1994) argues that if the Uruguay Round of GATT envisaged restructuring is achieved, food prices for urban dwellers would possibly be reduced on a short-term basis. However, according to Goldsmith it would also mean that approximately 2 billion people living from the land would become redundant in the long term, thereby creating mass migrations to urban slums and profound social instability on a global scale.

The impact of the Uruguay Round negotiations on the 'Third World' also extended to tariff concessions and the potential long-term benefits of the liberalization of the trade in goods and services. According to an assessment by the GATT Secretariat, tariff concessions offered at the end of 1993 amounted to an overall future improvement of 38 percent in market access. However, the increased market access for the products of so-called developing countries was only 32 percent, whilst the so-called least developed countries received only 19 percent. The United Nations Human Development Report (1992) estimated that the GATT agreements on tariffs controls would cost 'developing' countries $250 billion or more per annum in lost revenue. The benefits of early 1990s negotiated tariff concessions and liberalization of the trade in goods and services were very unequally distributed. Madden and Madeley (1993) estimated that the 15 percent of the world's population living in the advanced industrialized countries would in the long term obtain about 67 percent of the potential benefits, with 85 percent of the world's population sharing the remaining 33 percent of the trade benefits with the poorest region in the world, namely Sub-Saharan Africa, worse off than before.[50]

There are three general reasons for the disparity between the 'advanced' and 'least developed' countries in relation to the Uruguay Round negotiations, particularly in regard to the poorest continent, namely Africa. Firstly, African farmers are not able to compete with grains and other agricultural goods produced in the advanced industrial countries. This is partly due to the ongoing, and often indirect, government subsidization of agricultural products by the advanced industrial countries, the continued existence of quotas and non-tariff barriers, as well as vastly different production technologies. Whilst the universal reduction of tariff barriers addresses an important aspect in this regard, African countries at the same time lost some of the relative comparative advantages they enjoyed under the Lome Convention of preferential access to the European market.[51]

Secondly, most African countries lack a strong manufacturing base, and consequently require some protection for new manufacturing and service industries in order to be competitive in the selectively regulated global markets.[52] Thirdly, the dynamics of trade and foreign investment between countries and macro regions decisively affect their relative competitiveness, especially in the light of the increased importance of open access to large, integrated and affluent markets such as the European Union.[53] African countries have a very limited influence on these negotiations and consequently struggle to secure access to affluent markets.[54]

These developments in the relationship between the African continent and global capitalism, as well as the particular changes in monetary policies and management, are examples of the changes that shaped the *new global financial environment* (NGFE). The emergence of the NGFE towards the end of the twentieth century is, however, a culmination of developments in trade and monetary exchanges since, at least the 1870s (i.e., in relation to the four periods; 1870-1913, 1918-1939; 1945-1970, and the 1980s) as discussed above.

The emergence of a new global financial environment

The composition of the new global financial environment, and the *pari passu* globalization of money and the valorization of speculation, are two central aspects of the new global financial environment.

The composition of the new global financial environment

The emerging NGFE is characterized by the increased integration of private and public interests and institutions. The major active participants in this public/private hybrid global financial environment are private global enterprises and banks, multilateral financial institutions (e.g., the IMF), multilateral cultural-material agreements and institutions (e.g., the North American Free Trade Association [NAFTA], the European Community [EC], the Asia Pacific Economic Conference [APEC], and the G7),[55] and local and global public institutions (e.g., national governments and the United Nations). In combination, these participants structure the global financial environment and regulate/deregulate the global movement of money, goods, services and labor.[56] Within this new global financial environment, private and public interests are integrated into a complex web of shared influence. During the last part of the twentieth century, governments in the advanced industrialized world attempted to balance their general loss of control over financial markets and other social activities by means of increased integration with other states through bilateral and international collaboration. This strategy is, for example, embodied in the formation and restructuring of the global and regional structures governing global trade. The increased influence of private interests, especially transnational corporations, is arguably the quintessential feature of the new global financial environment.[57]

During the 1980s governments not only changed their policies on Foreign Direct Investment (FDI), but also turned FDI into a competitive terrain as a source of capital and technology. Some of the general changes in regard to FDI regulations include the following: (i) the number of activities and industries closed to FDI, or with major restrictions on FDI, has been considerably reduced; (ii) compulsory joint ventures with governments and/or local private enterprises are now limited to a small number of strategic activities; (iii) the establishment of global legal standards which offers protection to foreign investors, particularly in the areas of expropriation and state contracts; (iv) entry authorization requirements are being eliminated and replaced by registration aimed at facilitating the repatriation of capital and remittances of profits; and (v) fade-out requirements have virtually disappeared.[58] These changes to the management of FDI have led to dramatic increases in FDI. The FDI of transnationals quadrupled between 1985 and 1995, and increased by 40 percent in 1995 alone.[59]

During the 1980s, around 97 percent of all outward direct investment consistently originated from companies 'based' in one of only ten countries.[60] Whilst there were no major changes in the geographical origin of outward direct investment, the geographic destination of FDI has, however, changed considerably. For example, until 1960 the 'Third World' received about half of the total FDI flows. By 1966 this percentage had declined to one third, and to one quarter in 1974. By the late 1980s it had dropped to 16.9 percent, with more than half of this figure going to the regions of East, South and South-East Asia.[61] Africa's share declined to less than 2 percent during the 1990s due to a substantial loss of investment.[62] By the mid-1990s, 91.5 percent of FDI flows went to the more advanced industrialized countries comprised of 28 percent of the world's population.[63]

Generally speaking, investment and trade liberalization, as negotiated mainly through various rounds of GATT and the

WTO, diminished the influence of local policy tools, such as tariffs and quotas. The capacity of governments to protect domestic producers and domestic workers consequently declined. Governments started to compete with each other by offering a range of incentives for businesses, such as tax cuts, export subsidies and a plethora of short-term production and business-enhancing schemes. For example: the French government subsidized a quarter of the cost of the recently developed Mercedes-Benz plant in Lorraine; Mercedes-Benz paid about 55 percent of the start-up costs for a new plant in the comparatively poor state of Alabama; and the American electronics corporation Advanced Micro Devices received DM800 million, or 35 percent of the outlay costs, from governmental subsidies for a microchip factory in Dresden.[64] Governmental subsidies to private corporations is not a new development. However, current state incentives to private corporations tend to be more short term and hands-off. Furthermore, state incentives are informed by global competitive factors and the global mobility of corporate business.

The growth in global money markets constitutes an important aspect of the current denationalization of exchange activities. This development is particularly observable in the changes that occurred in exchange activities over the last twenty years. In this period, the international financial structure changed from a series of nationally-based credit systems, linked through the buying and selling of credit across nationally controlled exchanges, to an integrated global system.[65] Whilst exchange controls still exist in many countries, their administration presently follows the logic of the global market and the practices of transnational enterprises, rather than the letter of local laws since money, in a variety of guises, straddles across national boundaries.[66]

Without exception, interviewed Zem managers regarded the skillful management of the 'gray areas' between governmental regulations and company objectives as an important part of their international business success. These 'gray areas' were mostly defined as protectionist laws that still exist, but may not be enforced by governments, or that could potentially be circumvented by transnationals. A Zem manager articulated these issues as follows. "Politicians and bureaucrats in almost all countries in the world are today faced with the reality of the global economy. This gives them an insight into the problems, and potential solutions, of their own economy. They know that they have no choice but to open their economies to multinationals. Without the money and technological investments of multinationals in their economies they will perish. ... Their biggest problem is often to convince their population of this reality. Knowing that they cannot succeed in doing this they leave protectionist laws on the lawbook, but they do not enforce those laws. The contracts between multinationals and governments are so complex the general population in any case do not understand them" (Zem manager).

The importance this so-called gray area of governmental regulations and laws regulating transnational transactions is particularly transparent in the light of increasing world trade in relation to world production since the Second World War. For example, in the period from 1950 to 1975, the volume of world production increased by 220 percent, whilst world trade expanded by about 500 percent during those years.[67] In 1965, the total value of global exports was US$94 billion; by 1986 this had increased to US$1,365 billion. This growth was fueled mainly by the trade and production activities of transnational enterprises.[68]

The technological barriers to foreign direct investment and transnational transactions in general have largely been broken down during the 1990s, thereby making it more difficult for national governments to control the transnational flow of money, goods and information. In addition, many of the traditional domains of state intervention were undermined by the increased global interconnectedness and its control by private enterprises due to accelerated technological advances (e.g., in the transportation and mobility of goods, services and communications) which made trade over long distances and across national boundaries easier, faster and cheaper, and more difficult for national governments to manage. The latter is especially the case with regard to the exchange of informational and financial products.

New technologies currently facilitate the dissemination of detailed information to every financial center around the globe in real time. This leads to the integration of almost all major financial and banking centers into a single financial network. At the same time, contemporary money flows are not only more global, but also more autonomous *vis-à-vis* the actual performance of so-called national economies, as the control of the movement and value of currencies are increasingly controlled by a new breed of global financial specialists, consisting of the financial analysts of major banks, transnationals, pension and mutual funds.[69]

The *pari passu* globalization of money and the valorization of speculation

Under Fordism surplus monetary values were mostly created in heavy industries and agriculture. In many advanced industrial spaces the primacy of heavy industries and agriculture to surplus creation is declining at present. For example, according to the chief executive of Siemens, Heinrich von Pierer business at Siemens is no longer dominated by production, as was the case up to a few years ago. "Today, software, engineering, and services are the backbone of our business – and the key to success. They already comprise over 50 percent of our value added – and the share is steadily growing" (Von Pierer, 1999:11).

The decline of the primacy of production activities also coexists with the increasing centrality of the fiscal structure through which monetary values are created, realized and generated. In addition to the changes in the functional operation of financial markets, the forms, margins and locational position of surplus within the commodification cycle (i.e., production, exchange, consumption, appropriation and accumulation) are changing at a rapid pace. One of the areas in which this change can be observed is the emergence of speculative trading and speculative lending.

A combination of various factors contributed to the increased valorization of speculation. They included: (i) excess capital due to monetary surpluses, such as the 1970s petrodollars; (ii) a dearth of traditional investment opportunities due to decline in the profitability of projects during the 1980s recession in the advanced industrialized world; (iii) the over-production of mass products,[70] (iv) the deregulation of financial markets; (v) the monetization of more and more social exchanges; (vi) the extension of valorization activities beyond the production and marketing of goods,[71] as well as the related increased creation, realization and generation of monetary values in both the pre-dominantly value adding (i.e., so-called production) and mainly monetizing (i.e., so-called exchange) spheres of activity; and (vii) technological developments which engendered a vast range of financial innovations, including the evolution of more and more valorization opportunities at the intersection of exchange and consumption processes through speculative trading and other electronic exchanges.

Electronic valorization (i.e., the electronic creation, realization and generation of monetary values) takes place mainly through the trade in currencies, equities, bonds and derivatives. Between 1980 and 1990, the volume of cross-border transactions in equities grew at a compound rate of 28 percent per annum, from US$120 billion to US$1.4 trillion. International bank lending increased from US$324 billion to US$7.5 trillion, and the international bond markets rose from US$259 billion to US$1.6 trillion.[72] From 1980 to 1992, the size of world financial markets increased threefold to an estimated US$43,000 billion per day.[73]

Presently, more than a trillion dollars of currency exchanges flow through the electronic arteries of the global financial network every day. This is more than the total foreign exchange reserves of all the major central banks in the advanced industrial countries.[74] Up to 40 percent of the profits of the ten largest 'American' and 'British' banks are today derived from trade in currencies and securities (i.e., stocks, bonds and options).[75] The daily volume of foreign exchange trading now exceeds the volume of traded goods at a ratio of 100 to 1, with the gap widening by about 10 percent per annum.[76]

The financial innovations of latter part of the twentieth century were essentially due to technological advances. However, the impetus for these technological developments came from the need of global financial institutions and transnational enterprises to protect themselves from the rapid changes in interest and exchange rates during and after the 1980s, as well as by their endeavors to circumvent state regulation in financial markets more easily and profitably.[77] Corporations employ various risk management strategies, such as hedging and securitization, in addition to derivative transactions, production loci diversification and offshore capital management in order to intervene in volatile money markets.

The standard characteristic of a hedge fund (e.g., the establishment of a contract in which there is a commitment to buy or sell currency at a specific price, regardless of the exchange rate on the day the contract is signed, or on the day it takes effect) is that it attempts to neutralize market risk by buying and selling at the same time. Whilst minimizing risk is central to hedging, it, nevertheless, creates additional speculative opportunities and valorizable risks in the money market. Speculators buy or sell so-called forward contracts. The profit, or loss, made with these contracts is, for example, dependent on changes in the relevant exchange rates.[78]

During the 1990s there has been a massive increase in transnational liquidity, the separation of financial flows from exchanges in goods and services, and finally to altered forms and margins of profits. The differentiation within global markets has blurred the financial activities of banks, insurance enterprises, security dealers and transnationals. Insurance and capital market activities are also taking place in an ever closer proximity to each other, especially in 'alternative risk transfer' (ART) activities, such as finite risk contracts. Similarly, mutual and pension funds are bypassing securities firms and are making direct equity investments. In addition, the digital transfer (via fibre optical cable or satellite) of goods such as software programmes, information, music and videos direct from their producers to end users who pay digitally, lead to new forms of personal disintermediation[79] of the industrial financial chain.[80]

The financial operational strategies of transnational corporations illustrate the convergence of traditional risk transfer, traditional financing, insurance activities and capital markets. While they are still producing and trading goods, they are also operating as quasi financial institutions. Similarly, their profitability and survival is also increasingly dependent on global financial markets, and on the financial management of their assets in these markets. So-called non-financial institutions now overtly focused on monetization management as a major area – to complement, or even supersede, the traditional production of goods – in which monetized surplus could be created, realized and generated. The transnational corporation Siemens, for example, earned more from its financial transactions than from its acclaimed products during the 1990s.[81] In the past, the ascendancy of financial engineering *vis-à-vis* classical productive engineering was most often seen to be an indicator of the decline of the specific industry. This is no longer the case.

A Zem manager articulated this general trend and the shift in the relationship of exchange *vis-à-vis* production processes in relation to transnationals as quasi financial institutions, as follows. "Not long ago [circa fifteen years] the profitability of our business was mainly dependent on our products and our business acumen in the production of goods. ... Financial markets, and the management of our funds in financial markets, are now an equally important aspect of our business. Often it is better for us to invest our money in financial markets than in production plants" (Zem manager). The ways in which transnationals now operate as quasi financial institutions are also illustrated by their debt management strategies. For instance, in the past transnationals tended to finance their debt and growth mainly through bank loans.

Presently, they increasingly borrow money through the issue of equities, with banks underwriting share issues. The process of loan selling in which the payment of debt is underwritten, is called securitization. In essence, securitization enables financial and 'non-financial' institutions to trade in debts and debt payments as they convert relatively illiquid assets into tradable securities.

A similar process of financial restructuring characterizes the forms of long-term capital raising used by corporations by means of issuing debentures (i.e., bonds traded on the open market without specified collateral or assets as a mortgage, but secured by all the unencumbered assets of the issuer) instead of bank loans. As corporations became less dependent on commercial banks for their short-term financial needs they are able to operate with much lower current ratio's (i.e., current assets divided by current liabilities). For example, in the 1960s it was thought that the current ratio of a corporation should not be less than 2:1 or 200 percent, since this level of liquidity allowed for substantial billpaying ability even if major debtors or customers failed to meet their obligations promptly. Presently American manufacturing corporations operate with a current ratio of 1.40 or even lower.[82] These kinds of strategies increase both financial risks and the importance of financial management.[83]

Trading in derivatives has risen enormously since the early 1980s. In 1986 the total outstanding value of derivatives markets was about US$1 trillion; a decade later this amount had risen to about US$20 trillion.[84] Derivatives include various financial instruments which acquire their value from underlying securities such as bonds, bills, foreign currencies, bank deposits, futures, forward contracts, options and swap contracts (i.e., the exchange of one type of loan, such as a fixed interest rate loan, with a floating interest rate loan). The complexity of derivative transactions has also increased. For instance, in September 1999 the Chicago Mercantile Exchange started to trade weather-linked derivates (to protect individuals or companies against adverse weather) with values varying with the temperature as measured by an index of warmth in the four largest American cities. An estimated US$4 billion of weather-related financial deals were concluded over the past few years.[85] In some financial markets, futures trading now outstrips trading in the underlying cash security.[86]

The role of futures markets for non-financial organizations can be observed in the way gold-mining companies are affected by the current gold price crisis. For example, during 1999 the spot price for gold was around US$270 per ounce. Many gold-mines could not extract gold at or below this price. However, by not selling on spot markets, but selling forward using futures markets to hedge production, many gold-mines continued to operate profitably. For example, the Australian gold company Sons of Gwalia has not sold gold on spot markets for 10 years. Whilst the gold spot price was below US$300 per ounce, Sons of Gwalia was delivering at US$650, Ross Mining at US$530, Newcrest at US$633, Normandy at US$596 per ounce during the first quarter of 1999.[87] Smaller gold companies usually do not have the same access to hedge tools due to financial restrictions, resulting in gold companies delivering gold at dramatically different prices due to their financial management strategies.

Complex derivatives transactions have led to some spectacular financial disasters during the 1990s. In 1995, for example, Orange County, California lost US$2.16 billion on interest-rate derivative contracts entered into by its treasurer (Robert Citron). Similarly, in 1995, a 233-year-old British merchant bank, Barings, collapsed because of the activities of a single trader in Singapore (Nick Leeson), who lost US$1.78 billion with options on the Japanese Nikkei Index. In 1996, the Japanese trading company Sumitomo lost US$3.3 billion through the electronic gambling activities of one trader (Yasuo Hamanaka).

The electrification of the contemporary techniques, forms and patterns of valorization affects not only global corporations and direct investors (e.g., shareholders in transnationals, banks, etc.), but also a large section of the so-called working and middle classes, whose shares, savings, investments and pension funds increasingly flow in the electronic arteries of the global financial system. For instance, in the mid-1970s, 75 percent of private savings in the United States were held in savings accounts or fixed-interest securities. By 1985, bank deposits had declined to 50 percent,[88] and presently about 75 percent of savings are invested on the Stock Exchange.[89] Whilst stockmarkets have an inherent element of risk – in reality no form of investment is without risk – the limited liability aspect of stock is a key factor in both the organization of contemporary corporations and the management of surplus money owned by individuals. Corporations are organized as legal persons, entering into contracts and taking on debt in their own name. Should a corporation fail to meet its obligations, it may go bankrupt. However, the corporations' owners (i.e., the stockholders) are not liable for any debt incurred. The shareholders loss, and thus risk, is limited to the amount paid for their shares, leaving their other assets untouched.

Contemporary speculation also extends beyond the neo-classical areas of speculative trading, such as the Stock Exchange, as there is a movement of productive capital into fictitious investment based accumulations, such as real estate, currencies and art. For example, at the Kasumigaseki Country Club in Japan, golf membership fees are about US$2 million. This amount is based on the present trade value, and members generally agree that it is far above the real value of the membership.[90] The present trade value is primarily based on the same principle which dominates speculative trading in general: borrowing occurs at very low rates – if possible – in order to make investments against the often inflated value of a specific investment. The expectation is that the appreciation (i.e., the trade value at a specific moment in the future) of the investment would be faster than the combination of inflation and the cost of the borrowed money. If this is the case, the difference between the appreciation value, inflation and interest on the borrowed money, constitutes the profit.[91]

The general movement of savings, investments and pension funds into the spheres of global speculation alter the pressures for 'financial globalization' (e.g., maintaining liberal and deregulated markets for finance and trade). These pressures reside not only within the dominant fractions of corporate capital with overt global interests. They also stem from a broad spectrum of the population in the advanced industrialized world whose money circulate in global financial markets.[92] The electrification of valorization processes affects the short-term financial viability, employment compositions and labor relations of transnational corporations. For example, on the day BHP announced the planned restructuring and downsizing of its Australian steel works with a loss of at least 8,000 jobs in 1997, the markets responded and the market value of BHP immediately increased by AUS$1 billion.[93] Whilst it is clear who the winners (shareholders) and losers (workers) are, neither party is forced, or has the opportunity, to confront the other.

Money, profits and social destituteness are all increasingly virtual and faceless entities. For those who participate, directly or indirectly, in the global financial markets there is no longer a need to retain money as a productive commodity within the social relationships of the nation-state. Exchange activities are increasingly oblivious to the historical constraints of time and space on monetary flows. This contributes to the transition of money from a fetishized productive — mostly national — resource, as was the case during the phase of regulated and nationally controlled currency markets, to a fetishized post-national commodity in itself. This solidifies the global interests of those individuals who participate in global financial markets, and undermines the national sovereignty of states as money is no longer retained as a productive resource within the social relationships of the nation-state.

The denationalization and globalization of money contribute to the privatization of the self interests of those who participate in the global financial markets.[94] For these 'global insiders,' national and geographical monetary solidarity is becoming obsolete and dysfunctional. The solidification of global financial participants by money as a fetishized post-national commodity is one of the consequences of the social transformation of money.[95] For example, the IMF (1991) estimated that individual investors from the so-called Third World have invested an estimated $165-200 billion dollars in the global financial markets between 1975 and 1985 alone. Given a choice, these people will rather invest in the global markets than in their 'own' national markets or 'own' national productive activities.[96]

The incessant increase in the number of people in advanced industrialized spaces owning equity in listed companies, is not only a symptom of the changing patterns of personal financial management, but also of the creation and concentration of wealth and financial authority. For example, an investor who correctly perceived the trend towards fast food consumption and bought 100 McDonalds' shares in 1965 for US$2,250, would have owned 37,180 shares worth US$1700,000 by 1995 if the investment was left untouched for 30 years and all dividends were reinvested.[97] Even more dramatic, an US$20,000 investiment made in 1992 in AOL, Dell or Nokia would have increased to US$1000,000 in only seven years. However, these kinds of statistics hide the concentration of wealth. For example, although more than 40 percent of Australians now own shares, 90 percent of shares are owned by the richest 10 percent of the population and almost two-thirds of this 90 percent is owned by the richest 1 percent of the population.[98] Wolff calculated that 86 percent of the total profits made on the financial markets since the early 1980s is concentrated in the hands of 1 percent of the population.[99]

The financial markets also restructure financial authority through a variety of more and less complex practices, such as through different classes of shares and weighted voting rights. For example, the Ford Motor Company has two classes of shares and whilst the Class B shares owned by the Ford family and certain key officers constitute only about 6.4 percent of the shares with voting rights, these shares are weighted to allow them to control about 40 percent of the votes. If the shareholders then vote as a block, as they always do, it becomes highly unlikely that the vast majority of other shareholders could determine a different policy direction.[100]

Despite these statistics the general simplification, level of sophistication and partial democratization of participation in the state-of-the-art spheres of capitalism cannot be denied. During the unfolding of Fordism, entrepreneurs such as Henry Ford had to develop innovative new products, establish new production methods, create new consumer needs, etc. in order to be successful. For this reason, very few people could actively participate as entrepreneurs in the state-of-the-art spheres of capitalism at that time. This is no longer the case. Today about anyone (irrespective of age, or gender, or intellectual capacity, or work-ethic), with some or a lot of surplus or borrowed money, can – merely with a modem and a mouse click – be part of the state-of-the-art spheres of capitalism and wealth creation. Seen in this contexts, the electronic valorization of speculation is a modernization process *par excellence*.

Conclusion

"The truth is that there is no longer any such thing as money. At least not in the sense required by monetarism and its siblings" (The Economist, 19/9/92:30).

In this chapter some of the central twentieth century developments in the internal and global dynamics and management of monetized exchange processes were outlined. Particular attention was given to the developments that constitute and shaped the post 1970s. Overall, a new and important subsystem of global financial management, organized by and around currency markets, has emerged in response to financial deregulation, the partial demonetization of gold, the end of fixed currency exchanges, disintermediation, the opening of domestic financial markets and currencies, and new computer and information technologies. The increasing gap between profits in the production of goods and services, and rents generated in the sphere of circulation, facilitated important shifts in mainstream investment strategies and the movement of world savings into global and electronic financial spaces.

Monetized exchanges have been an important part of

modernity ever since money was exchanged for goods centuries ago. Later money, especially surplus money, was also exchanged in relation to production and accumulation processes. In other words, inactive capital was transformed into active capital as deposits were recycled by financial institutions as loans, which, in turn, were used in the production of goods. During the latter part of the twentieth century monetization became a valorization activity in itself, as one form of money is now sequentially exchanged for other forms of money (e.g., in currency and derivative transactions) in global financial markets. These sequential transactions, in which money is created, realized and generated *en masse* in the processes of electronic and virtual money circulation, are part and parcel of the hypermodernization of risk. Whilst money itself is a symbol and a tangible form of the systematic standardization of social exchanges, contemporary valorization processes have made risk – as, for instance, a tradable commodity in derivative transactions – an intrinsic part of the monetization of social exchanges.

The sequential, rapid and electronic circulation of money also valorizes time in new ways. A significant portion and growing number of financial transactions (e.g., futures, options and derivatives) are based on the principle of capturing future time in present transactions. These new financial innovations increase the mass of nominal capital *vis-à-vis* bank deposits and assets so dramatically that there appears to be an abstract digression of time and money in which future money is indeed created, realized and generated by time, as well as by the virtual circulation of money.[101] These electronic valorization processes are taking place regardless of the traditional restrictions of space and time through the skillful manipulation of the intersections of real and virtual spaces, times and monies by electronic entrepreneurs.

Managing and understanding global financial flows and their impact on social spaces and peoples, is arguably one of the most complex and difficult tasks facing politicians and social theorists today.[102] The evolution of systematically standardized monetized exchanges has expedited trade between localities across space, standardized exchanges over time, transformed work into wage labor, and generally solidified the emergence and development of the modernist epoch. Only time will tell whether the current wave of changes in monetary exchanges will result in similarly profound repercussions for the organization of future social life.[103]

The changes in monetized exchange processes and relations are perhaps the most unequivocal indicators of contemporary globalization. The emergence of fetishized electronic capital, electronic valorization, the amplification of risk, electronic entrepreneurs and the current forms of valorization, as well as the electronic virtualization of monetary surplus are some of the most important, and far-reaching, social changes of our time. It could be argued that the gravity of the globalization-valorization-marginalization triangle today resides more and more in the valorization sphere. It also stands to reason that the increased monetization of the social world has a significant impact on the modernist landscape, and that the contemporary techniques, forms and patterns of valorization are instrumental to the increased market-interceded rearticulation of global social relations. These issues are addressed in the following chapters.

Chapter 2
The Organization of Production Processes

"By means of electricity the world of matter has become a great nerve, vibrating thousands of miles in a breathless point of time" (Hawthorne, 1851, quoted in the Australian Financial Review, 16-17 January, 1999).

At the beginning of the twentieth century, the principles and practices of the scientific management movement, generally referred to as Taylorism and Fordism, dramatically restructured the organization of production and of the workplace in Europe and America.[1] Taylor (1964) argued for a greater technical division of labor by fragmenting the production process into its component parts. The aim was to simplify job descriptions by reducing shopfloor activities to a single, simple, repetitive and low knowledge task. Taylor divided the work tasks of each worker into the smallest identifiable operational components, then, using a stopwatch, measured each task to ascertain the best possible time attainable under optimal performance conditions. This calibration of worker performance focused on even the most minute aspects of performance. In order to save as much time as possible, work tasks were also structured to confine the movement of workers, keeping them stationary and reducing pockets of non-productive time. In addition, organizational autonomy was removed from the shopfloor by introducing hierarchical organizational and management structures. Taylor argued that the greater specialization and the deskilling of workers would increase efficiency, reduce labor costs and undercut the negotiation power of workers. Ford (1923) further rationalized work organization by introducing mechanized mass production. This led to dramatic increases in productivity and in the volume of mass produced standardized items.[2] Under the Fordist production regime, work and production were organized around the semi-automatic assembly line, fixed-purpose machinery, and producer networks clustered around heavy industries with large concentrations of semi-skilled workers.

The organization of the production processes of twentieth century global capitalism has been pivotal to the ways in which resources, goods and work were systematically standardized and valorized. In combination with hierarchical global divisions and supply zones for both labor and raw materials, the specific Fordist technology and labor regimes formed the backbone of global capitalism throughout this century. However, since the 1970s the Fordist backbone has become brittle, particularly in the advanced industrialized world. This chapter deals with some of the important contemporary changes related to the reorganization of global production processes. Particular attention is given to: drastically reduced product development time and product life cycles; the ascendancy of automation technologies; and the proliferation of corporate strategies and new management theories in relation to the global repositioning of organizations.

Drastically reduced product development time and product life cycles

"This company has changed more in the last three years than it did in theprevious 50 years" (Heinrich Von Pierer, Chief Executive, Siemens in the Financial Times, 20/4/98:8).

Until the 1970s new product development tended to be a linear, stage-by-stage and cumbersome process characterized by a lengthy time-lag between technological innovations and the full-scale production of a product. For example, whilst the electrical engine was developed in the 1880s, it only really had an impact on productivity from the 1920s onwards.[3] Presently the effective time needed to develop, manufacture, market and use a product, and the conventional time-lag between technological innovations and the full-scale production of a product has declined substantially. Current product life cycles have been reduced from a human generation cycle (e.g., model T-Fords) during the first half of the twentieth century, to years, months, and even days. Contemporary electronics, in particular, facilitate multi-dimensional, precipitative product, and 'stage-in-stage' development and production processes. A Zem manager described 'stage-in-stage' production processes as "the separate, but simultaneous development of several stages as several engineers in different locations work independently on smaller parts of a bigger project integrated by our computer network" (Zem manager).

The post 1970s implosion of production time was essentially a consequence of accelerated technological developments, including mechanization and automation, within production processes. These technological advances were, however, also driven by important changes in the social architecture of the Fordist regime. Throughout the twentieth century Fordist technological advances and production gains were related to, and driven by, changes in the patterns of mass consumption. Fordist growth and expansion relied on a symbiotic relationship between simultaneous increases in mass production and mass consumption. The specific distribution of surplus between capital and labor was crucial to the expansion of manufacturing activities. Absolute profits thus co-existed with the diffusion of relative surplus to labor.

Fordist mass commodification processes[4] were furthermore underpinned and sustained by the monetization of many social exchanges, by middle- and working-class patterns of mass consumption, as well as by high levels of income security (and thus employment) and relatively high wages. As such, mass-production as a profitable undertaking relied on the extraction of relative surplus value in the production of goods, and the creation of surplus in 'economies of scale.' Within this framework, production cost per unit is relative to the quantities produced in standardized mass production processes.

On the one hand, this mass-production system is dependent on the continuous and uninterrupted expansion of market demand for the same product in order to compensate for increased labor productivity and technological efficiency. On the other hand, this kind of mass-industrial production does not cope well with cyclical recessions, increased competition, product diversifications, nor with changing market demands. The demand for a greater variety of diversified and customized goods, as well as increased 'reflexive consumption practices' (Lury, 1996) in specialist market niches, meant that consumer needs became unpredictable in terms of quantity, quality and content from the 1970s onwards. These changes in the social architecture of Fordism meant that single purpose production equipment became too slow, too rigid and too costly in relation to the consumption needs of their prime markets.

The importance of speed in product development and manufacturing cycle increased particularly since the mid 1980s. For example, in 1985 more than 50 percent of the worldwide sales of the transnational company Siemens came from products and systems that were more than five years old. Ten years later in 1995, two-thirds of the company's worldwide sales came from products and systems less than five years old.[5] Within Zem a corporate strategist estimated that from the year 2000, approximately 80 percent of Zem manufacturing employees will produce products requiring different, or even very different, skills within cycles of around, or less than, 3 years. Based on these kinds of estimates, another Zem corporate strategist reasoned that if Zem were to stop all research and development of new products for a twelve-month period, approximately 50,000 Zem employees world-wide would lose their jobs during the following year. This would be the result of the redundancy of their current activities and the lack of new activities based on new product lines. The general compression of product life cycles, and the specific *need for speed* in production processes are central to the current ascendancy of new kinds of automation technologies.

The Organization of Production Processes

The ascendancy of automation technologies

"The initial cost of developing fully automated systems used to be uneconomically high. New computer technologies are making this a financial possibility. The obvious benefit of full automation lies in the reduction of our labor requirements, especially of workers in non-managerial positions. ... Full automation will, however, also enable us to develop totally flexible manufacturing systems. ... In other words, we will improve our performance to both our shareholders and to our customers" (Zem manager).

The technological reorganization of work through labor-saving technologies has been central to capitalism since its inception. Corporate strategists most often explain the contemporary developments in labor-saving technologies, and 'productivity-through-automation,' as strategies to deal with the "excessive labor market regulations and wage rigidities" (Zem corporate strategist). This notion of politicians 'forcing' companies to reduce the relative size of the labor force in advanced industrialized spaces via automation and spatial reorganization, permeates most of the articulated 'productivity-through-automation' and 'core-de-industrialization/periphery-industrialization' logic within Zem. Consequently, Zem corporate strategists and managers most often argue that the 'excessive labor market regulations and wage rigidities' made them, and other companies, reluctant to increase their labor force, especially in Europe. "For us to increase our productivity we had to develop very expensive technologies in order to reduce our European labor costs. .... Without these excessive regulations we would have created more jobs and less technologies" (Zem corporate strategist).

This automation rationale underlies other, almost identical strategies which are used under very different conditions. For example, the manager of an African textile mill explained the automation strategy as follows: "[It is] because African labor, unused to industrial work, would make mistakes, whereas automated machinery does not make mistakes. The quality standards demanded today are such that my product must be perfect to be able to find a market. Surely my task is to

81

eliminate the human factor" (Anonymous African textile mill manager, quoted in Lang and Hines, 1993:77). Even in the poor South African village of Spoegrivier, the majority of small farmers (i.e., any person with access to some land to grow produce or owned more than 5 cattle, or 10 sheep/pigs, or 100 chickens) indicated that the increased mechanization and partial automation of their activities was the single most important issue affecting their abilities to produce a surplus. "At the moment I am too poor to afford to hire a tractor. This means that I and three helpers plough the land with donkeys. ... We also harvest by hand. This is a lot of work. Sometimes one of my helpers is sick, or lazy, then we cannot do much. With a tractor I can plough all my land myself at the optimum time because it all happens within a day or two of good weather [the first good winter rainfall]. With the hand we still plant three weeks after the good weather. Often this is too late, and we get a small crop. ... And at the end of the day I must still pay my three helpers as well. That is why I have nothing left for myself. ... Access to tractors and other machines are the only way I can produce more, without having to divide my income" (Spoegrivier farmer).[6]

Throughout the historical development of industrial capitalism automation strategies attempted to surplus by systematically reducing the real and potential costs of human labor relative to production output. The current emphasis on automation strategies within transnational corporations is a result of: the increased global spread of production facilities which accentuates the need for standardized technology; the increased technical complexity of valorization processes which reduces the influence of mass labor *vis-à-vis* sophisticated technologies and virtual resources such as time; and low global interest rates compared with generally high labor costs, making equipment cheaper relative to labor. Present automation strategies are furthermore characterized by three important objectives, namely: (i) to reduce the bargaining power of labor *vis-à-vis* capital; (ii) to reduce the size of the labor force *vis-à-vis* productive output; and (iii) to develop new 'technologically created' products.

Reducing the bargaining power of labor vis-à-vis capital

Technological advances continue to contribute substantially to the restructuring of work relations. The automated enhancement and fragmentation of production processes, and the superior speed of Technological Production Process Innovations (TPPI) relative to retooling practices are two of the most important developments in this regard. The automated enhancement and fragmentation of production processes are characterized by contemporary automation technologies which engender new forms of production process flexibility. Examples in this regard include, programable machines that control their own operations, and the ability of management to centrally control and electronically monitor labor functions and task performance. Companies are continually experimenting with new methods to optimize the interface between employees and their work tools, such as computers. For example, in order to maintain and increase the speed of work tasks, companies can, and often do, program visual displays to give the operator a specific time limit to complete the task before it disappears, or is recorded. Consequently, operators experience increasing levels of stress when the time limit approaches. "From the eleventh second [for a task programed for seventeen seconds] they begin to perspire, then the heart rate goes up" (Rawlence, 1985:39).

The automated enhancement and fragmentation of production processes are also characterized by the well documented general reorganization of work processes into smaller and semi-autonomous work groups which often leads to increases in worker autonomy and self management in certain areas of work.[7] However, the reorganization of work into smaller and semi-autonomous work groups have also resulted in a selective decline in human-centered forms of team work and the fragmentation of the functional organization of workers as a working collective and/or as a working class.[8] The *pari passu* increases in both worker autonomy and management control/worker disorganization have led Kotthoff

(1998) to argue that contemporary work practices constitute a form of 'selfdirected Taylorism.'

The superior speed of TPPI relative to retooling practices is a new and unique feature of work reorganization that emerged during the 1980s. In the past, both technological innovations and retooling practices had been incremental procedures. In contrast, contemporary technological innovations occur at such a rapid rate that incremental retooling practices are often an expensive option compared to the development of a completely new production site. The tempo of change in technological inputs renders single-purpose production equipment more and more obsolete and provides corporations with unprecedented process flexibility. New production sites most often allow corporations to simultaneously reduce their labor component and the collective organization of workers by closing a site with collectively organized labor, and by opening a new site where workers are employed on individual contracts. The threat of plant closures, accompanied by the technical and financial advantages of new plant developments elsewhere, also increased the relative competition between governments in order to lure companies to their countries or cities. This means that transnationals can confidently negotiate with governments for tax reductions, subsidies, and low-cost infrastructures.

A Zem manager argued that the present technologically induced movement flexibility of transnationals decreases the abilities of national governments to act parochially and unilaterally. "In the past, new site developments were most often too expensive in relation to the upgrading of old sites. Now new technologies often make upgrading too expensive in relation to the development of a new site. ... This has an important consequence for the way we do business. For example, why should we pay forty percent tax [in Germany] if we can pay ten percent in Ireland. ... No, this does not mean that paying tax has became a voluntary activity. It only means that the days of governments expecting big companies to bankroll their ideological fantasies are over. ... The fact is that companies are undermining these national ideologies. We

[Zem] are becoming more globally orientated and we [transnationals in general] are forcing political leaders to accept that all people – irrelevant if they live in Europe or Asia or wherever – should have equal access to compete for jobs" (Zem manager). In general, the speed and scope of technological innovations relative to retooling practices, as well as the new technologically induced movement flexibility of transnationals, expands the options open to corporations *vis-à-vis* collectively organized labor and decreases the state's control of production processes.

Reducing the size of the labor force vis-à-vis *productive output*

The social foundations of industrial labor processes and relations developed *pari passu* with European colonialism. Colonial rule transformed the social organization of production and social exchanges. Subsistence networks were smothered by the extensive disposition of indigenous land, and by new monetary exchanges and taxes, forcing peasants to grow cash crops in order to, for example, pay their taxes.[9] These displacements provided the core with urban and settler-controlled colonial wage labor forces. Within Europe a similar, but less violent and more subtle process of peasant displacement took place. Later, during the growth phases of Fordist industrialism, urbanization supplied an optimum mixture of varied skilled, cheap and surplus labor. Presently, increased levels of urbanization and the changing needs of commodified production, have led to large-scale redundancies and unemployment in urban centers around the world.[10]

Current mechanization and automation strategies need to be evaluated in the light of the global unemployment trends, whilst also taking into consideration the population projections for the first 20 years of this century. The inclusion of a high proportion of the world's population into the orbits of global capitalism provides it with billions of potential workers, as well as with billions of potential unemployed workers. This could jeopardize growth and social stability. In the early 1990s, the global labor force stood at 2.8 billion people, which is about half of the total population of the world. Of the 2.8 billion people, about 800 million (30 percent) were not productively employed, and more than 700 million were underemployed.[11] According to Simai's (1995) analysis of the population projections of the United Nations, the number of people in the working age group will increase by 1,360 million people in the years up to 2010. Of the total increase, only about 60 million (i.e., less than 5 percent) will be in the so-called developed world, with 1,300 million people (i.e., more than 95 percent) in the so-called developing world.

If current levels of employment, underemployment and unemployment were maintained over the next twenty years, the relative number of people underemployed and unemployed will increase by about 30 to 40 million people per year. In real numbers, this would mean a 50 percent increase over the next 20 years. However, current trends and projected trends in both the 'developed' and 'developing' parts of the world suggest that even maintaining present employment levels in the foreseeable future could be a very difficult task indeed.[12] Agriculture technologies, particularly in the 'developing' world, have the potential to radically restructure the global work force by increasing the relative percentage of unemployed people. For example, farming mechanization and automation in core industrial countries led to the reduction of the farming population from approximately 60 percent in the 1850s to less than 3 percent in the 1990s.[13] Almost half of the world's population still makes a living by farming the land today. The livelihood of a large section of these currently productively engaged people is threatened by mechanization and automation.[14]

The dynamics and various aspects of global capitalism (e.g., the increased technological valorization of more and more social activities) contribute to the unabated mass urbanization, the productive redundancy of many people, and substantial changes to the patterns of productive redundancy in the late twentieth century.[15] The South African village of Spoegrivier is a micro example of these phenomena in a 'Third World' contexts. The percentage of Spoegrivier residents primarily and actively involved in agricultural activities was about 70 percent in the late 1960s. Whilst 77 percent of these people were strictly speaking unemployed, they were, nevertheless, actively absorbed into the productive spheres of rural agricultural activities when they became temporarily or permanently redundant in the industrial sector. By the mid 1990s the percentage of people actively involved in agricultural activities had declined to 26 percent of which only 19 percent were strictly speaking unemployed. Technological developments as simple as a tractor, hired from white farmers, meant that whilst production increased, the reserve army of labor was no longer absorbed into productive activities, and consequently suffered a much greater social dislocation. In the 1960s less than a quarter of unemployed people were not absorbed into rural productive activities; by the 1990s this figure rose to more than three quarters of the unemployed. As a result, the experience of unemployment in Spoegrivier was very different in the 1960s compared to the 1990s with regard to social integration *vis-à-vis* social dislocation, and in terms of exclusion from active participation in productive activities.[16]

In addition to the impact of technological advances on rural and subsistence agriculture communities, some important changes in the general patterns of urban unemployment can be observed. During the last three centuries, those laborers who were displaced by new technologies were mostly absorbed by new emerging sectors. This does not seem to be the case today. Currently the only important emerging new sector is the small so-called 'knowledge sector.' This sector consists mainly of a small group of industries and professional disciplines related to new high-tech, high-skill and selectively automated activities. Rifkin (1996) extensively analyzed the developments in this sector over the last two decades. Rifkin argues that whilst the numbers of these so-called symbolic analysts or knowledge workers (from the fields of science, engineering, management, consultancy, teaching, marketing, media, and entertainment) will continue to grow, their absolute numbers will remain small "compared to the number of workers displaced by the new generation of thinking machines" (Rifkin, 1996:35).[17]

In contrast to the period from the 1960s to the 1980s, the service sector is also no longer absorbing the large numbers of workers who became redundant in the industrial sector.[18] On the contrary, even within the service sector, computer-based and telecommunications processes, accompanied by electronically integrated work, exchanges and consumption practices, drastically reduce the human labor component. For example, in advanced industrialized spaces electronic banking and other changes in commercial banking endanger the immediate employment of 30 to 40 percent of workers in this service sector.[19] As the real costs of automation technologies, and their costs relative to labor costs, continue to decrease, automation technologies seem likely to substantially increase unemployment and underemployment in the foreseeable future as automation technologies continue to decrease enterprise's relative dependency on labor in general, and on mass labor in particular.[20] Furthermore, it is often those people who are socially the most vulnerable, such as unskilled and underskilled workers, women, migrants, blacks and peasants, whose job categories are most affected by automation technologies, thus exacerbating their marginalization from productive and social activities.[21]

The development of new technologically created products

New real and virtual transport, communication and information technologies, such broadband fiber optics, are central to the reordering of the dominant production processes. Extended and sophisticated communication networks are not something new *per se*. The Mongol Yuan Chinese dynasty of the fourteenth century operated an extensive message network involving 70,000 people and 40,000 horses. In the eighteenth century, the French constructed an optical telegraph network, using visual signaling with telescopes. In the same era, Russian technologies could relay messages over a distance of over 1,100 mph within two hours.[22] The major breakthrough with regard to speed, accuracy, volume capacity and the spatial reach of communications occurred with the progressive advent of electricity and electronics. As information technology developed certain work areas and work processes were automated through the rationalization of simple tasks, as was the case with batch-processing automation.

Until the 1970s, robotics electrified specific areas of the production process. However, these areas were isolated within certain parts of the production cycle. Presently, the chain of electrification extends throughout production cycle as companies automates accounting, manufacturing and inventory control.[23] It also engenders its own products by transforming knowledge and information into products and raw materials for both mass and specialized consumption.[24] The emergence of information as a product and a raw material is a consequence of a fundamental change to the role of information in the production process, as well as in the relationship between information and technology.

Contemporary information technologies consist of the integration of two originally distinct technologies, namely communications technology (i.e., dealing with the transmission of information) and computer technology (i.e., dealing with the processing of information). Consequently, information-saturated automation processes are no longer restricted to discrete tasks, nor are they exclusive to certain parts of production processes. The entire idea-design-development-production-marketing cycle is now rationalized, primarily through the information of work practices and the relative increases in the knowledge component of work processes. Within these 'work informating processes' (Zuboff, 1988) large quantities of previously unavailable information are created, distributed and utilized by organizations.

The linear structure of the idea-design-development-production-marketing cycle, characteristic of Fordism, is becoming obsolete as multi-dimensional 'stage-in-stage' and precipitative product development processes become more prevalent due to: the increased real time integration of information from different and spatially dispersed sources; the standardization of the physical and technological languages of information (i.e., English and computer languages respectively); and the advent of information as an important raw material in production processes, especially in high-tech industries.[25] The dramatic increases, standardization and real time dissemination of knowledge and information, also make it possible for corporations to redeploy their production activities in a more geographically dispersed manner, whilst maintaining rigorous quality controls.

A Zem manager articulated the general implications of the new techniques of the production cycle for Zem as follows. "From the initial assessment of the needs of the customer to the final product delivered and installed used to be a very stretched-out process with many separate stages and many people working on the project one at a time after each other. One broken link in the chain could delay the process since nobody really knew at which of the twenty odd stages the project was at any one time. This is the way in which our organization used to operate, and it is still the way in which the majority of our employees think – linear stages, not integrated processes. The cultural revolution in Zem is to use the available information technology and new management strategies to eliminate linear stages, to make the relevant information available to all people participating in the integrated process of product definition, realization and marketing at all times. ... The standardization of technical communication through information technology enables us to have highly productive cross-functional teams, and to replace separate linear stages with a single integrated process. Sales representatives and software developers, for example, can now productively communicate and even understand each other" (Zem manager). Overall, developments in computer automation technology have made a major contribution to organizational restructuring, the proliferation of corporate strategies and the global repositioning of private enterprises.[26]

The Organization of Production Processes

The global repositioning of organizations

"I use the term [globalization] because I don't like the word multinational ... If it means a company with many nationalities then that is not Sony. Sony is global" (Morita, Sony executive, quoted by Cope, 1990: 53).

The above developments in the production dynamics of advanced industrialized spaces proceeded *pari passu* with the growth of global corporations and the proliferation of new corporate strategies and theories used by corporations in order to manage their global activities. Since the mid 1980s transnational corporations directly or indirectly control the following activities on a worldwide basis: about 30 percent of the gross domestic product of the world's market spaces; more than 25 percent of the world's activities aimed at commodified trade outside their so-called home countries; between 50 and 70 percent of the world trade in manufactured goods and in services; and about 80 percent of the world's cultivated land where crops are grown for export. In addition, transnational corporations control approximately 80 percent of the trade in technology and the overwhelming majority of world technological innovations. Currently, the world's 15 largest transnational corporations have gross incomes that are larger than the GDP of the poorest 120 countries. More specifically, the largest 300 transnational corporations account for 70 percent of the total FDI and about 25 percent of the world's capital. In monetary terms, 51 of the world's 100 largest 'economies' are today private corporations, accountable only to their shareholders as transnationals are able to exert enormous influence over labor, the state and the international state system. [27]

Transnational corporations not only exert an important influence on global technological and production processes, they are today also shedding their national and transnational identities. A Zem manager articulated the increased detachment of transnationals from nationalist projects as follows. "Sixty years ago the German government and

91

German people expected from Volkswagen, BMW, Mercedes Benz, and so on, to be German companies. ... After the war, up until the late 1970s, the government, the company, our workers and Germans in general, expected us to play an active role in the German economy and German community. For the management of Zem, this was both a business and a moral issue. ... In my office [during the 1960s] there was a sign stating that our two most important responsibilities were towards Zem and our community, meaning our German community. How true this was I do not know. But we believed in it. It influenced the way we did business. ... Today? Today our responsibilities are towards Zem and 'yourself'. Neither the company, nor the workers feel morally responsible for a local or a German community. The company and the workers look after themselves, and that is similar for companies and workers not only in this country, but all over the world" (Zem manager).

The changes in the self-perceived identities of corporations, as well as the rearticulation of their relationships and moral responsibilities towards national collectives and the communities in which they are based, dramatically affect the way transnationals approach exchange processes.[28] In the words of another Zem manager: "[w]e no longer calculate shareholder value only in Deutsche Marks, but in dollars, yens, pounds, marks, etc. We provide our shareholders, so to speak, with a voucher. It is up to the shareholder to decide what currency they will exchange this voucher for, and where they will invest or spend the money. ... The days of this company thinking in terms of the DM [Deutsche Mark] are over. Our interest in exchange rates are today purely for business reasons – and business has no nationality" (Zem manager).

The perception and reality of business globalization inform the ways in which private and public organizations more overtly reinterpret their identities *vis-à-vis* the spatial dynamics of the global social environment. In particular, the interrelationship between *the local* and *the global* is today becoming both more obvious and tangible, as well as more elusive, fragmented and contested. In addition, it is also increasingly beyond the control of collective institutions, such as the state and trade unions. Organizations cannot escape from these general social spatial changes as the operational infrastructures of organizations are integrated more comprehensively into global networks. The organizational identities of corporations and the corporate world in general are today saturated with the ambiguous semantics, and the real and virtually fragmented boundaries, of local and global spaces.

A post-1970s semantic genealogy reveals part of the paradigm shift that occurred as those organizations operating across national borders, evolved from international, to multinational, to transnational, and finally to global enterprises. This does not mean that private global enterprises now have homogeneous global identities. Even within the same corporation, organizational identities vary across space and time. The public image of organizations has become more overtly and proudly local (e.g., Australian) and at the same time, more overtly and boldly global. The specific emphasis on either of these electives depends on aspects such as their target markets, local legislation and product specifications. In the global media, the connection between the local and the global is often made through the careful use of semantics in relation to the target audience and nationalistic undertones. For example, Newsweek once carried a cover story in America called 'Japan Invades Hollywood,' with the Statue of Liberty clad in a kimono. In the Pacific the headline of the same issue read 'Japan Moves into Hollywood,' whilst in the Japanese-language edition the same story was called 'Sony Marches into Hollywood.'[29]

Another important aspect influencing the global repositioning of organizations, is the changing context in which the interface between the state, local conditions and private enterprises takes place. This 'production influence triad' has been extensively problematized by social and business analysts in recent times. Generally speaking, these analysts can be divided into two categories. Porter (1990), for example, argues that the state and local conditions continues to

Globalization for Sale

be pivotal, even paramount, in relation to the influences of the global operations of private enterprises. This category will be referred to as the 'context scenario.' The other school of thought (e.g., Ohmae, 1990) asserts that the center of influential gravity within the 'production influence triad' increasingly resides in private enterprises. This category will be referred to as the 'private enterprise scenario.'

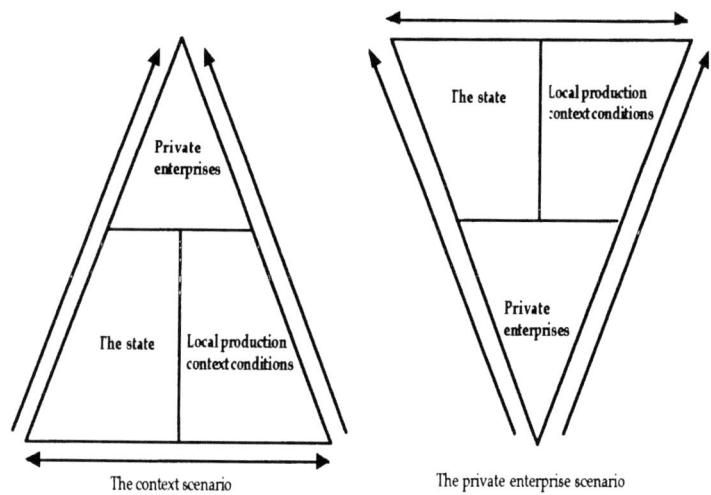

The production influence triad

Porter's (1990) work focuses on competitive advantage as defined by the relationship between transnationals and their 'home' environments. For Porter, the increased globalization of business enhances, rather than deflates, the importance of nations and the local national environment. Porter argues that it is the national business environment which determines the competitive advantage of corporations. Porter's argument is based on two premises. Firstly, that the performance of corporations is decisively influenced by the nation-state as the primary supplier of infrastructure, and the main regulator of markets, financial market conditions, financial flows, taxation policies, and legal rules.

The Organization of Production Processes

Secondly, Porter reasons that domestic conditions have a dramatic impact on the global competitiveness of a corporation. These conditions include local factor costs, cultural resources, work practices and technical skills, as well as quality of home demand, the intensity of domestic competition, and the geographical concentration of competition. For Porter, the geographical concentration of rivals in a single city or region exacerbates competition, forcing low cost and product innovations. Examples given by Porter of geographical competition concentration include Italian jewelry firms in Arezzo and Valenza Po, cutlery firms in Solingen (Germany) and Seki (Japan), pharmaceutical firms in Basel (Switzerland), motor cycle and musical instrument firms in Hamamatsu (Japan), minicomputer firms around Route 128 in Boston (America), and advertising agencies in Madison Avenue, New York (America). "In such an environment, popular luncheon spots are patronized by executives from several companies, who eye each other and trade the latest gossip. Information flows with enormous speed. Though any one firm must move fast to sustain its advantage, the whole national industry is dynamic and sustains, or even widens, its advantage over foreign rivals who lack the same structure. Domestic rivalry not only creates advantages but helps to avoid some disadvantages" (Porter, 1990:120).

Porter's research illustrates that national boundaries, laws and regulations indeed continue to substantially influence the global activities of transnational corporations. As such, national governments and local social environments continue to play an important role in shaping global capitalism. Porter's research also highlights the contradictory elements, due to paradoxical global and national forces, present in the processes of denationalization in which transnationals engage. As a result of the interplay of these contradictory elements, corporations tend to have a chameleon national/global identity. For example, during the 1980s the advances in computer aided design and manufacturing technologies made it profitable for transnationals in certain industries, such as electronics and textiles, to relocate some of their activities back to their 'home' countries. However, this has been a very limited practice, influenced by a variety of other factors such as taxation rates, collective bargaining (or the lack thereof), subsidies, etc. In addition to these specific issues, Porter outlines the ways in which transnational corporations continue to psychologically and sociologically 'belong' to their home base, despite the global reach of their operations. For Porter "social and political values and norms are linked to nations and slow to change. ... [In the final instance it is thus] the combination of national and intensely local conditions that fosters competitive advantage" (Porter, 1990:158).

Porter's work has made an important contribution to the reassessment of social and cultural factors impacting on global capitalism. However, a major weakness of Porter's work is the atheoretical conceptualization of an ideal-type state consisting of a conglomerate of bureaucratic structures. States, as organizational entities, are embedded in the dominant social practices and relations of their space and time. An understanding of the operation of the state is dependent on much wider frames of reference, the influence of external social forces and the active social agency of the state in relation to other institutions and social actors.[30] A second limitation is the a priori acceptance of competition as an inherently positive value without serious consideration of the related social, moral and environmental costs which accompany it under certain circumstances. In general, 'contexts' protagonists do not problematize the impact of private enterprises on national and social environments. It is on this aspect, which is discussed in the next section, that 'private enterprise' theorists tend to focus.

The global restructuring of firms and the increased influences of private enterprises

It is difficult to isolate the relative influences of the state, local conditions and private enterprises in a meaningful way. Nevertheless, at least five major trends can be observed. These trends contribute to the global restructuring of firms and the increased influences of private enterprises *vis-à-vis* the influences of local conditions and collective organizations, including the state.[31] These trends relate to: the relationship between transnational enterprises and so-called national economies; the declining importance of variable-costs and 'economies of scale;' transnational labor reorganization; the decline of absolute location in relation to relative location; and the ways in which organizational space is managed in relation to other corporations.

The relationship between transnational enterprises and so-called 'national economies'

The current global spread of transnational enterprises makes it difficult to draw a meaningful distinction between the nationality of the ownership, including the work force involved with value-adding activities, or the nationality of the beneficiaries of specific value-adding activities. It has thus become less relevant to analyze transnational enterprises as national entities (i.e., as an American, Australian, German, Japanese, etc. company). The relationship between the national identity, ownership, and production, profit and tax locations are increasingly polylithic. For example, Ohmae (1990) argues that it is very difficult presently to classify corporations in terms of rigid national criteria. "Is IBM Japan an American or a Japanese company? It's work force [in Japan] of 20,000 is Japanese, but its equity holders are American. Even so, over the past decade IBM Japan has provided, on average, three times more tax revenue to the Japanese government than has Fujitsu. What is its nationality? Or what about Honda's operation in Ohio? Or Texas Instruments' memory-chip activities in Japan? ... What is the nationality of these products or of the operation that makes them?" (Ohmae, 1990: 10).[32]

Juergen Dormann, the chairperson of the world's largest chemicals company, Hoechst, argues that Hoechst is "not merely a German company with foreign interests, one could almost say we are a non-national company" (Dormann, quoted in The Asian Wall Street Journal, 21 February

1997:24). According to Dormann there is today very little German left in Hoechst since "... our biggest single market is the United States, our Kuwaiti shareholder holds more shares than all our German ones put together, and our research area is international"(Dormann, quoted by Martin and Schumann, 1997:128).

The nationality of the beneficiaries of specific value-adding activities is also increasingly clouded with anomalies as manifested in developments such as the calculation of trade deficits. For example, in the early 1990s more than one-third of Taiwan's trade surplus with America came from the activities of so-called American enterprises, exporting goods from Taiwan to the United States.[33] A former Japanese prime minister, Yasuhiro Naka, once responded to American concerns about its trade deficit with Japan, by urging all Japanese to buy $100 of American goods. However, the majority of 'American' goods in Japan are produced in Japan, Taiwan, Hong Kong, Europe, etc.[34]

The decline in the importance of variable-costs and 'economies of scale'

In general, companies are today no longer technically or financially able to develop and keep all technologies inhouse as, for example, General Motors did in the 1930s and the 1940s. The augmentation of potential global markets and areas of profitable valorization has also altered business strategies in general and competitive strategies in particular. Consequently corporations are moving away from a variable-cost environment which emphasized the cost reduction of inputs, such as materials and wages. Instead, there is a tendency to focus more on a short-term fixed-cost environment, which accentuates the importance of sales and product distribution, exchange and electronic valorization networks.[35]

The interrelatedness of interfirm technological dependency and global market augmentation constitutes the rationale for cutting edge technological development co-operation between Zem and some of its most prominent rivals. "Within an

The Organization of Production Processes

environment which I will call overnight innovation and overnight reverse engineering joint [interfirm] R&D [research and development] carries fewer risks than going it alone. ... Furthermore, in most cases there is today such a fast potential market for the right product that it is better to hit the target [develop a 'right' product] and share the profits, than to develop many wrong [commercially not viable] products. No single company can today satisfy demand of a widely wanted product. ... Over the last one hundred years the potential market of [the products] of our company grew from a couple of thousand people to millions – say fifty years ago – to billions today. That is globalization. ... So, what I am saying is that there are two main factors that contribute to our need, and willingness, to share R&D. Firstly, it is the only way we can stay at the cutting edge of new innovations. Secondly, our potential markets are today so vast that we can survive and even flourish more if we had fifty similar size competitors world-wide. In contrast, after the war [Second World War] a handful of companies [such as ours] satisfied demand" (Zem manager).

Most managers within Zem's high-tech businesses consciously subscribe to the notion that competitive interfirm co-operation stimulates innovation and the market simultaneously. The perception is that co-operation between researchers from different 'national and corporate cultures' lead to the development of more globally generic products. At the same time, it is assumed that the increased competitive focus on certain high-tech products will lead to more demand, especially if the social environment is bombarded with advertising and ideal high-tech mediated lifestyle projections. It is difficult for individual companies to create the proliferated technological interfaces with other products, the social needs for these products, as well as to promote the lifestyle of that product in isolation from other companies. For example, the direct competitors of, for example, McDonalds (e.g., Burger King, KFC, Hungry Jacks, etc.) inadvertently benefits from McDonalds advertising since the latter not only promotes specific products, but also specific lifestyles.

The interrelatedness of technological interfirm dependency

and global market augmentation has made the national measures of concentration and market share less relevant to business success. As a result, transnationals today are less concerned with seeking resources, and show a declined interest in 'economies of scale,' especially as a *global digitally networked economy* leads to 'diseconomies of scale.' Instead, transnationals seek to capture the 'economies of integration, differentiation and diversification' as they become more interested in strategic assets in the context of a global diasporic production environment.

Transnational labor reorganization

Transnational labor reorganization is an important part of the social architecture of competitive forces in the production cycle. The global reorganization of production loci places transnationals in an unrivaled position relative to labor as the latter category is unable to organize itself globally at the same rate and ease as transnationals. For example, the new Jaguar X400 will be built in Halewood/Merseyside (England). This decision was made by Ford, the owner of Jaguar, after they negotiated more than 50 million British Pounds of public subsidies for the 400 new jobs (plus some more in the supplier industries), and several concessions from the trade unions. The context for these negotiations was set a year before they started when Ford shifted the production site of the Escort model from Halewood to the Ford plants in Belgium and Spain, causing 1,300 layoffs.[36]

The geographical movement of labor and global employment compositions is indeed a major consequence of the internal re-organization of private enterprises. For example, in 1994 Hoechst employed 172,000 workers worldwide, of which about 47 percent (80,000) were based in Germany and approximately 53 percent (92,000) were based outside of the 'home country.' Within three years this changed dramatically. Hoechst now employs 150,000 workers worldwide. Only about 30 percent (45,000) are based in Germany, and approximately 70 percent (105,000) are employed elsewhere.[37] These

The Organization of Production Processes

examples are by no means isolated cases, but symptomatic of a general global trend as more than a third of the 300 largest transnational enterprises now produce more than 40 percent of their output from foreign subsidiaries.[38]

The decline of absolute location in relation to relative location

The increased active and often real-time global co-ordination of production has resulted in a situation where relative location (i.e., how an enterprise is connected to the global network of production, distribution and consumption), becomes more important than actual or 'absolute location' (Brunn and Leinbach, 1991). The global reorganization of the division of labor and product configurations are particularly observable in the partial de-industrialization of the core in relation to the selective industrialization of certain parts of the periphery. The emergence of new and cheaper centers of production as major competitors went hand in hand with the partial demise of the manufacturing sector in core spaces since the 1970s. For example, while manufacturing was responsible for 24.5 percent of Australia's GDP in 1969-1970, by 1990-1991 it only accounted for 14.5 percent of GDP.[39] Importantly, this decline is relative to the phenomenal pace of industrialization and growth in manufacturing jobs in areas such as the Asia-Pacific region.[40] These new centers of manufacturing often 'outperform' the traditional manufacturing centers in many areas of mass production in regard to competitive cost advantages.

The traditional distinction that existed between central plants with advanced/dominant production configurations (e.g., relatively high levels of R&D and technological innovation, new and specialized products, high wages, relatively stable and transparent employment relations, etc.) and peripheral plants with shoestring copied/submissive production configurations (e.g., relative low levels of R&D and technological innovation, older and non-specialized products, low wages, mostly heterogeneous and opaque employment relations, etc.), is indeed changing at a rapid rate in many corporations.[41] In the words of a Zem manager, production facilities in the old periphery no longer "play in the second league that only recycle our dated European ideas, products and methods. ... Our people no longer go to Asia to teach them how to do things, but to learn from them, to bring innovative ideas back to Germany" (Zem corporate strategist). Within Zem the current wave of spatial and internal organizational restructuring is characterized by an emphasis on the global synchronization of production configurations across the traditional core-periphery divide.

The global co-ordination of productive activities not only includes the global organization of production plants, but also transnational mergers, acquisitions and collaborative ventures involving so-called foreign direct investment (FDI). More than half of the world's commercially traded goods and services now depend on global planning, design, production and marketing strategies.[42] These global strategies are essentially a response to changes in the structure and balance of production costs. For example, changes in design and technology brought about substantial savings in communications and transport, amounting to approximately a 40 percent relative saving on raw materials in the period from 1974 to 1984.[43] There has also been a substantial reduction in the cost of transmitting information during the latter part of the twentieth century, making it more accessible to a wider network of users. For example, the annual cost of an Intelsat telephone circuit was more than US$60,000 in the 1960s; in the 1980s, it was US$9,000, and by the 1990s it had dropped to less than US$5,000.[44] These input cost reductions coexist with the present escalation of research and development expenses. This increases the imperative to spread the cost of research and development between sector related firms through mergers or less formal links, such as strategic alliances.[45]

The ways in which organizational space is managed in relation to other corporations

The final consequence of the global reorganization of

production for transnational enterprises relates to the management of the corporate organizational space in relation to other corporations, as companies redefine their identities and operational strategies. In general, the global repositioning of private enterprises is essentially a movement away from an incipiently local or national self identity. Beyond the self identity and the articulated public image of companies – which are dependent on, for example, marketing strategies – lies the reality of simultaneous and often contradictory connections to various local and global spaces. In general, three forms of contemporary management of organizational space can be identified: interfirm co-operation, intrafirm competition/ collaboration, and suprafirm collaboration.

Interfirm co-operation

There are two basic types of competitive advantage: lower cost and differentiation.[46] A lower cost strategy focuses on reducing the design, production, and marketing cost of a product comparable to those of its competitors. Selling the product at a similar price to its competitors means that lower cost translates into superior returns. Korean steel and semiconductor producers are good examples of this strategy. Essentially, these enterprises produce comparable products at very low cost. This is achieved by employing low-wage but highly productive labor and advanced process technologies, purchased or licensed from foreign suppliers. A differentiation strategy focuses on a variety of provisions, such as a unique product (e.g., Kao), special features (e.g., Apple computers), superior value (e.g., Toyota), outstanding product quality (e.g., Mercedes Benz), good and responsive after-sale service (e.g., Nilfisk), or aggressive marketing (e.g., Nike). High prices are demanded for these differentiated products and services. If costs are comparable to those of competitors, profitability levels increase.[47]

Presently, transnational enterprises seek to spread the development costs of products, speed up the development process and reduce the turn-around time of the idea-design-development-production-marketing cycle. This enables transnationals to gain a competitive advantage by combining both 'lower cost' and 'differentiation' in selective competitive co-operation strategies. A Zem manager articulated the importance of selective competitive co-operation strategies to the reduced product-development-time and product-life-cycle environment as follows. "We are increasingly having less time to develop new products. As a result, we now often have to work closely with our competitors in developing new products at an accelerated rate, and in developing new markets. This means that our competitive advantage margins are getting smaller and smaller" (Zem manager).[48]

Interfirm co-operation strategies are central to re-organization of organizational space. Corporations form new strategic alliances in order to maximize profits and to reassert their control over their organizational spaces and spheres of influence. These strategies include interfirm strategic alliances and networks, strategic alliances built around supplier-client relations, joint ventures and mergers, as well as new sourcing strategies (e.g., global sourcing, out- and insourcing). Strategic alliances may include joint ventures for a range of purposes, including new product development, marketing agreements and subcontracting arrangements. It is not always easy to distinguish between alliances where there is no, a minor or a major equity cross-ownership. For example, whilst General Motors owns Opel, it continues to publically manage Opel as a separate entity whose public identity continues to be an extension of its own historical identity. Prominent examples of strategic networks areas include the airline (e.g., British Airways-Qantas; KLM-Northwest-Air New Zealand; Ansett-Malaysian Airlines-South African Airlines-Lauda Air; etc.), automobile (e.g., Ford-Mazda; etc.) and telecommunication (e.g., Deutsche Bundespost Telekom-France Telecom; etc.) industries.[49]

In the period before the 1990s, most forms of interfirm co-operation were based on practices such as the formation of cartels and other oligopolistic agreements. In contrast, present co-operations are much more specific in terms of target products, markets and processes, and they include competition in areas which may not be specifically covered by the agreement. Consequently, specific interfirm co-operation does not entail the end of competition between the firms involved.

A Zem manager articulated this phenomenon as follows. "Working closely with your strongest competitor [in a strategic alliance] can be nerve-racking, but this is often your best chance to leave the rest of the competition far enough behind for both of you to prosper in that area [of the new product]. Working with a strong competitor in one area on a specific product might also help you to understand the strategies, work practices, culture, etc. of this competitor better. This understanding can help you to outcompete them in other areas. Or for them to outcompete us. This is the law of the free market; the strongest survive. ... Even in showing your willingness to co-operate with them, you intimidate your competition" (Zem manager). Given the focus on research and development, many joint ventures are concentrated in high technology industries. However, in addition to technology development and acquisition motives, joint ventures are also driven by competitive commercialization factors. These factors include access to new markets, increased market concentrations, decreased product development and turn-around time, the sharing of costs and risks, the expansion of product portfolios, and the circumvention and satisfaction of local laws and requirements.

In general, five types of new strategic organizational network restructuring can be identified.[50] Firstly, there are producer networks which include arrangements that enable competing producers to combine their production capacities, financial and human resources in order to expand their product portfolios, customer base and geographic coverage. Secondly, customer networks are established and include the linking of manufacturing companies with distributors, value-adding resellers and end users. Thirdly, standard coalitions are used by firms to lock-in other firms, including potential competitors, into their proprietary products and interface standards. Fourthly, technology co-operation networks are created in order for companies to gain access to various technologies, and to share the costs of developing new products. Fifthly, supplier networks are formed between the focal company and its suppliers. These networks include subcontracting, OEM (Original Equipment Manufacturing) and ODM (Original Design Manufacturing) arrangements.[51]

Unlike smaller firms, larger transnational enterprises are most often able to subcontract more effectively on a global scale. Global subcontracting and outsourcing to enterprises based on the island of Saipan, in the Philippine Sea of the Western Pacific, is an example of these practices. The Commonwealth of Saipan is an American territory and the islanders are American citizens. In the early 1980s, new American federal rules for the garment industry allowed for duty free, and virtually quota free, imports from Saipan into America. Enterprises with subcontracting operations in Saipan include Arrow, The Gap, Montgomery Ward, Geoffrey Beene, Liz Claiborne, Eddie Bauer, and Levi Strauss. Whilst these exports make up only a small percentage of all clothing imports into America, they, nevertheless, account for roughly 20 percent of sales of some large American clothing companies. Saipan is exempt from American federal minimum wages, yet its products carry a legitimate 'Made in USA' label.[52]

The case of Nissan Motor Manufacturing (United Kingdom) is a further illustration of the current subcontracting and outsourcing practices in a specific company. In the past, Japanese companies have often been accused of establishing 'screwdriver' manufacturing plants outside Japan. These plants relied heavily on parts imported from Japan, but were able to circumvent import restrictions since the imported parts were used in local manufacturing processes. As transnationals became less dependent on 'boosting production at home,' both in real and imaginary terms, the nature of direct foreign investment changed considerably. By 1994, the local content (i.e., European Union) of Nissan's new product ranges increased from 60 percent in 1988, to 80 percent in the United Kingdom. Nissan's Sunderland plant now uses 197 European

The Organization of Production Processes

suppliers, accounting for an average annual expenditure of £850 million. About two-thirds of these suppliers are located in the United Kingdom, with other major component suppliers based in other European countries, such as Germany, France and Spain.[53] Furthermore, Nissan UK is now the United Kingdom's largest car exporter, exporting over 80 percent of its annual production to more than thirty countries, including Japan.[54]

Intrafirm competition/collaboration

The next area of the reorganization of corporate organizational space, consists of intrafirm competition and intrafirm collaboration. Two of the most important forms of these practices include the deconstructed conglomeration of large companies, and specific global insourcing strategies. The deconstructed conglomeration of large companies is an extreme example of a form of intrafirm strategic alliance. The major advantages of these practices include labor, sourcing and production flexibility, as well as increased tax mobility. Asea Brown Boveri (ABB), a so-called Swiss-Swedish company, is the world's largest power-engineering group and an example of a global deconstructed conglomerate. ABB has annual revenues exceeding US$30 billion from its circa 1,200 'companies.' Each of these 'companies' employs about 200 people. In the process of deconstruction, the headquarters staff in Zurich was reduced from 4,000 to less than 200. Around 90 percent of ABB sales are generated from outside the host countries.[55] For CEO Percy Barnevik, ABB is not a global business, but "a collection of local businesses with intense global co-ordination" (Barnevik, quoted in Naisbitt, 1994:14).

Specific global insourcing strategies constitute the second form of contemporary intrafirm competition and intrafirm collaboration. Global insourcing strategies have two main purposes. Firstly, they aim to optimize production costs through the global segmentation of the different production spheres according to local cost, skill, efficiency, infrastructure and available technology. The conceptualization, design, financing, manufacturing and distribution of single products are consequently more and more strung together globally.[56]

The second main purpose of insourcing relates to the 'international' manipulation of costs and profitability levels in order to take advantage of differences in national tax systems and special national tax reduction incentives. This is achieved through, for example, 'transfer pricing,' where subsidiaries, branches and departments trade with each other in un- or semi-finished products, services, royalties, licenses, etc. Since no comparable market prices exist for many of these items, subsidiaries, branches, departments and even other firms, are able to vary the costs to one another substantially. As a result, the expenditure of corporations tends to be the highest in high tax rate countries, and high profits are moved in such a way that they are 'based' in low tax rate countries. For example, whilst the car manufacturer BMW does not produce cars in Belgium it now makes up to a third of its total profits in Belgium, which has relatively low taxes compared to Germany.[57]

Within Zem, tax transfer practices are also used to shift costs to businesses, such as R&D (Research and Development), which qualify for tax reductions or subsidies. A Zem manager explained this particular insourcing strategy as follows. "In the case of specialized and customized high-tech products a high portion of the costs relates directly, or maybe indirectly, to R&D, for which some government assistance is sometimes available" (Zem manager). With specialized and/or small batch products or components, it is often very difficult to establish the boundaries between R&D and production costs. This provides businesses, inadvertently, with some "leeway to make optimal use of the tax incentives" (Zem manager).

Suprafirm collaboration

The third area of post-1970 reorganization of corporate organizational space management consists of suprafirm collaboration. This kind of collaboration often defies existing organizational patterns and legal systems. The contemporary forms of countertrade are examples of suprafirm collaboration. This practice refers to sets of cross-border contracts, linking a seller's exports to imports from the buyer, and covers activities ranging from direct exchange (e.g., barter) to long-term buyback contracts. Countertrade transactions can usually proceed immediately, making speed – saving time – a major advantage of this practice.

One of the common features of countertrade deals is their complexity, as illustrated by the following examples cited by Kreinin (1993). "ICL, the British computer manufacturer, provided components to Poland for building portable televisions to Western European standards and then acted as a sales agent for the TVs in the West. The Poles then purchased ICL personal computers in kit form with the hard currency received for the TV sets. These machines were customized for the Polish market and sold locally for zlotys, which were then used to subsidize production of more televisions that ICL sold in the West. 3M Corporation set up a Swiss subsidiary to negotiate deals with Eastern Bloc countries. The proceeds from selling 1 million dollars' worth of Polish nails were deposited in a Western bank and the Polish government drew on the account to buy 3M healthcare products" (Kreinin, 1993:104).

Corporations engage in countertrade for various reasons. It allows them to circumvent credit and foreign exchange controls, and to alleviate shortages of foreign exchange reserves. At the same time, firms gain access to otherwise closed markets, and are able to hide price cuts and/or inflate sales. Countertrade also enables them to disguise business agreements, or a certain part thereof, as prices need not be made explicit in the contract. In this way, discounts, special offers, and trade violations (e.g., anti-dumping, fair trading practices or national or United Nations trade sanction laws) can be concealed.

Overall, the dominant organizational model of large, vertically integrated firms is being superseded by more decentralized internal/external networks and strategic intra- and interfirm alliances. In the context of the contemporary global repositioning of corporations, the organizational space of corporations has been re-articulated via project specific conglomerates, which include strategic alliances, interfirm networks and an expanding number of contingency interfirm relations and co-operations. Flexible organizational spaces constitute an important strategic variable and a critical vehicle for gaining a competitive advantage in global markets. Strategic alliances, and the various forms and practices they facilitate, can lead to an increase in industry concentration, despite the fact that there are no formal changes in ownership structures. This has a number of serious implications for various areas of public governance, such as national antitrust laws and policies, and international monetary agreements and policies which can be circumvented by complex private enterprise strategies.

Conclusion

Modernity gave birth to three colloquialisms: space is endless, time is money and knowledge is power.

This chapter addressed some of the central aspects of the re-organization of globally integrated production processes in the post-1970s era. Attention was also given to the fragmentation of the socio-technical reorganization of production and the partial demise of Fordism in certain parts of the advanced industrialized world. Whilst all of the discussed changes have a considerable and direct impact on the general organization of daily social life, they also carry within them the seeds to change fundamental aspects of modernity itself. This is particularly the case in relation to three fundamental changes in the socio-technical architecture of production processes, namely the closely related deplosion of space, implosion of time and explosion of information.

In the context of production processes the deplosion of space includes four important dynamics. Firstly: physical space disintegrates as production processes are more and more strung together irrespective of physical distances. Secondly, corporations are rearticulating their organizational spaces via

The Organization of Production Processes

project specific conglomerates, strategic alliances, interfirm networks and an expanding number of contingency interfirm relations and co-operations. Thirdly, there is a dual process of simultaneous spatial fragmentation and electronic integration which leads to the emergence of electronic and virtual spaces – saturated with information – as central, even interactive, components of production processes. Finally, there is a diasporization of space through the emergence and valorization of cyberspaces (e.g., online shopping), virtual spaces (e.g., via new communication technologies) and supranational spaces (e.g., the commercialization of the deep seabed and extraterrestrial space).

The implosion of time is embodied in, for example, drastically reduced product life cycles brought about by accelerated technological developments and changes in the Fordist consumption practices. These developments meant that the tempo of change in technological inputs renders single-purpose production equipment obsolete – it is too slow, too rigid and too costly in relation to the consumption needs of their prime markets. On a practical level these developments facilitated the general compression of product life cycles, as well as an incremental movement away from mass production and towards short run batch-type production aimed at customized markets and specialized reflexive consumption.

On a theoretical level, time was historically an essential component of labor costs within the production cycle. The relevance of time-saving technologies were consequently almost solely related to the labor-time component. The general compression of product life cycles and reflexive consumption practices contribute to the emergence of time as an independent variable no longer predominantly attached to labor costs. Time is now a resource and valorizable entity in itself. This can be observed in the emphasis placed on the manufacturing of time – that is, making products that will save consumers time relative to using comparable products to perform the same function. The specific *need for speed* in production processes means that the everyday saying, *time is money* can indeed be applied literally, and is pivotal to all aspects of the production cycle.

The explosion of information is the result of the *pari passu* electrification, computerization and informatalization of production processes. Generally speaking, contemporary electronics free communication from the constraints of space and time, and the limitations of physical transport. Optical fiber and satellite technologies, computer-aided design and manufacturing systems, and the standardization and technologization of communication through information technology, are all important components of contemporary production processes and their increased real and potential geographical dispersion.

The application of information technology innovations in, for example, the computerized automation and informating of work and work processes also facilitates a transmutation of the functional, technical and social composition and nature of information. Information no longer exists as an entity separate from technology, used in order to act on technology, as was the case ever since the Industrial Revolution. Instead, information, technology and information technology are now scarce resources and scarce products in their own right. Information in particular is no longer predominantly a means to an end, but also an end in itself.

The speed and scope of technological innovations and the new technologically induced movement flexibility of transnationals, enlarge the options open to corporations *vis-à-vis* collectively organized labor and collective institutions. The potential social impact of the new wave of electrified computer technologies is only starting to unfold, as the technologically created cyberspace emerges as a new space of cultural mediation. Already, conventional modernist boundaries of institutions (e.g., the nation-state) and social conglomerates (e.g., space, place and time) are made obsolete in certain areas. This is particularly the case in global financial markets, and in regard to the global segmentation of different production spheres as single products are strung together electronically and globally. Fundamental changes to production processes have substantially altered the industrial techniques of valorization (e.g., through increased electrification and computerization) and refigured the interdynamics between valorization and globalization. The impact of this refiguration is particularly apparent in relation to concurrent developments in productive relations and social identities, which are the focus of the next two chapters.

Chapter 3
The Recomposition of Production Relations

"Just as the Industrial Revolution brought people together in factories, the Information Revolution is pulling us apart" (Barten, 1999:49).

During the nineteenth century jobs became a way of organizing work in the wake of the Industrial Revolution. The first wave of the Information-Technology Revolution, the spatial reordering of global commodification processes, and the contemporary refiguration of the interplays between globalization and valorization in relation to exchange and production processes have disposed of neither jobs nor work. These developments are, nevertheless, having a dramatic impact on the recomposition of jobs, the reconstruction of the forms of work and on production relations in general. In this chapter these issues are discussed. Particular attention is given to the social redefinition of the social organization of labor processes by organizations, and the recomposition of the global technical division of labor.

The redefinition of the social organization of labor processes by organizations

"The growing asymmetrical power relationship between labor and capital strengthened the bargaining leverage of the capitalists vis-à-vis *workers. Firms in the age of globalization can tame unions with the*

threats of capital flights and unemployment" (Im, 1995:14).

Since the sixteenth century the dominant pattern of capitalist expansion was based on the global division and interdependence of production and labor. In general, this interdependence took the form of the peripheral supply zones for both raw materials and labor, a differentiated division of core/periphery labor, and the industrial manufacture of completed goods in the core, mostly for core consumption with surplus production – included so-called cultural goods – exported to the periphery. European cultural exports to colonial spaces, or in Barber's (1987) words 'cultural dumping,' included cultural interaction modes (e.g., the transposition of European languages), intellectual ideas (e.g., European philosophies), spiritual modes (e.g., European religions) and the visual arts (e.g., film and later television productions).[1] The introduction and incremental enforcement of the cultural practices of European monetization processes – including the separation of use and exchange values, and the extension of the monetization of goods to also include land, labor and aesthetic artifacts – was arguably the central cultural intervention.

During the colonial era, the physical location of national resources and cheap, unskilled, semi-skilled and skilled labor were pivotal to the spatial organization of the global division of labor.[2] The increased importance of private global corporations *vis-à-vis* the state in the post-colonial world,[3] the current changes to valorization processes, as well as new methods of production, production materials and technologies have reduced the geographical constraints on global capitalism and contributed to the reorganization of the contemporary global division of labor. These issues inform the organizational management of labor processes by private corporations, their application of the ideology and practices of selective flexible specialization, and the relative decline in their bureaucratic hierarchies.

The ideology and practices of selective flexible specialization

Fragmented low skill and knowledge, repetitive work practices, vertical and hierarchical organizational structures and national production boundaries were central features of the Taylorist and Fordist production regimes. This is no longer universally the case, since flexibility in production processes emerged as an important post-1970 strategy in large parts of the advanced industrialized world. The ideas of flexible specialization were generally translated into selective flexibility in production processes, and flexible organizational and labor market management practices. In essence, selective flexible specialization is an attempt to combine high volume standardized production with specialized, and sometimes customized, production processes. Corporations thus aim to deal with market fluctuations in a profitable way, capturing both so-called 'economies of scale,' and 'economies of scope,' in order to utilize the speed and flexibility advantages of contemporary Technological Production Process Innovations (TPPI). Two of the most important aspects of selective flexible specialization are so-called cultural intervention strategies and internal organizational rationalization.

'Cultural intervention' strategies

From the early 1980s, management theorists and corporations generally increased their focus on the micro-sociology of work relations and organizational culture. The focus on technology as an important comparative advantage variable now became part of more inclusive work organization strategies. These new strategies placed a renewed emphasis on innovative work organization, skill transformation and social relations.[4] In order to translate the speed and flexibility of technological abilities of TPPI into the production cycle, organizations redefined the social organization of production and labor processes. It is in this environment that 'culture' emerged as a critical variable in the organization of work processes. The articulation of culture was infused into a specific prognosis related to the philosophies of rationalist monetarism. The protagonists of this view of culture included politicians, such as Margaret Thatcher, who intended to transform Britain into an 'enterprise culture;' and intellectuals, such as Hammer and Champy (1994), Naisbitt (1994, 1995), and Peters and Waterman (1982), who generally hailed organizational culture as central to the re-emergence of *laissez faire* capitalism.

Within Zem, the infusion of 'cultural intervention' strategies into worker training programs includes a focus on, and the advocation of, labor processes which partially reverse some of the practices central to classical labor process theory and its hierarchical organization of work processes. For example, in Zem's efforts to encourage the integrated use of intellectual, manual, organizational and social skills, they strongly advocate multiskilling in many work areas. This multiskilling in specific areas is mainly achieved through the integration of production processes which are organized around a process, rather than a task.[5] During the 1990s Zem increased its efforts to create a more horizontal and less hierarchical structure for both the organization of production and for management itself. One of the major consequences of this restructuring was an often dramatic decrease in middle management levels. For example, in some business units hierarchical levels of reportage went from more than 20 in 1992 to less than 5 in 1997.

'Cultural' restructuring strategies are not restricted to Zem. Since the early 1980s, 'Western' corporations began to introduce 'Japanese' organizational practices, such as Toyotism, into the ideological and practical nexus of the social organization of production.[6] These organizational practices sought to achieve high degrees of flexibility in producing specialized variants of basically mass-produced goods. This was done in order to differentiate between essentially similar commodities, and to respond to rapidly changing markets seeking more specialized and customized goods.[7] Prominent features of these post-1980 managerial practices include the 'just-in-time' system of supplies, and 'total-quality-control cycles.' The just-in-time system of supplies aims to substantially reduce costs by suppliers only delivering their goods to the production site when it is required in the production process. Total-quality-control cycles aim to minimize defects, and achieve relative worker shopfloor autonomy with more decentralized worker participation in the organization of work practices and processes. However, in practice greater worker shopfloor autonomy often co-exists with sophisticated electronic mechanisms used by management to centrally monitor and control the performance of workers.[8]

During the 1990s, various so-called cultural intervention strategies, such as Flexible Specialization (FS), Total Quality Management (TQM) and World Best Practice (WBP) were introduced in tandem with TPPI in order to increase and accelerate the diffusion of labor-displacing technological and organizational innovations. During Zem workshops, cultural interventionist strategies are most often explained by applying the principles of, for example TQM, in conjunction with state-of-the-art technological procedures. A Zem manager articulated the rationale behind this practice as follows. "The very rapid technological changes [in the production process] over the last 10 years or so, exposed our organizational weaknesses. For example, we now had new technologies, but we could not really use them because of our outdated organizational culture. ... Strategies such as TQM, are nothing more than attempts to effectively deal with the opportunities that new production technologies have opened up for us. ... Organizational culture, organizational practices and organizational production methods and technologies are different dimensions of a single process" (Zem manager).[9]

Current production processes generally require progressively fewer specific professional skills and more human, organization centered and company specific skills in order to produce high quality products. The increased focus on company specific skills also has the advantage that they are less of a transferrable and portable commodity owned by individual workers. Inhouse professional training is not only costly, but also increases the accredited marketability and mobility of the trained worker. In contrast, a Zem corporate strategist argued that cultural intervention strategies tend to selectively "improve the value of a worker within the specific organizational structure of Zem, without improving the value of the worker in the open labor market. ... The cost investment of training a worker is thus tied to us [Zem] and not to the worker, as is most often the case with professional [inhouse] training" (Zem corporate strategist).[10]

Internal organizational rationalization

From the early 1980s, the rationalization of the external capacity was a macro-organizational strategy that resulted in the so-called 'lean' and 'flexible' organization.[11] As a result, this period was characterized by organizational job rationalization, or job liquidation. The largest 500 transnationals, for example, have shed over 400,000 workers each year from the mid 1980s to the mid 1990s.[12] Between 1980 and 1993, the 4.4 million jobs cut by the Fortune 500 represented a quarter of their previous work force. During the same time, the sales of these companies increased 1.4 times and their assets 2.3 times.[13] These job cuts are also part of a micro-organizational process of internal rationalization. Potentially externalized work activities range from low-skill, repetitive to high-skill and research activities.

Organizations generally aim to identify the pockets of unproductive time which form part of full-time employment, and reduce costs by paying only for the tasks performed successfully. Work is exported to outside sources, and workers who used to performed these tasks are dispensed of, or re-employed on a casual or part-time basis. Inhouse activities are thus replaced by subcontracting, outsourcing, offshoring, and downsizing. In order to eliminate or minimize unproductive pockets of labor and/or products, organizations tend to focus on a smaller or more specific part of the value-added chain. This means that labor in general, and work security in particular, are externalized and individualized. Parts of the value-added chain are sourced out to worker configurations, such as individuals or small firms, which overtly undermine collective worker organization and job security within a particular firm. The work externalization chain is nearly endless, since subcontractors themselves often subcontract work out.[14]

In 1997, the managers of the six largest business units of Zem in Australia projected that they would export between 10 and 40 percent of their current inhouse activities over the following 10 years, mostly by outsourcing and subcontracting. The main reasons given for this strategy were labor cost savings (e.g., in terms of wages, superannuation contributions and redundancy payouts), flexibility (e.g., to extend their abilities to elicit specialized skills for the duration of specific projects only) and to strengthen strategic alliances and relationships with other firms (e.g., suppliers) and individuals who could expose Zem employees to new ideas and business practices.

Organizations particularly focus on externalizing necessary but costly work activities which have a high percentage of potentially unproductive labor, or work activities in which worker controlled time buffers are difficult to monitor against time. This latter development can, for example, be seen in the decline of face-to-face customer relations in the wake of the growth of call centers. Call centers are becoming an important component of customer service for a variety of business transactions (e.g., ordering take away food, banking, airline reservations, payment of bills, and software support). By replacing face-to-face counter service, call centers reduce unproductive labor pockets. For example, research in Australia indicates that each call center attendant handles an average of 94 calls a day.[15]

Traditional call centers offered call routing, queuing and reporting, whilst interactive voice response, agent scripting and fax handling were added on overtime. The next phase of call center development involved web, online and e-mail facilities, followed by online shopping and complete customer services.

The Recomposition of Production Relations

This changed the nature of call centers from complaints departments to telemarketing and complete customer care centers[16] as accounting, sales, distribution and after sales care are integrated into a single division. Around 60,000 people in Australia are presently employed in call centers, and this figure is projected to rise to between 300,000 and 350,000 by 2004.[17] American call center employment currently stands at 1.5 million.[18]

In addition to the time effectiveness, call centers are also distance neutral and can be located to areas with lower labor and operating costs, as well as lower staff turn-over rates. The Sydney call center of the US corporation Cisco Systems is an example of distance neutrality. This specific center serves as the only direct-dial hotline for Cisco Systems customers worldwide for 6 hours every day. Lufthansa's Asia-Pacific call center in Melbourne serves Australia, Hong Kong, Japan, Singapore, New Zealand and out-of-hours calls from North America and Europe. The distance neutrality of call centers is an important strategy to counter the escalation costs in a 24-hour business environment, as well as part of the wider processes of internal work rationalization and exportation.

The relative decline in bureaucratic hierarchies

The new patterns of selective flexible specialization during the 1990s have contributed to a number of important changes in restructuring bureaucratic hierarchies and the related labor relations. These changes include: the redefinition of work organization processes; vertical organizational disintegration and work polarization; and the evolution of an increasingly bipolar labor force.

The redefinition of work organization processes

Contemporary TPPI and selective flexible specialization practices have enabled corporations to redefine work organization processes and job classifications. New technologies require different kinds of skills, knowledge and decision-making from workers. A Zem corporate strategist argued that the greatest single challenge facing Zem in relation to its workforce is "to change the attitude of our workers towards learning new skills quickly. ... Our engineers, managers, etc. have to create the new products and new work processes, but our workers have to implement them. Practically, this means that a worker learns a new skill today, implements it tomorrow, and discards it next week when he needs to learn a new skill. This is a very threatening thing for workers since they have to be very flexible, and their job security is no longer guaranteed by the [professional/technical] skills they learned as apprentices" (Zem corporate strategist). In America those starting their working careers today can expect to change jobs at least 11 times in the course of their working lives, as well as changing their skill base at least 3 times.[19]

The need for continued worker re-skilling relates closely to the *pari passu* partial vertical disintegration of corporations and the so-called re-engineering of the sequential (Fordist) organization of work.[20] In 1995 work organization specialists in Zem estimated that an uncomplicated order for an existing product proceeds sequentially through approximately 25 'control points or levels' (e.g., individual, departmental or process levels). This sequential organization of work processes is cumbersome, time-consuming and fraught with breakdown points which are likely to cause delays. With the aid of TPPI and SFS, Zem consequently started to reduce their work processes to only three sequential levels. These levels are definition, realization and marketing. Within this system, most work processes are integrated simultaneously rather than sequentially.

In Zem workshops and inhouse publications, the following explanation was given to its world widework force in regard to the system of simultaneous work integration. "... [E]very work process between the customer's wish and customer's satisfaction is newly structured. Here specialists work together to solve the problems instead of having them worked on by a series of departments. Everyone in the team works as a specialist with authority and responsibility. What he says, goes

The Recomposition of Production Relations

– without lengthy consultation or needless fuss. In our example case from the production sector, the work process is composed of three teams. First, the definition team: Here all who are directly concerned with providing the products and services the customer requires sit down together. Everyone commits to achieving the goals which are set. Problems are jointly discussed from the start and solved with as little red tape as possible. Second, the realization team: Here the guidelines are independently implemented on the team's own authority. How the team members achieve the agreed goal is up to them, they are the specialists. Third, the marketing team: Here everything revolves around the matter of how to get the product to the customer on time. How this is to be accomplished is worked out by the specialists themselves. Finally, it always comes down to one thing: the team" (Zem inhouse publication, distributed to employees world wide).[21]

Vertical organizational disintegration and work polarization

Production relations affected by the relative decline in bureaucratic hierarchies and the new patterns of labor market flexibility have contributed to the partly vertical disintegration of corporations. This has had a major impact on work relations and classical Fordist polarizations of production relations in regard to the relationship between employees (i.e., the so-called workers) and management (i.e., including employees in managerial positions and shareholders) of a business. As a result of the decline of work hierarchies, individual workers tend to be more mobile, both upwards and downwards in terms of occupational positions within an organization. This renders worker-worker and worker-management alliances more open, fluid and contested.[22]

A Zem manager articulated the new ambivalent management-worker shopfloor relations as follows. "What is a good worker? In the past it used to be somebody that worked hard, similar to a person having a workout in a gym – lots of sweat and blisters [on their hands]. ... As managers, we were aerobic instructors, telling people what to do, how to do it, etc., and pushing people to work faster and faster. Today we [managers] are organizing our workers strategically and tactically into teams, we are now coaches, and our workers are the main players – like in football. ... Our technology, work processes and practices now require workers to think about what to do, think for themselves and make important decisions on their own. One of these days they will be more important than me" (Zem manager).

At this relative early stage of selective flexible specialization and flexible labor regimes (including the flexible hours and part-time work), one can only speculate about their long-term impact on organizations and workers. However, it is foreseeable that workers may experience vastly different levels of work participation during their working lives in the future. More specifically, large sections of the work-force may possibly have multiple-careers, with some careers existing concurrently (i.e., people being fully qualified and working part-time in more that one job, for example, as a nurse and as a hairdresser).

The decline of the classical caste type of structured hierarchical Fordist work and class relations is paving the way for less structured and less overtly polarized management-worker relations. The general technical disorganization of workers as a class has far-reaching organizational and identity implications for the working-class. Touraine, Wieviorka and Dubet (1987) argue that the traditional mechanisms used to form a working-class identity have been undermined by changes in the organization of work and the forms of capital control. For Touraine, Wieviorka and Dubet the contemporary working-class does not only have to grapple with the definition of its own identity, but it also has to contend with identifying its direct adversaries. These issues are complicated by the new forms of direct management-worker shopfloor relations which are less overtly polarized, and by the increasing real and symbolic distance evolving between physical production and virtual valorization locations.[23]

The increased symbolic and/or spatial distance between those who contribute to the creation, realization and generation of monetized surplus (e.g., workers), and those who appropriate a relative disproportionate quantity of monetized surplus (e.g., owners, management, stockbrokers and shareholders), also co-exists with the greater spatial proximity of workers and customers. The increased service orientation of most industries means that the work environment is progressively saturated with additional emotional labor at the interface of more direct customer relations.[24] In addition, the customer base is augmented due to the increased number of business deals within (e.g., insourcing) and between corporations (e.g., outsourcing).[25]

At inhouse Zem workshops, customers were mostly defined as all people with whom an employee has an exchange relationship, irrespective of the type of exchange (e.g., monetary, information or social), or whether the other person was also a Zem employee or not. This working definition of Zem customers intentionally defines Zem employees as entrepreneurs. In the words of one Zem corporate strategist, this complements "the symbolic disintegration of work hierarchies, and is one of the first steps in the direction of the real disintegration of work hierarchies" (Zem corporate strategist).

During the mid- to late 1990s (1995-1997), these ideas tended to translate into the continued centralization of major business decisions at executive level, more participation of low level workers in regard to procedural aspects, and a decline in the role and decision-making powers of middle management. A tangible example of these practices can be found in the bonus reward structure of Zem in Australia at that time. The bonuses of the executive managers (e.g., business unit managers) were mainly determined by the performance of their business units, and to some degree, by peer evaluation. The bonuses of middle-level managers, however, were also determined by the evaluation of their performance by their subordinates.

Overall, the selective disintegration of work hierarchies caused a great deal of uncertainty amongst middle-level managers in terms of their role in the organization and job security. One of these middle-level managers articulated this as follows. "Zem has been democratized from the neck downwards only. All the really important decisions are still made in the office with the soft leather chairs [CEO] by ... [the CEO] and the other senior managers. This is no different from the past, but in the past we [middle managers] made the next round of decisions, the people working directly under us the next round, and so on until you reached the most junior worker. Now these rounds of decision-making are disappearing. ... My ability to make decisions has been eroded, I now have to consult much more with my subordinates. That is why I say that we now have an organization with an autocratic head and a democratic body. ... My role [as middle-level manager] has been eroded and will probably disappear in the next couple of years if things continue down this path" (Zem manager). This was a typical response from a middle-level manager to the above changes. In all the countries in which Zem was studied, this group of managers generally consisted of men aged between 40 and retirement age, with few prospects of retraining or redeployment within the company.[26]

The evolution of an increasingly bipolar labor force

The evolution of an increasingly bipolar labor force is the third major aspect related to the relative decline in bureaucratic hierarchies, the new patterns of labor market flexibility, and state-of-the-art work information technologies. One the one hand, the emerging labor force is composed of a skilled, highly paid, full-time, unorganized and semi-permanent core of information-based 'symbolic analysts' (Reich, 1992), or knowledge workers. For Zuboff (1988), contemporary information automation 'informates' work processes and practices, and increases the importance of occupational positions with a high information and knowledge content. This change in the content and occupational structure of the production process has a dramatic influence on the organization and reward structures of work.

Productivity gains and increased profit margins have always

been distributed disproportionally between non-managerial and managerial workers. Despite the partial disintegration and decline of bureaucratic hierarchies from the early 1980s onwards, income distribution differences continue to mount. Frank and Cook (1995) argue that the changing distribution of opportunities since the 1970s is one of the reasons for the increasing inequality of salaried incomes in America. Frank and Cook regard the technological changes in information processing and transmission to be largely responsible for this shift. Authority, creative power and valorized opportunities (e.g., large salaries and shares) are centralized in a small portion of top positions.[27] Consequently, the reward structure typical of entertainment and sports, where thousands compete for a handful of big prizes at the top, now permeates most spheres of monetized activities.[28] For example, from the 1950s to the 1990s the executive compensation in America increased from 22 to 61 percent of corporate profit. During the 1980s the average income of American CEOs increased from being 29 to 93 times higher than the average factory worker.[29] In 1999 this ratio balooned to 419 to 1.[30]

On the other hand, the emerging labor force also consists of low-skill, low-paid, disorganized, and often underemployed prosaic implementors. These prosaic implementors constitute a disposable circumference of workers who can easily be hired and fired, and whose labor can be automated, externalized or offshored depending upon market demand and labor costs.[31] This new reserve army of just-in-time workers reduces labor costs, and provides new kinds of labor flexibility.[32] During the 1980s, the fastest growing categories of work in the advanced industrialized spaces were temporary labor and part-time work, growing by about 30 percent during that time according to the OECD (1994b).[33] While new jobs are created in the advanced industrialized spaces, they are concentrated in the low-paying sectors and in temporary employment. For example, in Britain about 57 percent of the workforce is presently in full-time employment, while 43 percent consists of either part-time, temporary or contract workers. In 1999 only 36 percent of Australian employees work a so-called standard, full-time 35-

40 hours a week,[34] whilst casual workers account for 26 percent of all employees. Indeed all net employment growth in Australia in the 1990s has been in casual jobs.[35]

The trend of more part-time work co-exists with a general increase in working hours. For example, Rifkin (1996) found that Americans are now working longer hours than what they did forty years ago when the information-technology revolution started. Rifkin argues that this seems to be a general trend in advanced industrialized spaces. "If current trends in work continue, by the end of the century American workers will be spending as much time at their jobs as they did back in the 1920s" (Rifkin, 1996:223).[36]

In general, labor market flexibility is playing a substantial role in the recasting of corporations as partially hollow or virtual organizations. In its extreme form, as exemplified by corporations such as Benetton, Nike, and Ikea, these hollow or virtual corporations perform an intermediate function between product development, production, financing, and marketing with a relatively small core of inhouse workers. A closer look at Nike, for example, illuminates the labor practices of the hollow or virtual corporation, as well as some of the general global employment externalization trends. During the 1980s, Nike relocated most of its production offshore to so-called developing countries, such as South Korea, Indonesia, Malaysia, Taiwan Province of China, Thailand and China. In 1997, Nike employed only 9,000 people directly, mainly for the purposes of product design and development, marketing, and general administrative co-ordination. The absolute majority of labor-intensive tasks was subcontracted out to 'independent' subcontractors. This included the subcontracting of 100 percent of manufacturing activities. In total, about 75,000 people were employed by Nike subcontractors.

In an attempt to achieve both flexibility and stability, Nike has an organizational structure with clearly differentiated supply relationships with different subcontractors and with different categories of subcontractors. The most important of the three categories of suppliers in Nike's network is the 'development partners,' mainly located in South Korea and Taiwan Province of China. This category participates in joint product development and concentrates on the production of the latest product designs. The second category is that of 'developing sources,' located mainly in Indonesia, Thailand and China. These developing sources generally offer lower labor costs and provide Nike with the opportunity to diversify their assembly sites. The third category is comprised of the 'volume producers,' consisting of large-scale factories which are not exclusively tied to Nike.[37]

The other major aspect of the Nike business approach focuses on marketing, media and image strategies. In this realm, Nike has simultaneously captured a central aspect of contemporary monetization processes, namely the hypervalorization and aestheticized commodification of individualized identities. For instance, by monetizing the image of Michael Jordan, the person Michael Jordan is also valorized.[38] In other words, Micheal Jordan both as a worker (i.e., as a paid basketball player) and as an image (i.e., as an identity icon) becomes a valorizable entity. This form of individual valorization is usually accompanied by both increased monetary wealth and social status for the valorized individual. However, it also constitutes a form of postmodern serfdom. The monetized icon individual is indeed sold to the public with the price difference between, for example a pair of Air Jordans and non-iconed basketball shoes, constituting the partial selling price of Micheal Jordan. With this purchase the buyer, and the public at large, acquires some ownership of Micheal Jordan, turning his private life into public property (with ownership rights accomplished and enforced, for example, via the media).

The new forms of individual valorization also feed into the contemporary hypervalorization of the privatized self and the related human-value-equals-net-value syndrome. By infusing the image of Michael Jordan into the identity of Nike, the identity-product can be sold to the public as a package deal. Consumption of the product becomes a functional activity (i.e., acquiring a pair of shoes), molded by an aspired aestheticized identity. By wearing the Nike swoosh, one publically displays membership of the Nike cult, thereby worshipping the cult's heroes and heroines and appropriating part of their images, ideas and identities.[39] Nike's combination of the practices of labor market flexibility and the processes of individual and image valorizations, makes it one of the new breed of private modernist empires, standing in contrast to the national and colonial empires of the past.

The post-1970s work organization is characterized by management theories extolling the importance of 'people empowerment.' However, this development coexists with the 'hollowing out' of organizations, whereby employment becomes more precarious for many people within the realms of selective flexible specialization, employment externalization and the growth in flexible labor practices, such as part-time employment. The savings of focused labor externalization are generally obtained at the direct expense of outside sources, such as a pool of underemployed workers and other businesses, and at the indirect expense of the social welfare nets as organizations seek to lower the social spending component of their labor costs (e.g., superannuation payments for full-time workers). This occurs at a time when states in the advanced industrial world are generally less willing, and many so-called 'developing' states even less able, to provide social welfare safety nets.[40]

The recomposition of the global technical division of labor

"There are informational agriculture, informational manufacturing, and informational service activities that produce and distribute on the basis of information and knowledge embodied in the work process by the increasing power of information technologies. What has changed is not the kind of activities humankind is engaged on, but its technological ability to use as a direct production force what distinguishes our species as a biological oddity: its superior capacity to process symbols" (Castells, 1996:92).

Presently, there are several factors which contribute to the recomposition of the spatial dynamics of the social and global

Endnotes: The Recomposition of Production Relations

technical division of labor.[41] The augmentation of knowledge-based production practices and processes is arguably the single most important recent development. The primacy of industrialism is today supplemented, and even partially replaced, by informationalism in the production cycles.[42] Information technologies are critical to the mobility of capital, the versatility of labor and the aestheticization of goods and production processes. Information and knowledge, in both technological and human intellectual forms, are becoming important valorization aspects and activities. Within production processes, a divergence is occurring between so-called knowledge workers and prosaic implementors.

A Zem manager articulated the direct impact of the emergence of a knowledge-based bipolar labor force within his business unit as follows. "Within this business unit I have 200 odd workers who every night clock off and leave all the tools of their trade here in this factory. If any one of them does not come back tomorrow, then we hire someone else who can press the same buttons, follow the same procedures. ... This person might not work as hard or as efficiently, but basically they can immediately do the same job, because the job stays here in this building. ... But then I have a handful of workers who take my factory home with them every night. No, no, no, I do not mean they take their work home. No, I mean that they take home with them not the way things work – for that we can, and do, write detailed procedures – but the ability to come to work tomorrow and do something different, ... to move beyond the existing detailed procedures" (Zem manager).

As the influences of information technology on valorization activities increase, the technology-based division of labor also has an expanding impact on the restructuring of labor markets. At the turn of the century, production activities were dominated by natural resources. For example, in 1900 the twelve largest companies in America consisted of the American Cotton Oil Company, American Steel, American Sugar Refining Company, Continental Tobacco, Federal Steel, General Electric, National Lead, Pacific Mail, People's Gas, Tennessee Coal and Iron, U.S. Leather, and U.S. Rubber. Ten of these companies were natural resource companies.

In contrast to the beginning of the twentieth century, the present growth areas include microelectronics, biotechnology, telecommunications and computer electronics, all of which are high knowledge, and low natural resource industries in which virtual valorizations (e.g., the progressive replacement of extractive natural resources – such as oil – by time as arguably the most precious contemporary non-renewable resource) are important components.[43] The trend towards the increased importance of electronic valorization is also observable in the fact that a company such as Yahoo is today worth more than Boeing, and American Online (AOL) more than General Motors. In market value AOL also outranks companies such as Disney, Du Pont, Chase Manhattan and McDonalds.[44]

The labor cost distribution through the production cycle has also shifted. For example, in 1920 about 85 percent of the cost of car manufacturing was shared between production workers and investors. In 1990, this share declined to less than 60 percent, with knowledge workers (e.g., designers, engineers, stylists, planners, strategists, financial specialists, lawyers, advertisers, marketers, etc.) accounting for the rest. The recomposition of rewards in the technical division of labor is particularly clear in the high technology industries.

Reich (1992) calculated that less than 3 percent of the price of a semiconductor chip is advanced to the owners of the raw materials and energy, about 5 percent to those who own the equipment and facilities, and 6 percent to routine labor. The small minority of knowledge workers, including electronic entrepreneurs, and those holding patents and copyrights, receives the remaining 85 per cent of the cost. These knowledge workers use state-of-the-art information technology to enhance their business acumen and to manipulate valorization activities optimally. Specific high knowledge job categories include: electronic entrepreneurs (e.g., investment bankers, currency dealers, financial and tax consultants); R&D engineers; human relations specialists (e.g., management consultants, lawyers, and, strategic planners); software developers; marketing specialists; technology and

The Recomposition of Production Relations

biotechnology researchers; certain media and certain so-called culture workers (e.g., television, film, print and music artists/producers/writers); and high-tech informational activities in general.

The recomposition of the dominant forms of the technical division of labor can be classified into a number categories (see Table 4.1 below). All typologies are simplistic generalizations and this one is no exception. However, the purpose of the 'categories of a general technical division of labor' table is to visually summarize the relative importance of various work attributes in relation to the various job categories by ranking them relative to each of the other categories. The technical division of labor categories consist of raw material creators/symbolic analysts (e.g., knowledge workers); co-ordinators (e.g., middle management); raw material extractors/producers (e.g., miners, farmers) and volume producers (e.g., automated workers). Under the Fordist regime, there was considerably less technical specialization, and a fusion between the raw material creators/developers and the co-ordinators categories, as can be observed in the industrial empires established by creative inventors. The raw material extractors/producers category was often closely integrated with the Fordist developing co-ordinators category.

The impact of the recomposition of the technical division of labor within advanced industrialized spaces has important implications for the restructuring of both private organizational and global/regional spatial labor relations. Dunning (1993) argues that for transnational corporations the significance of the labor time and value-added ratio has increased dramatically over the last two decades, and consequently corporations have tended to focus on reducing labor costs relative to other expenses. This accentuated the importance of knowledge work and contributed to the diminished role of semi-skilled labor in production processes.[45] On the one hand, corporations generally try to specialize more and more in low labor, high value-added activities.[46] On the other hand, due to the high wages and cost of knowledge workers, corporations also aim to reduce the

Table 4.1 Categories of a general technical division of labor existing in the dominant production processes which are globally integrated[1]

Technical labor categories / Attributes	Raw material creators/ 'symbolic analysts'	Co-ordinators	Raw material extractors/ producers	Volume producers
Industry/ Activities	Knowledge /cultural/ post-industrial	Management	Traditional industrial /agricultural products	Automated
Raw material: (i) Information/ Knowledge	Highest	High	Low	Lowest
(ii) Concrete	Lowest	Low	Highest	High
Labor specialization/ Mobility	Highest	High	Low	Lowest
Automation of labor input	Lowest	Low	High (2)	Highest
Value added	Highest	High	Low	Lowest
Labor cost	Highest	High	Low	Lowest
Labor-time/ value added ratio	Highest	High	Low	Lowest
Final product: (i) Information	Highest	High	Low	Lowest
(ii) Concrete	Lowest	Low	Highest	High
Job stability	High	Highest	Low	Lowest

---

1 Examples of jobs in the different categories could include; raw material creators/developers – product developers, research engineers, software developers, etc.; co-ordinators – factory managers, managerial consultants, specialized service workers, etc.; raw material extractors/ producers – miners, farmers, housewives, etc.; and volume producers – production line workers, general service workers, etc.

2 The one major exception in this regard is in the domestic sphere were automation is extremely low to high.

relative percentage of these workers compared to prosaic implementors. A Zem manager articulated this as follows. "Without these [knowledge] workers there would be no future for this business. And they know it, so we have to pay them well. For this reason, we must keep the ratio of these [knowledge] workers, compared to the 'button pushers,' as low as possible. ... We have to find the right team balance between innovators/ people with ideas ... who are sort of payed what they ask for, and those workers who follow, and sometimes contribute to procedures, who are paid what we offer them" (Zem manager).[47]

The contemporary spatial recomposition of the technical division of labor is proceeding *pari passu* with the selective transfer and implementation of 'advanced' technologies between different production loci. The impact of the contemporary technology package (i.e., processes and labor divisions) on the labor requirements of capital has affected various parts of the old periphery in different ways. The social organization and spatial dynamics of the global division of labor are undergoing fundamental changes. Presently, the historically defined core and periphery relationships tend to be redefined across national boundaries and geographical spaces. Hoogvelt (1997) argues that the contemporary global division of labor is "bringing on board within the core, segments of the [so-called] Third World, and relegating segments and groups in both the traditional core of the system and in the [so-called] Third World to peripheral status. Core-periphery is becoming [more overtly] a social relationship, and no longer a geographic one" (Hoogvelt, 1997:145). This unbundling of the 'Third World,' or so-called developing countries, is illustrated in a comparison between the Asian Pacific (characterized by what can be labeled 'peripheral production industrialization') and African (characterized by what can be labeled 'peripheral de-production valorization') regions.

In 1913 the 'Third World' captured half of global trade,[48] by the 1990s this figure had declined to less than a quarter. This relative reduction is exacerbated by the fact that two-thirds of the manufacturing exports of the 'developing world' presently come from the Asian Pacific region.⁴⁹ A similar pattern characterizes foreign direct investments (FDI). For example, in the first half of the 1990s, FDI in the 'Third World' almost tripled. It is significant to note, though, that about 60 percent of this FDI was concentrated in Asia, and particularly in China, Singapore, Malaysia, Thailand, Hong Kong, Taiwan, and Indonesia.⁵⁰

The post-1970s peripheral production industrialization of the so-called newly industrializing countries, entailed a general structural transformation of production processes.⁵¹ The emphasis of labor processes shifted from labor-intensive to capital- and technology-intensive goods, centered around high value-added products.⁵² During this period, public and private entrepreneurs operating in the Asian Pacific region, fastidiously rearticulated the technical and social organization of production and labor processes. This rearticulation was based on a predominantly Fordist social organization of production and labor within a neo-Keynesian structural framework in which national spaces were diligently controlled by strong central governance. Whereas the European Keynesian welfare state attempted to restrain market rationality in order to protect the most vulnerable groups from the vagaries of the market, Asian Pacific states tended to restrain market rationality in order to accelerate industrialization *per se*. This contributed to the rapid production industrialization of the Asian Pacific region from the 1970s onwards.

In contrast to the Asian Pacific peripheral production industrialization, the peripheral de-production valorization of the African region represents another aspect of the re-invention and rearticulation of the spatial dynamics of global capitalism in the post 1970s era. From the sixteenth century onwards, the expansion of global capitalism was characterized by dependency relationships between the core and the periphery. The core produced goods for domestic consumption, whilst the periphery acted as supply zones for raw materials and cheap labor, as well as absorbing some of the surplus production of the core. Three post-1960s developments characterize the changed production-labor relationship between the core spaces of global capitalism and the African region.

Firstly, new investments and production ventures presently require an appropriate mix of both low and high labor skills. This is partly due to the diminished significance of the absolute costs of labor as a competitive factor and the related increased importance of sophisticated production technologies. Since African colonial education specifically aimed at low skill manual labor for centuries, and considering the low educational spending in contemporary Africa,[53] most Africa spaces cannot readily supply the required labor skill mix. Consequently, Africa's labor markets are becoming partially obsolete to the spheres of competitive global production. In addition, global investments are no longer defined to the same extent by geographical location, so-called 'economies' of scale, and semi-permanent investments, such as stationary production plants and restricted financial movements, as was previously the case. These changes have undermined competitive advantages previously held by the African region *vis-à-vis* other regions.

Secondly, colonial African production concentrated on primary products and commodities from extractive industries and agriculture. From the 1960s onwards, the relevance of the primary production model started to fade, mainly due to a declining demand for many raw materials, and the development of artificial and biotechnological substitutes. In 1970, the proportion of trade in primary products and commodities consisted of more than 52 percent of Sub Saharan Africa's total exports, and more than 70 percent for Northern Africa.[54] At the same time, primary commodities formed 7.2 percent of world trade. However, the world trade share of primary products and commodities dwindled to 5.5 percent in 1980, and to only 3.7 percent a decade later.[55] This decrease contributed to the erosion of Africa's share in world exports from 2.4 to 1.4 percent during the 1980s. For many African countries this decline was dramatic. For example, Nigeria's share of agricultural exports plummeted from 86 percent in 1960, to 4 percent in 1975, and to a mere 1 percent in 1980.[56] After correcting for inflation, natural resource prices have fallen almost 60 percent from the mid-1970s to the mid-1990s.[57]

Most African governments responded to these changes by embarking on a process of rapid industrialization in the manufacturing sector, and the commercialization of the agricultural sector. This restructuring was essentially financed by foreign public and private financial institutions. However, these industrialization and commercialization processes were mostly misplaced since African countries do not today have the skilled labor, the transport or the communication infrastructure to be competitive in world markets. African spaces also lack the ecological, environmental and population stability required for competitive export manufacturing and commercial export agricultural sectors.[58] Neither do African-based enterprises have the puissance to negotiate the required open and regulated access to affluent markets. Consequently, new dependency relations were created, and the control of private global interests on public African affairs increased substantially.[59]

The third development in the production-labor relationship between the advanced industrialized spaces and the African region concerns the reconstruction of dependency relations. The increased wealth of the advanced industrialized spaces substantially raised its own labor costs, making it too expensive as a production location in relation to the relative and absolute impoverishment of most of the African continent. Africa's general impoverishment and its post-1970s debt crises also meant that it could no longer afford to absorb the surplus production of the advanced industrialized world. Although its mechanisms changed, the net transfer of wealth from the African periphery to advanced industrialized spaces did not cease.

The new mechanisms for the unequal exchange patterns reside mainly in the institutions of market governance, such as WTO (GATT), the IMF, the World Bank, and in the deregulated global financial markets. For example, since the early 1990s, African debts exceed the combined GNP of all

African states. Sub-Saharan Africa's total debt servicing amounts to $10 billion annually, four times the amount spent on health and education.[60] In comparison, African debts amounted to 28.5 percent of GNP and about 10 percent of export earnings in 1980. From the early 1970s to the late 1990s, Africa's share of world markets has been reduced by half, while its debts have been multiplied by twenty, equalling its total GP (gross product) during the 1990s.[61] Even in real terms, financial flows continue to move out of Africa.[62]

The growing imbalance between exports and imports also exacerbates Africa's debt cycle. During the 1980s export/import growth rates declined from 11.2 percent and 1.9 percent to 3.8 percent and 0.3 percent respectively. In the same period, balance-of-payments deficits increased from US$3.9 billion to US$20.3 billion, foreign debt increased from US$4.3 billion to US$257 billion, and debt-servicing obligations amounted to between 40 and 100 percent of export earnings for highly indebted African countries.[63] The expectation that developing countries would 'grow their way out of debt' (Cline, 1984), was not fulfilled. Although some growth was evident in Latin America during the early 1990s, the same is not true for the majority of African countries. A sizable portion of loans made to African countries no longer consists of new loans, but merely of rescheduled old debt.[64] At the same time, the continent's exports are declining in quantity, relevance and access to the production and consumer markets of the world's affluent spaces. Africa's people depend increasingly on foreign loans, aid and imports as the continent's level of self-sufficiency continues to decrease.[65]

The most evident link between large parts of Africa and global capitalism is now based on indebtedness. This stands in stark contrast to the dynamics of colonialist expansion, during which Africa was closely integrated into the global division of labor. The spatial dynamics which forcefully integrated many parts of the world into the European network, have become considerably more selective. At present, many African countries are too dependent, and have too little to offer to be of continued importance to the production spheres of global capitalism. Overall, Africa's relevance to global capitalism is shifting from the production sphere to a sphere of valorized electronic capital as embodied in the post-1980s development of debt-peonage.[66] As a result of the peripheral de-production valorization of the African region, African workers are no longer the macro geographical reserve army of global capitalism. Following centuries of forced inclusion, the impact of structural exclusion from the production and social spheres of global capitalism is extremely severe for people living in Africa.

Conclusion

"If you had a choice to buy a bread at one of the following two shops, which one would you choose? The first shop belongs to a rich man who sells a loaf of bread for 5 marks. The second shop belongs to a large poor family who sells the same loaf for 3 marks. Where would you buy your daily bread? Not only would it be stupid to buy from the rich man, it would be a bit immoral. Similarly, our company is doing sensible, and morally justifiable, business in areas such as China. ... In China we today use state-of-the-art technology, provide jobs, produce good-quality products and make good profits. ... There is no business, or moral, argument against our strategy to produce and create jobs in poorer parts of the world when the opportunities are there" (Zem corporate strategist).

This chapter addressed some of the selective flexible specialization trends in the social and technical division of labor, and the spatial restructuring of global labor relations. Based on this discussion, four general trends in contemporary production relations can be identified. These are: the reorganization of work practices in the advanced industrial world; the coexistence of overtly less polarized direct management-worker shopfloor relations with an increased symbolic spatial distance between those who contribute to the creation, realization and generation of monetized surplus, and those who appropriate a relatively disproportionate quantity of monetized surplus; the decline of the real industrial spatial separation of work and home, as well as the rigid separation

The Recomposition of Production Relations

between work and private time; and the redefinition of the classical core-periphery relations.

The first general trend relates to a substantial reorganization of work practices in the advanced industrial world in relation to at least four major features. Firstly, the computerized electrification of production processes enables companies to globally integrate dispersed production loci for the production of a single product. It also facilitates improved work integration of workers within a single location, reintegrating (in relation to Taylorist and Fordist practices) the often cumbersome sequential organization of the activities of different workers around a process, rather than a task. This increases turn-around times and general levels of organizational efficiency.

Secondly, there is an acceleration of flexible automation technologies, accentuating the importance of information in production cycles, knowledge work and multiskilling in specific work areas. In job categories with a high knowledge component, flexible automation technologies generally reduce labor-time relative to labor-value added. At the same time, flexible automation technologies also contribute to a decrease in the craft content of work, a decline in the creative content of work activities in lower work categories, and a diminished role, and employment opportunities, for semi-skilled workers.

Thirdly, there is an increase in the segmentation and externalization of work activities. This leads to the partial replacement of inhouse activities by subcontracting, outsourcing, offshoring, and downsizing. Working conditions and working hours are increasingly more flexible, varied and less standardized. The segmentation and externalization of work activities contribute to the emergence of a bipolar labor force, consisting of a core of knowledge workers (i.e., skilled, highly paid, full-time, unorganized and semi-permanent) and a circumference of prosaic implementors (i.e., low-skilled, low-paid, disorganized, often underemployed, and disposable).

Fourthly, there is a decline in work organization hierarchies as both the organization of production, and the management of corporations become more horizontal and less hierarchical.

The second general trend in contemporary production relations is the co-existence of overtly less polarized direct management-worker shopfloor relations with an increased symbolic spatial distance between those who contribute to the creation, realization and generation of monetized surplus, and those who appropriate a relatively disproportionate quantity of monetized surplus. In the past, the hierarchical divisions of work practices, processes and relations were central to the formation and maintenance of class-based social and labor movements. During the twentieth century, class-based social movements were also clustered around geographical locations. The reorganization of work and its electrification have dispersed the large concentration of workers found around heavy industries during the Fordist growth phase. At the same time, changes in transportation and housing patterns have scattered class-based urban populations, leading to a spatial disorganization of the working class.[67]

The general lack of transnational organizational structures also curtail the labor-force's capacity for global collective organization. Whilst the global flows in goods, production loci and capital continue to occur with greater ease, labor markets remain segmented by gender, level of skill, and geographical and physical location. In relation to the progressive mobility of goods, production loci and capital, labor remains relatively immobile, particularly with regard to transnational labor flows.[68] The general re-ordering of work relations (e.g., more horizontal and less hierarchical, less structured and less polarized management-worker relations) and the global spatial recomposition of production processes, further decrease the ability of labor to organize collectively.

During the twentieth century the development of the welfare state systematically undermined the class struggle as an important force for social change.[69] However, it is unlikely that the present demise of the welfare state (see Chapter 4) will reinvigorate class struggles as a social force. As a result of technical, spatial and organizational changes to production processes and work relations, the contemporary social environment is no longer conducive to mass and collective

The Recomposition of Production Relations

work mobilization through mass trade unionism, labor-centered political parties and class-based social movements.

The third trend in contemporary production relations is the decline of the real industrial spatial separation of work and home, as well as the rigid separation between work and private time. This occurs in conjunction with certain central aspects of selective flexible specialization such as flexi-hours, around-the-clock trade, longer local business hours, teleworking, combining more than one part-time career, etc.. However, the decline in the real industrial spatial separation of work and home, and work and private time, co-exists with the increased spatial proximity of workers to customers, including fellow workers as customers.[70] The increased service orientation of many work activities also means that the work environment is progressively saturated with additional emotional labor at the interface of more direct customer relations. This is particularly the case in certain areas, or certain types, of work where workers are in direct contact with each other or with outside customers. These areas of intense social interaction, however, co-occur with certain types of work mediated by the electronic integration of work, private spaces and times. For workers predominantly dealing with other workers or outside customers by means of electronic communication technologies, work can thus be a process of intense social isolation.

The fourth trend in the reorganization of production relations is the present redefinition of the classical core-periphery relations. The impact of the contemporary social-technology package (i.e., work practices, processes and labor divisions) on the labor requirements of global capitalism, has had a different effect on various parts of the old periphery. On the one hand, peripheral production industrialization strategies, such as applied to the South-East Asian region, mainly entailed a structural transformation of production processes. On the other hand, peripheral de-production valorization, as applied to the African continent, essentially shifted Africa's relevance to global capitalism from the production to the exchanges spheres of valorized electronic capital, as embodied in the post-1980s development of debt-peonage.

Structural marginalization and active production dislocation is, however, not unique to people in the pre-1960s geographical periphery of the then advanced industrial core. There is substantial indication that, despite some important differences related to geographical location, we are presently in the midst of a large scale global diasporization of wealth and social dislocation from production activities, as well as the general refiguration of contemporary marginalization dynamics and the spatial re-ordering of these dynamics. These changes have important implications for social integration, and form part of the influences on the composition and narration of contemporary social identities.

Chapter 4
Social Identity Compositions and Narratives

"Back in the mid-1980s, when the Labor government was trying to whip up a little national enthusiasm to compensate for its embrace of the dictates of economic rationalism, Bob Hawke used prime-time television to nominate four Australian heroes: Paul Hogan, Joan Sutherland, Greg Norman and Ben Lexcen. ... Of the four nominees, three were living overseas at the time, and all four were working in post-industrial markets organized in the Northern hemisphere ..." (Hogan, 1996:279).

"Things are more confused now. A scratchy recording of the Norwegian national anthem blares out from a loudspeaker at the Sailor's Home on the bluff above the channel. The container ship being greeted flies a Bahamian flag of convenience. It was built by Koreans working long hours in the giant shipyards of Ulsan. The underpaid and the understaffed crew could be Salvadorean or Filipino. Only the Captain hears a familiar melody" (Photographer Alan Sekula in relation to 'Fish Story,' a photographic project on harbors, cited in Bhabha, 1994:8).

In the film, 'Bananas' Woody Allen bemoans the fact that he dropped out of college. When asked what he would have accomplished had he finished his course, he answered. "I don't know. I was in the black studies program. By now I could have been black."

This chapter focuses on some of the central aspects of contemporary identity compositions and narratives in relation to modernist marginality, within the context of the dominant global social dynamics. The three quotes above highlight aspects of the intricate cultural mosaic of contemporary social identities in relation to changes in the spatial dynamics of the global social environment and the proliferation of social relations which exist across classical modernist space and time constraints.

On the one hand, contemporary social identities are today shaped by the structural influences of the state and capitalism. The diasporic nature and the increased neo- and post-industrialized valorization processes of contemporary global capitalism, in particular, have the ability to stretch social relations across space and time. These structural influences constitute a contemporary form of valorized subjugation – as illustrated by the Norwegian navigational allegory and the Australian heroes metaphor.

On the other hand, social identities are today also more overtly mediated by individual agents who reflexively and selectively appropriate parts of their identities.[1] These agent-centered processes could be described as a contemporary form of existentialist liberty – with the post-structuralist Woody Allen becoming black as an extreme example. This chapter deals with both of these aspects of contemporary social identity compositions and narratives. In the discussion particular attention is given to the reconstellation of socially composed practices, interpretative mechanisms and the construction, representation and circulation of meanings.

Generally speaking, modernist social identity compositions and narratives can be classified into two broad categories, namely those that tend to be supra-modernist (and often quasi biological) such as gender and race, and those that tend to be more specific and unique to the modernist epoch, such as nationality and class.[2] During the twentieth century, the specific modernist identity compositions and narratives were primarily mediated by the state through nationalist identities, and by productive relations, via class identities. Industrial technologies also contributed to modernist identity narratives through the reorganization of social relations via numerous technological interventions, such as the social compression of time and space.

Towards the end of the twentieth century, some notable changes are occurring in the interdynamics of the globalization-valorization-marginalization triangle, and in the

Social Identity Compositions and Narratives

ways in which these changes inform the specific modernist identity compositions and narratives. In order to address these developments – which include the phenomenon referred to by Robertson (1992) as the 'global valorization of particular identities' and the 'universalization of particularism' – the co-existing, contradictory and complementary influences of states, technologies and productive relations are discussed. These influences on social identity compositions and narratives occur at the following social intersections: state *vis-à-vis* private capital influences; machine *vis-à-vis* virtual technological influences; and production *vis-à-vis* consumption influences.

State *vis-à-vis* private capital influences

"The official justification is that government bureaucracies are holding back development. What's good for business is good for the whole community, for free trade is the rising tide that lifts all boats. But, in practice, this means the deregulation of economic activity, the privatization of functions once public, and the commercialization of activities once social. In short, it means a net transfer of power from governments and the people to transnationals and private wealth" (Brand, 1996: 14).

From the nineteenth century onwards increased working-class organization contributed to the rearticulation of the relationship between the state and class interests. Within the parameters of nationalism, social security evolved as an important aspect of the state's relation to civil society. The state forged a symbiotic relationship between the vox populi, different classes and the state. Over time, a complementary link was established between mass mobilization for national security and a collective social security network. Within its own borders, the modern nation-state consolidated its power in a centralized bureaucracy as it acquired effective control over a number of state apparatuses, and also monopolized the means of legitimate violence which it could use to manipulate or force compliance.

The translation of haphazard social control and power into a systematic form was dependent on the nation-state expanding its administrative and coercive state apparatuses. In order to build up its apparatuses and their respective institutions, the state developed ways of extracting resources from, as well as dividing resources between, its citizens. This was primarily achieved through effective administration and taxation. During the twentieth century the welfare state also engaged in numerous social organizational activities. The state managed social and national security, mediated the social integration of its citizens, controlled the distribution of collective goods between interest groups, and engaged in the practices of nationalism.

Over time nationalism evolved into a central organizational mechanism and primary influence on social identities. By providing social security (i.e., free education, unemployment and pension benefits, etc.), social democracies internalized the costs and organization of existing and potential class conflicts through active state intervention in the market. The welfare state tended to promote market competition within a national integration framework which had institutional barriers, regulating the commodification of certain social relations and social services (i.e, certain aspects of mass education, health care and transport). This protected workers from some of the worst vagaries of the market, and also infused the class struggle into the national project, in part 'nationalizing the working class.' The integration of mass mobilization and social security into the national project enabled twentieth century welfare states to achieve a national class compromise by engendering a coalescence of the interests of the state, capital and labor.[3]

After the Second World War, a number of important global developments occurred which affected the day-to-day operation of the state as an organizational agent. During this period, the global social landscape was dominated by the formal dissolution of the European colonial empires, the emergence and termination of the Cold War, as well as the construction, and later the disintegration, of post-war empires (e.g., the Soviet Union). In addition, the institutionalization of transnational governance (e.g., via the Bretton Woods

Social Identity Compositions and Narratives

agreements), and its subsequent partial denationalization and reprivatization (e.g., via GATT agreements), significantly influenced global relations.[4] These global events contributed to the reorganization of the social structural influences of the nation-state, its management of valorization processes and affected its organizational operation *vis-à-vis* global capitalism. In this regard, eight general contemporary trends can be observed.

The end of the Cold War

In the post-Second War period, the Cold War had an important impact on transnational macro-cultural identity narratives. During this time, the East/communism was juxtaposed against the West/capitalism, resulting in 'them and us' narratives, which were rendered obsolete with the demise of communism and the end of the Cold War.[5] This undermined the specific articulation of the 'national capitalist project' that emerged during the Cold War period. It is more difficult to sustain the idea of a national capitalist project without a juxtaposed, and often vilified, other existing outside of both the specific national and general capitalist projects. This discord in the narrative of a coalescent national capitalist project is exacerbated by the mounting number of people who are socially dislocated and marginalized within the advanced industrial world. The potential social instability resulting from the polarization of poverty and wealth across and within nationally defined spaces, poses new challenges for the state in regard to the management and control of crime, social inequality, and large scale visible famine, as well as for its narration of collective national identities.[6]

Post-war mass mobilization

Since the Second World War nation-states have generally become less dependent on an integrative collective national identity, as their legitimation and security needs have changed in relation to mass mobilization and mass participation. The atom bomb, chemical and biological warfare, accurate long-distance missiles, as well as other advances in military technology, not only altered the dynamics of interstate warfare, but also the relationship between specific states and their own citizens. The military capacity of the state has come to increasingly depend on sophisticated technology operated by small numbers of highly trained professional soldiers, rather than on the mass participation of its citizens. The importance of the link between mass mobilization and military security (i.e., mass participation in security and military issues) is thus diminishing. As a result, states are today less dependent on the national mass project for their functional military operation. Since the dependency of the state on mass participation for its functional military operation was one side of the 'Faustian welfare state bargain' (the state providing a social security network being the other side), the decline of this dependency inevitably alters the context in which the state 'renegotiates' the national class compromise in practice.

Global interrelatedness

The coexistence and interspersion of different levels of decision-making and modes of social organization undermine the praxis of the nationalist project. As many contemporary global social realities have become part of the daily populist intellectual diet, only a few examples are given here. For instance, the 1973 oil price increases demonstrated the vulnerability of national spaces to changes in global markets, even in regard to a single product; decisions to increase/decrease American interest rates often influence major policy changes in other countries, such as in Australia; low American home mortgages are partially dependent on high prices for Tokyo's real estate, which are also essential to prevent a collapse of the Tokyo stock exchange; an earthquake in Japan (Kobe) which caused the American dollar to fall, had an immediate effect on German car exports to America since it affected the price of German imports to America; and the decision of the Australian treasurer Peter Costello to sell

Australian gold reserves in 1997 had an immediate and potentially long-term impact on the lives of two million South Africans, whose livelihood is dependent on the operational viability of South African gold-mines (i.e., a world gold price above a certain level).

A number of ecological disasters also contributed to the emergence of a global ecological consciousness.[7] These disasters included: the Chernobyl nuclear disaster which affected people and the ecology far beyond the Russian border; the destruction and burning of forests in parts of South America (e.g., Brazil) and parts of Asia (e.g., Indonesia), contributing to the problems of stratospheric ozone depletion and climatic changes; and big dam projects in India that caused flooding in Bangladesh. Global social and ecological realities more and more impact on the abilities, as well as on the moral space of national governments to act unilaterally, either through intervention or abstention, in regard to the social and natural environment. At the same time, these contemporary social realities of global interrelatedness also augment the real, potential and perceived dependence of individuals on the global social environment *vis-à-vis* the national social environment.

Pluralization of sovereignty

Whilst national governmental decisions still have a major potential impact on the daily lives of people the world over, the ability of governments to control the direct and indirect effects of decisions over which they have no authority has decreased substantially. Transnational forces and global processes are increasingly orbiting outside the organizational reach of all nation-states. Consequently, the organizational capacities of states are more restricted, forcing them to collaborate not only with one another, but also with a variety of other organizations and cultural constituencies. As a result, there is an interspersion of different categories of decision-making and a pluralization of organizational options. The developments in the actual and nascent global social realities undermine the relative sovereignty and independence of nation-state *vis-à-vis* other nation-states, transnational forces and global processes.[8] The present disjuncture between particularistic and universalistic pressures seems to lead to a simultaneous increase in global integration and local disintegration.[9]

Within the interconnected global network, many of the traditional domains of state activity, as well as new domains of responsibility (e.g., ecological issues), can no longer be fulfilled without increased international and transnational collaboration.[10] This global collaboration takes place through plural authority structures (e.g., the OAS, OAU, APEC, WTO, G7 and the D8), transnational security networks, and global media conglomerates. In order to counterbalance the destabilizing consequences of global compression, states are increasing their integration with other states, and non-governmental organizations including public and private agencies and interest groups. Many areas of modernist state responsibility (e.g., defense, health, etc.) are currently co-ordinated on a supra-national basis as states surrender sovereignty to larger organizational units (e.g., the EU), multilateral treaties (e.g., OPEC), or international organizations (e.g., the UN). Consequently, sovereignty is today divided among a number of agencies – national, regional, international and supra-national - and limited by the very nature of this plurality of organizational options.[11]

The changes in the contemporary global social environment have led to a re-classification of the categories of global 'political' organization. Bretherton (1996) divides the issues constituting contemporary global 'politics' into three categories.[12] The first category consists of national issues which were traditionally considered to be the responsibility of individual sovereign states. They involve transnational collective responsibility on a regional or global level in areas such as security and human rights. The second category comprises of issues which are transboundary or worldwide in scope or effect, including crime, control of infectious diseases, transport, communication and transborder pollution. The third category contains issues which are global in scope and require global co-operation if they are to be effectively addressed. They include areas associated with the global 'economy,' development, population movements, as well as the more specific problems of stratospheric ozone depletion and climatic changes. A fourth category, namely that of virtual or supra-geographical issues, can be added to Bretherton's typology. Virtual or supra-geographical issues encompass the emerging diasporization of space (i.e., supra-national spaces, cyberspace, social non-space, etc.), and the contemporary coalescence and fragmentation of real time, mobile and virtual geography.[13]

Erosion of rigid national boundaries

Keynesian management strategies were dependent on the existence of rigid national boundaries and focused on the infusion of private accumulation into the realm of centralized state power. This was achieved through the social integration of the complementary, yet often contradictory national (i.e., particularistic social) and capitalist (i.e., particularistic individual) projects within the welfare state as a 'economic' unit in the international system of states. The post-1970s structural erosion of Keynesian certainties through the growth and electrification of supra-national exchange and production processes, tends to undermine both the internal state apparatuses and the intra-state Keynesian policy instruments.[14] The inclination of governments to relinquish their control over national boundaries (e.g., through GATT – i.e., transnational agreements on trade liberalization) further undermined the complementary coalescence between the nation and capital projects. At the same time, the decline in Keynesian controls exposed core spaces to cyclical market fluctuations. It also engulfed nation-states in a structural crisis of legitimacy, as the vagaries of market-driven capitalism could no longer be effectively counterbalanced by national-social-democratic interventions and welfare state strategies, thus undermining the twentieth century coalescence of the interests of the state, capital, labor and the *vox populi*.

Taxation changes

The relative ascendancy of the social influences of capital *vis-à-vis* the social leverage of the state also relates to developments in taxation.[15] These developments include a shift in the tax burden from corporate capital to individuals, various forms of tax mobilization, and the private recycling of profits. The shift in the tax burden from corporate capital to individuals is, for example, illustrated in the concurrent reduction of corporate tax rates and the introduction of more selective individual consumption and general sales taxes.[16] Corporate tax mobilization strategies include the movement of profits and certain operations to countries with low taxation rates, or to countries which offer tax advantages related to research, development or the establishment of plants. Based on the same principles, companies centralize their expenditures in countries with high tax rates. Other tax mobilization techniques used to legally circumvent paying tax include 'transfer pricing' (e.g., the uncontrolled or uncontrollable trade in unfinished goods and services within companies, between subsidiaries, or between companies), the use of subsidiaries and offices in low tax locations, investments in foreign assets, and numerous tax concessions to those who own mobile assets (e.g., the United Sates of America allowing foreigners to have tax free savings accounts).[17]

The extent of tax mobilization is extremely difficult to measure. However, it is a widespread practice amongst those with mobile assets as more and more countries avail their national spaces to low and very low (even zero) tax addresses to which incomes earned elsewhere can be channeled. For example, the German Inland Revenue office estimated that in the mid-1990s so-called German companies were using the Irish governments' special tax concessions to reduce their German tax burden by about 25 billion marks.[18] In the early 1990s Siemens paid nearly 50 percent of its profits in tax to the 180 countries in which it operates. By the mid 1990s, this profit-tax ratio had shrunk to about 20 percent.[19]

The private recycling of profits also takes place through the tax benefits on interest payments incurred through mergers, acquisitions and loans. Surplus capital such as profits is increasingly 'invested' and/or 'borrowed' as part of a tax minimizing debt management scheme. For example, in the 1950s American corporations paid US$4 in taxes for every US$1 in interest. By the 1980s, this ratio was reversed to US$1 in taxes for every US$3 paid in interest (with interest paid on borrowings subtracted before calculating net profits).[20] The profitability of this practice entails an element of risk for corporations, as it is dependent on a decrease in their acquired debt relative to increases in share values and inflation.[21]

It is likely that the new forms and mobility of digital money will also have a dramatic social impact as governments respond by moving from direct to indirect taxation at point of spending. Earnings, royalties, interest payments, etc. can today be transmitted to either off-shore tax havens via unregulated networks, or directly to individuals, with great ease. Direct digital money transfers reduce the role of traditional intermediaries such as banks, who report transactions to national tax authorities. It also reduces visible, and thus taxable, earnings. In a similar way, the viability of taxation at point of spending is also undermined by direct digital producer-customer networks.

Overall, technical (e.g., the increased electronic mobility of capital) and legal (e.g., the decreased governmental control on capital flows) developments in tax are eroding the abilities of the state to provide active (i.e., providing social security services) and passive (i.e., providing infrastructural services) social security networks vis-à-vis the increased commodification of social relations and social services. The increased international tax mobility of corporations and wealthy individuals vis-à-vis small businesses and less or poor individuals also contribute to a shift of the relative tax burden from the more to the less wealthy.

Globalization for Sale

The reconceptualization of the 'idea of civil society'

An apparent shift in the operational view of the state and civil society by the dominant and governing elites, including the large section of people with direct and indirect interests in global financial markets,[22] is manifested in the monetary policies adopted by governments of the advanced industrialized world in the post-1970s era, and especially since the 1980s. The state is no longer viewed by these governments, and those in government, as the organizational framework for social integration, social spending and the distribution of collective goods and benefits as was the case after the Second World War. This post-1970s desocietalization of public governance (i.e., the demise of so-called statism) is summarized in Margaret Thatcher's well-known expression that 'there is no such a thing as society – there are only individuals...' Within the Thatcherite rationalist philosophy, the notion of the 'individual' was furthermore equated with that of an 'entrepreneur.' Generally speaking, the monetary rationalism of the post-1980s attempted to create a system of public governance. This reduced state intervention in the productive spheres of global capitalism, privatized state enterprises which subsidized users (e.g., electricity, public transport, etc.), and progressively transformed state services (e.g., public education and health) into user-pays services. At the same time it still provided some infrastructural resources, the control required by private enterprises, as well as underwriting and enforcing private property.[23]

The desocietalization of public governance was supported strongly by managers at Zem, as illustrated by the following response of a German Zem manager. "After the war the international community, industry and the government took responsibility to rebuild Germany. All of us together were responsible for, and looked after all the Germans, or in France after all the French, and so on. In the global economy of today Germany consists of say 10 million entrepreneurs and 40 million workers (or potential workers), looking after 30 million

Germans. In other words, people were being subsidized just because they are German. ... We, the entrepreneurs, can no longer afford this. It is too expensive. The government must reduce the burden of entrepreneurs. Otherwise we cannot expand our production facilities in Germany. ... We then go elsewhere. ... The role of government today should be to create the opportunity for 80 million potential entrepreneurs, not provide welfare. This is the only way in which we can be competitive in the world today. That is the reality of the global market economy" (Zem manager).

At a workshop attended by twenty of the most senior Zem managers in Australia, the 'over regulation' of the Australian labor market – "by an old-fashioned welfare state" (Zem manager) – was unilaterally singled out as the most influential, yet potentially controllable factor restricting the long-term business growth of Zem in Australia. Despite these views of the prolonged emergence of a state "that minds his own business and lets business mind its own business" (Zem manager), the dominant twentieth century ideas of civil society are indeed changing. This is evident in not only the articulated rhetoric, but also in the large-scale privatization programs undertaken by governments over the last twenty years.[24]

Most often, the well-documented escalation of the maintenance costs of the welfare state is given as the reason for its demise.[25] However, the erosion of the active (i.e., providing social security services) as well as the passive (i.e., providing infra-structural services) welfare state is also closely integrated with monetary rationalism and general anti-collectivist strategies. These strategies include the post-1980s wave of deregulation, the dramatic reduction of budget deficits in relation to GDP,[26] increased labor flexibility and large-scale privatization programs.[27] Furthermore, the maintenance of the welfare state is not only difficult due to the escalation of costs, but also because of the increases in accumulated wealth in the advanced industrialized world.

Twentieth century wealth increases have generally proceeded *pari passu* with the polarization of wealth distribution within and across nationally defined spaces.[28] In the long term, this has the potential to increase the relative number of people depending on social security. In addition, the relative price effect created by wealth raises the general cost of living, making it more costly for un- and underemployed people to survive. This means that social security costs also expand relative to wealth increases. In the final instance, late twentieth century wealth polarization also co-exists with increases in technological mediated individualism which undermines the incentives for collective sharing as embodied in the welfare state.[29]

The desocialization of social technologies[30]

Modernity is generally characterized by the transformation of everyday life through the expansion of instrumental rationality and the social use of technology. These social technologies include communication technologies which dissociates communication practices from physical transportation, personal identification numbers, address codes, international dialing codes, banknotes, the metric system, standard time, decimal numbers, etc. The global influences of social technologies expanded dramatically from the nineteenth century onwards. Thompson (1995) argues that the foundations of the global spread of communication networks were based on the development of underwater cable systems by the European imperial powers, the establishment of international news agencies and their division of the world into exclusive spheres of operation, and the formation of international organizations concerned with the allocation of the electromagnetic spectrum.

During the nineteenth and twentieth centuries, states by and large monopolized control over new technologies. These technologies often played an overt socially integrative role within the 'discourse of nation-building' during much of this time. For example, national television, as a social technology *par excellence*, is one of the great icons of the twentieth century state-controlled nation-building phenomenon. Many countries have very similar footage of their first television broadcast. It usually involved the national leader, framed by symbols of authority and nationhood, officially opening this new 'service' by reading a carefully drafted speech saturated with national pride. The dissemination of nation-building propaganda now became part of peoples' daily entertainment. However, the monopolistic state control over this modern instrument of nation-building, and over technology in general, was relatively shortlived.

The tempo of technological innovations, cost reductions, changes in public control and increased reflexive and aestheticized consumption, all contributed to the partial public deregulation of technological control. It also became increasingly difficult for governments to control the technological dissemination of information, eroding the informational sovereignty of the nation-state in this regard. As a result, there is a proliferation of opportunities for individualized and technologically interactive identity composition and narration.[31]

In the 1990s, the expansion of social technology continues, but its products are increasingly re-institutionalized, primarily by private organizations. The private spheres of peoples' lives are becoming more accessible to institutions such as banks, governments, communication providers, employers, etc. This has far-reaching implications for social control, especially given the fact that most of these institutions are privately owned. According to a report of the American Office of Technology Assessment, between 20 and 35 percent of all clerical workers in America are currently monitored by sophisticated computer systems in Orwellian-like electronic sweatshops.[32] In addition, the majority of new technologies are today developed and controlled by transnational corporations. During the 1990s transnational corporations were responsible for the development, trade and control of 80 percent of new general and advanced technologies.[33] As a result technological innovations tend to be primarily market driven.

Contemporary social technologies contribute to the acceleration of the privatization of accumulation practices and relations. Electronic valorization, for instance, means that capital accumulation is simultaneously more global and more indirect. Face-to-face shopfloor exploitation is partially being displaced by an electronic distance between work and accumulation processes. The symbolic and real distancing of electronic valorization accentuates the general shift away from mass work mobilization (e.g., through mass trade unionism, labor centered political parties, etc.) to individualized work mobilization practices. It also facilitates the relative ascendancy of financial management *vis-à-vis* production processes.

We are presently indeed witnessing the amelioration of the social influences of private capital *vis-à-vis* the social leverage of the state. This undermines the primacy of nationalist identity compositions and narratives. It also renders the socially dislocated more vulnerable to long term and structural marginalization, and impacts on the social environment in which the interplay between machine and virtual technologies, as well as production and consumption influences takes place. In the realm of contemporary social technology, Kranzberg's dictum: "Technology is neither good nor bad, nor is it neutral" (Kranzberg,1985:50), can be adapted to read: Social technology is both oppressive (as it expands privatized social control) and liberating (as it expands the opportunities for individualized identity self construction), as well as contentious (as it expands its saturation of the fabric of social life, and infiltrates more and more aspects of everyday life).

Machine vis-à-vis virtual technological influences

"Another sort of Disneyland hyper-real tour of the past is offered at the Holocaust Memorial Museum in Washington DC -- a 'theme park' stroll through genocide. On admission you are issued with an ID card, matching your age and gender to the name and photo of a real Holocaust victim or survivor. As you progress through 3 floors of the exhibition, you can push your bar-coded card into computer stations and see how well or badly your real-life subject is faring. Will you (like him or her) end up saved, shot, gassed, incinerated? You'll find extermination camp bunks on which inmates lay unspeakably crammed, dying of malnutrition and typhus. You'll see the ovens in which victims of Zyklon-B gassings were burnt. Worst of all is the endlessly re-run video footage of Einsatzgruppen mass-killing squads at work, shooting,

stabbing, filling ditches with piles of naked corpses. ... At the end, you'll find visitors' ID cards dumped in litter bins among the pop bottles and chocolate wrappers. Your hyper-reality tour is over" (Appignanesi and Garratt, 1995:122).

The industrial organization of social life fostered the incremental expansion of the technological co-determination of social identities and their narratives. The industrial mode was accompanied by specific modes of organizing, distributing and exchanging information (e.g., print, information services, radio and television), time (e.g., the clock), goods of value and wealth (e.g., physical money), communication (e.g., the telephone), and transportation (e.g., ships, trains, cars and on a limited scale airplanes). Over time, physical space and time were compressed as long-distance communications and travels, for example, became more common and remarkably faster.

Harvey (1989) refers to this development as global 'time-space compression,' and argues that it evolved gradually until the latter part of the twentieth century and then accelerated dramatically.[34] For example, between 1500 and 1840, the best average travelling speed for land (horse drawn coaches) and sea (sailing ships) was 10 mph. By 1930 it was 65 mph for steam locomotives and 36 mph for steamships, and by the 1950s aircraft traveled at up to 400 mph over relatively short distances, compared to speeds exceeding 800 mph over long distances today. Some of the most important contemporary manifestations of these technological developments are relevant to this study. They include the virtualization of class conflict, the emergence of real virtuality, the deterritorialization of space, and the dissemination of the ideas and values of liberty *and* subjugation by the media.

The virtualization of class conflict

The composition of social relations and social identities by concrete and directly observable social interactions was a central feature of the industrial organization of social life. This social environment is changing. For instance, face-to-face shopfloor contact and a clear distinction between 'workers,' who in part monetized create surplus, and 'management' (including owners, direct management, stockbrokers and shareholders) who appropriate a disproportionate large part (e.g., relative to labor time) of monetized surplus, is being displaced by an electronic distance between work and valorization processes. The rigid 'workers' and 'owners' categories have furthermore became blurred. As a result of the shifts in both exchange and production processes, direct confrontational labor battles are today partly superseded by either the social isolation of the individual worker, or by the virtual electronic battles of financial stockbrokers, currency dealers, etc.[35] The advent of electronic entrepreneurship in the global financial environment in particular, has engendered an important symbolic distance between the real, perceived and projected battlegrounds of capital.[36]

A Zem employee articulated this development as follows; "Over the last couple of years the value of the [Australian] dollar has [had] a greater impact on my job security and on how much I can earn than any action that we as union members can undertake. ... As a union we are more and more powerless to achieve anything. We can't blame the company or the bosses. All they say is that it is out of their control. Even the union leaders throw their hands in the air, 'there is nothing we can do mate, it's all due to globalization.' ... If only I could lay my hands on this bloody globalization I would strangle it to pieces" (Zem employee).

The symbolic distancing of electronic entrepreneurship makes it increasingly difficult for dislocated or disadvantaged social actors to grasp and articulate a social struggle. At the same time, it also accentuates the general shift away from mass work mobilization (i.e., through mass trade unionism, labor centered political parties, etc.) to individualized work mobilization practices. This virtualization of class conflict further undermines the existence and collective nature of classical capitalist class categories, and contributes to the social dislocation of workers.[37]

The emergence of real virtuality

The aestheticization of everyday life and aestheticized sign consumption[38] are prevalent, not only in the contemporary manifestation and articulation of social identities, but also in the market media's representation and virtualization of social acts, events and identities.[39] Whereas the media and mediated images (e.g., themed environments such as Disney World, Sun City in South Africa, the Holocaust Memorial Museum in Washington DC, etc.) tend to form part of an overtly hyper-reality, it can be argued that all social interpretations and narratives are in part a 'simulation' (Baudrillard, 1983). In the global media, the simulation of social reality is today often achieved through the merging of news, information, entertainment, social interaction and goods into a lineal sequence of real, fictitious, imaginary, symbolic and virtual images. These images instantaneously interrelate and synchronize different messages and forms of media (e.g., audio, audiovisual and print; news, information, advertising and entertainment; real, fictitious, symbolic and virtual cultural acts) and partially homogenize the cultural representation of simulated reality.[40]

Contemporary communication systems are generally organized around the electronic integration of various communication modes from the typographic to the multi-sensorial. In this digital and often virtual universe, the boundaries between the real, the fictitious, the imaginary, the symbolic, and the virtual are frequently blurred.[41] The development and augmentation of written communication and literacy spawned a mode of thinking and logic molded by lineal sequential arguments. The lineal blurring of images as a mass practice reverts back to some of the logical practices of a pre-literate world. It also transforms the semiotics of social life by converting images into a collage of simulated opinions. These simulated opinions are often reinforced or undermined, not by a dissection of the content of news events, but through the visual effigy and the seconds of media coverage (of, for example, 100,000 anti-Gulf war in comparison to 300 pro-war protestors in San Francisco on a given day – Brand, 1996) allocated to specific events. For Castells (1996) the most important consequence of the current electronic integration of various communication modes and its recreation of the social world "is not its inducement of virtual reality but the construction of real virtuality" (Castells, 1996:372).

The deterritorialization of space and the re-emergence of supra-national spaces

The acceleration of technological advances during the latter part of the twentieth century actively undermines the modernist spatial (i.e., space as a place) influences on social identity narratives.[42] Contemporary technologies have indeed created new social spaces which span and dissolve the conventional modernist boundaries of institutions and social conglomerates (e.g., space, place and time). As a result, social spaces are reconstituted in reference to wider and more encompassing frames of reference. Spaces as social locations no longer relate to physical places only (if indeed they did so previously), but also to symbolic, technological and virtual places. These new technologically created social spaces are accessible to a sizable proportion of people in the advanced industrialized world. Examples of these space-creating technologies and technologically created social spaces include: global financial markets and spaces; the virtual media universe;[43] global private mass communications (e.g., postal and telecommunication links); cyberspace (e.g., the internet);[44] extensive local and global transportation networks (e.g., international travel); and the re-emergence of supra-national spaces which can now be commercially exploited but lie beyond the jurisdiction of the nation-state system of spaces (e.g., the deep sea-bed and extraterrestrial space).

The re-emergence of supra-national spaces also relates to the general implosion of cultural forms mediated by electronic communication which facilitate – through the use of, for example, micro-electronics and broadband fiber-optics –

direct, instant and worldwide links between individuals and social groups.[45] These developments undermine the nation-state's geographical and social control over the dissemination of public information, whilst simultaneously strengthening the ability of the market media to influence, simulate and create social events. Consequently there is a diminution in the significance of territorial boundaries and state structures.

The dissemination of the ideas and values of liberty and subjugation by the media

The media's dissemination of the ideas and values of liberty and subjugation constitutes the fourth category of the technologically mediated virtualization of social identities. Contemporary communications technologies are today an important social co-constituent force and often the primary carriers of the cultural logic and values of modernism (e.g., democracy, individual human rights, existentialist liberty, perpetual commodification, etc.) to a global audience.

Thompson (1994) argues that contemporary 'political' activities, such as the deployment of American troops in South-East Asia and Central America, the suppression of demonstrations in China, Apartheid in South Africa or the West Bank, take place in a new kind of public space as state control over the flow of information and the construction of identities can be circumvented more easily (e.g., with the use of satellites, the internet, etc.).[46] Local events are witnessed simultaneously by millions of individuals dispersed across the globe, subjecting local actions to a new kind of global scrutiny. For Thompson this results in, and even creates, new forms of 'despatialized simultaneity' (Thompson, 1995). "Given the possibility of such scrutiny, political actions carry unprecedented risks and may expose a regime to international condemnation and to political and economic isolation. The visibility created by mass communication is a double-edged sword: today political leaders must seek continuously to manage it, but they cannot completely control it. Mediated visibility is an unavoidable condition of institutionalized politics in the modern era, but it has uncontrollable consequences for the exercise of political power" (Thompson, 1994:36).[47]

The global media's ability to control and create social events is transparent in an analysis of certain aspects of one of the major global events of the 1990s, namely the 1991 Gulf war. During this war, new communications technologies enabled the media to transgress beyond post-hoc reportage and representation. The media was now an active, real time participant in the unfolding events. Real life imploded into the hyper-reality of a television spectacle.[48] However, the simulation of reality presented to the world by CNN television in particular, did far more than just expand social actions across time and space, or aid the implosion of real life into hyper-reality. The media also co-composed a specific social identity for the war in their portrayal of the war as a sporting event, often labeled 'the showdown in the Gulf,' in which only a very few participants died. However, in (the other) reality, thousands of people (other than the few Americans) lost their lives.[49]

Generally speaking, the practices of the global media is characterized by the dissemination of the ideas and values of liberty, as well as those of subjugation. On the one hand, the global media has contributed significantly to exposing abuses in human rights (e.g., in Apartheid South Africa) and natural ecologies (e.g., Shell in Nigeria in the 1990s), as well as to informing global audiences of important developments (e.g., in 1989 when information about simultaneous events in Eastern Europe became an active part of the overthrow of Eastern European regimes and the fall of the Berlin Wall).[50] These kinds of activities have elevated the global media to one of the most important social watchdogs and mediators of social introspection of our time.

On the other hand, the global media also tend to be an accomplice to disseminating subjugation in two major ways. Firstly, news, stories and information about marginal people and marginal spaces are generally not created by them, but about them. In addition, marginal social spaces (e.g., Africa) often receive their local news (i.e., news about themselves) via the global news centers in the United States of America or Europe. Marginalized people and marginalized spaces often have no other choice than to look at themselves through the eyes, minds and interests of the global media, global advertisers and global capital. Secondly, the global media's transmission of images and messages to a global audience also includes those aspects, values and logic dealing with subjugation in relation to modernist social hierarchies such as race, class and gender. In this regard, the global media often perpetuate an underlying modernist semantic formula whereby essentialist differences and hierarchies are re-enforced.

This phenomenon can be observed in the global media's general classification and portrayal of perpetrators *vis-à-vis* victims, and perpetrators *vis-à-vis* saviors in situations of physical and structural violence. The media's images of these categories tend to perpetuate the historically fermented inequality between social hierarchies. For example, when Africans in Rwanda engaged in war and senseless violence in 1994, the media's coverage was particularly graphic in regard to the mutilated bodies of men, women and children. However, there is a tendency to cover up the savagery and the actual sight of mutilated bodies when Europeans (including the diasporas of European settlers the world over – i.e., the so-called 'Western' world) kill and mutilate on a similar scale as, for example, during the 1991 Gulf war. However, this latter example is not indicative of an inherent avoidance of mutilated white bodies. For example, when two American soldiers were killed by Africans in Somalia in 1993 their mutilated bodies were also depicted in detail on global television broadcasts on numerous occasions.

It could be argued that it is often the essentialist ontological status of those involved in structural or physical violence that seems to inform the classification, images and portrayal of perpetrators, victims and saviours of violence in the global media and so-called global culture industries (e.g., Hollywood). This is, for example, also observable in a kind of nostalgic triumphalism which tends to inform the portrayal of

Globalization for Sale

the colonial era and settler adventures – as typified in films such as 'Out of Africa' and 'A Passage to India,' as well as the general heroic portrayal of explorers such as Columbus, Dias, Da Gama and Cook whose voyages were pivotal to European colonial expansion. These notions continue to survive in the global media and 'culture industries' despite the well documented extent of the losses suffered by indigenous people, social networks and local ecologies during the colonial era. The essentialist ontological status of perpetrators and victims seems to often have a greater influence on the portrayal of dehumanization than the acts themselves, or the wider social issues spawned by these acts.

All in all, the emergence of virtual technologies as an important influence on the technical composition and narration of social identities, tends to accentuate both the existentialist liberty and valorized subjugation tendencies of modernity. New and virtual technologies also inform the production and consumption influences on contemporary social identity compositions and narrations.

Production *vis-à-vis* consumption influences

"Spinning webs of individuals across the globe, the post-modern market does not simply deregulate and privatize the economy, but deregulates and privatizes the social as well. This is a world where global subjects can form cultural spaces and identities that they may enter and exit freely but which never stand outside the market for very long" (Bainbridge, 1997:27).

The mediation of social identity compositions and narratives through market practices have been central to the modernist epoch since its inception.[51] After the emergence of industrial capital, production processes and relations dominated social stratification as well as individuals' integration into the social world.[52] The present forms of the co-mediation of social life and social identities through commodification practices include the fusion of the media and the market, the progressive equation between consumption capacities and social inequality, and the hyperculturalization of reflexive accumulation.

The fusion of the media and the market

Contemporary commodification practices are characterized by a symbiotic fusion of 'the media' and 'the market' in which the media becomes both the transposing instrument of the cultural genre of commodification, as well as the message of a specific product. This is not a new development. For example, the soap opera originated in the 1920s when Glen Sample, an American advertising agent, adapted a newspaper serial for radio production. The program, 'Betty and Bob,' was sponsored by a flour manufacturer. Sample used the same idea to promote Oxydol washing powder for Proctor and Gamble in a television series called 'Overtime.'[53] The so-called soap opera was born – a product of the 'media-market' fusion. Today, soap operas, media programs and films are scattered with overt advertisements and the quasi-natural consumption of specific brand names (e.g., James Bond on his BMW).

Private enterprises and global corporations saturate the social world with commodification images on a massive scale. For example, private enterprises spent over US$240 billion per year on advertising and a further US$380 billion on packaging, design and other promotions.[54] This amounts to a total of approximately US$120 per person around the world, exceeding the average annual earnings of the citizens in countries such as Sudan, Somalia, Mozambique, Tanzania, Ethiopia and Afghanistan.[55] The various forms and formats of advertising (i.e., products, lifestyles, values, soap operas, news broadcasts, films, etc.) are today complemented by a technological environment which continually expands the valorization opportunities in regard to the reproduction of symbolic forms, such as the use of credit cards to decode scrambled television programs.[56]

Two aspects of the interrelationship between advertising and marginalization warrant specific attention. Firstly, the work of Seabrook (1990) has drawn attention to the general social relationship between wealth and poverty, and the particular influence of the global media on the social construction of values and attitudes towards wealth and poverty. Seabrook argues that the images of 'remorseless luxury and overwhelming plenty' are central to the visual and auditory diet provided to the world by the global media where pictures of poverty are eclipsed and overlaid by images of well-being. For Seabrook the specific forms of consumption imagery are perpetuated by the media's projection of the consumption habits of the rich as the norm, leading to a decline in the perception of social differences. Seabrook writes that the omnipresence of scenes of comfort and ease "reinforce the idea that those who fail to avail themselves of their share of the eager capitalist cornucopia must, in some way, be defective individuals. ... They tell us that poverty and unemployment are not flaws in the system, but the problems of individuals. The implication is that there are no longer any socially-determined evils; only faulty people" (Seabrook, 1990:19).

Secondly, Domatob's (1987) work in Sub-Saharan Africa draws attention to the impact of contemporary advertising specifically on 'Third World' spaces. Domatob argues that advertising leads to a manipulation of poverty through the stimulation of consumption syndromes reflecting conspicuous wealth. For Domatob, advertising in Sub-Saharan Africa contributes to the uni-directional monetary flows towards the dominant production spaces (i.e., a drain on local and/or foreign exchange), as well as uni-directional cultural flows towards marginal spaces. Domatob reasons that poor people increasingly live 'imported [virtual] lives' (Domatob, 1987), molded by the global media and the advertising of 'First World' products and lifestyles.

Fieldwork done by the author found similarities in the rural African village Spoegrivier. In certain parts of South Africa there is an acute shortage of safe drinking water. A group of Spoegrivier schoolchildren was asked what they thought could be done to reduce their drinking water problem. A large number responded by saying that they wanted more and cheaper Coke. They then spontaneously enacted a number of

Coke commercials. At first this was taken in jest. However, according to the local store owner, undernourished and hungry children will indeed exchange food for a tin of Coke, "because it helps them to escape from their poverty to that other world" (Local store owner, Spoegrivier).[57] Their expensive virtual escape perpetuates both their own poverty and the wealth of 'that other world.'

The progressive equation between consumption capacities and social inequality

The progressive equation between consumption capacities and social inequality constitutes the second contemporary sphere in which social identities is co-mediated through commodification practices. Consumption relations are not only symptomatic of existing inequalities, but they are also central to the reproduction of inequalities between social groups and individuals in at least major two ways, namely through hierarchical credit structures and the buying of life chances.[58]

Hierarchical credit structures

Credit structures tend to be hierarchical and actively favor the wealthy. For example, it is not only much easier for wealthier people to acquire credit, but it is also cheaper for them than for poorer people.[59] This phenomenon also occurs on a macro scale. International interest rates are mainly determined by the credit rating given to countries by the analysts of Moody's Investors Service. This means that a 'B' ranking country such as Argentina pays approximately 4 percent more interest on its loans than a triple 'A' ranking country such as Germany. There is a general correlation between relative wealth of a country (e.g., in terms of GNP) and lower interest rates.[60] Whilst many of these practices may be financially sound (e.g., in terms of possibilities of debtors defaulting on a loan), they raise important moral questions, especially in a social environment in which monetized exchanges underpin an increasing number and scope of social

171

exchanges.

Buying life chances

During the twentieth century, the support base and the rhetoric of the welfare state used to be mass-based and included most sections of the population under the umbrella of nationalism. These states consequently attempted to provide more equal life opportunities to a large portion of their population through the social provision of education, health services, and the like. Presently, these practices are replaced by the rationalist management of social resources and services which discriminate overtly against social classes by increasingly deregulating the valorization of life opportunities (e.g., 'user pays' education).[61] The valorization capacities of capital are strengthened by the state-sanctioned commercialization of life opportunities. The rationalist management of social resources and services augments the social influence of consumption, not only as a symptom of existing inequalities, but also as a structural phenomenon which actively regulates access to life opportunities, such as education.

The expanding commodification of social life also highlights the hegemonization of a market driven by instrumental choices. When Henry Ford coined his famous dictum 'you may choose any car as long as it is black,' people may have had little choice in terms of car color. However, within the social environment of that era they had a real choice of viable, cheap or free transportation alternatives to the car. Presently, the proliferation of consumption choices co-exists with the dwindling of alternatives in goods and services which exist outside the commodified realm of capital, as public education, health, transport and physical spaces are commercialized *and* privatized.

The hyperculturalization of reflexive accumulation

The hyperculturalization of reflexive accumulation

Social Identity Compositions and Narratives

constitutes the third sphere of the contemporary co-mediation of social identities through commodification practices. Two categories of this phenomenon can be identified: the aestheticized commodification of identity (i.e., 'buying the self'), and the ascendancy of consumable globalism (i.e., 'buying the world').

The aestheticized commodification of identity

The aestheticized commodification of identity (i.e., 'buying the self') is a phenomenon primarily spawned by changes in the techniques, patterns and practices of valorization. During the Fordist era, capital extracted most of its directly monetized surplus value through the commodification of labor and the appropriation of surplus labor time in productionist or manufacturing industries.[62] Numerous social processes, such as the gender division of domestic labor, though pivotal to the appropriation and accumulation of surplus value, were not directly monetized. Over time, new parts of the labor chain were monetized through the expansion of service industries, and the escalation of the monetization of information, ideas, images and identities.

The contemporary surplus value chain extends potential valorization to more and more social activities.[63] Surplus value now consists of a fusion of directly commodified activities (i.e., being paid for a specific task − as a worker), the activities of commodified intermediation (i.e., as a consumer being paid − indirectly via the tax deductions made by advertisers − to watch television), and the objects of commodification (i.e., physical, abstract or virtual objects, with exchange value). As more and more social activities and objects are valorized, the role of objects as cultural mediators also tends to expand.[64]

Objects most often have use value and/or exchange value. In addition, objects acquire *and* signify cultural meaning in social exchanges. Historically, only a small aristocratic elite engaged in positional consumption.[65] The Fordist accumulation regime was generally characterized by a relatively strong focus on the production and consumption of use values.[66] Since the 1970s,

173

individualized positional consumption has increased at the same time as the acquisition of sign values, in addition to use values, gained momentum in the advanced industrialized world.[67] The growing emphasis on symbolic signs and aesthetic goods *vis-à-vis* products or physical objects with use-value is particularly prevalent in the proliferation of objects which possess a substantial inherent aesthetic component (e.g., pop music, art and sporting paraphernalia). This trend is also evident in the increasing component of sign-value, or image embodied in inherently physical objects with mostly use-value.[68] In response to these changes, manufactured goods are becoming more complex and a fragmented mixture of physical, cognitive, use and aesthetic content. The cultural aestheticization of goods[69] and the commodification of symbolic forms (e.g., the hypervalorization of brand names such as Nike),[70] not only occurs in sectors with an overtly high cultural content such as tourism and entertainment, but in most commercialized spheres. The monetization of symbols, images and meaning has indeed become central to valorization processes.[71]

For Dittmar (1992) capitalism, and consumer capitalism in particular, is presently moving beyond the consumption of goods and services to the consuming self. Dittmar articulates this relation between modernist identities and goods as a process in which the symbolic meanings of material possessions serve as expressions of group membership, as a means of locating others in the 'social-material' environment, and as a source of information about other people's identities.[72] The cultural agency of objects and the way in which they engage homo sapiens in cultural processes, is particularly noticeable in the clothing-culture industry. This industry is steeped in the visible display of brandnames, images and the omnipresent processes of bricolage in which objects and subjects acquire new meanings and identities through the recontextualization of objects within a specific social constellation.[73]

Pieterse (1994) argues that denationalization processes are related to the increased pluralization of cultural organization and a shift in the nexus of social identity composition processes, away from collective institutions towards the practices of individual social reproduction. The rapid and dramatic advances in technology which stretch social actions and relations across time and space, undermine the classical modernist links between nationally defined geographical spaces, social location and collective identities. Technological advances contribute to the manipulation of social imaginations, and initiate abstract interactions in a global symbolic, electronic and virtual environment as opposed to directly observable and concrete interactions which characterized the industrial organization of social life. In conjunction, denationalization, pluralization and virtualization processes are central to the simultaneous fragmentation and privatization of the social universe from which social agents accumulate, contextualize and articulate their social identities. It is today easier than before for individuals to make themselves temporarily and simultaneously available to several local, global and virtual organizational options and social identities. In these reflexive practices and processes, the 'sources of the self' (Pieterse, 1994) are amplified and diversified.

The reflexive immersion of the private self in a more encompassent collective is molded by a range of possible choices and motivations (e.g., social spatial location, self-interest, emotional, etc.). Whilst individuals still live local physical lives, the importance of virtual and phenomenal social lives is amplified by the electrification of time and space. As a result, individuals tend to compose and narrate their social identities with a much greater sensitivity to their temporal spatial locations. More specifically, individuals now often participate simultaneously in a number of overlapping social constellations, complicating and fragmenting their own social identities. Consequently, people more and more have multiple, partial and even several layers of social identities. Mort (1989), for example, argues that "we are not in any simple sense 'black' or 'gay' or 'upwardly mobile.' Rather we carry a bewildering range of different, and at times conflicting, identities around with us in our heads at the same time. There is a continual smudging of personas and lifestyles, depending where we are (at work, on the high street) and the spaces we are moving between" (Mort 1989:169).

It can be argued that social identity in advanced industrial spaces is no longer essentially a collective identity, but a privately self-collected and relativized identity.[74] It is today much easier for social actors to escape and challenge some of the constraints of unidimensional collective identities, as defined by nationalist hegemons, which are often intolerant of all so-called 'nonconformist' identities and their narratives (i.e., 'gays,' 'greenies,' etc.). This does not mean that current modernist social spaces are innately more tolerant of so-called 'nonconformist' identities, nor that alterity in itself is inherently more acceptable. However, pluralized identity spaces have been opened by the social ascendance of 'private free choice' market forces.

Both collective identities and the private self are no longer intertwined into a coherent, unidimensional, and often dogmatic, national narrative. Instead, alterity can now be articulated, displayed and even celebrated more openly and overtly. The renunciation or celebration of alterity in everyday life is, however, often dependent on the specific valorization opportunities, as illustrated by events such the Sydney Gay and Lesbian Mardi Grass festival.[75] This event, in which the celebration of so-called sexual preference alterity has been transformed into a major commercial venture, is an example of the sanctioned celebration of valorizable alterity. In these latter processes of social identity narration, the 'sources of the self' are amplified and homogenized by the market, and social identities are more overtly and hegemonically valorized. In the words of Friedman (1994), "[c]onsumption within the bounds of the world system is always a consumption of identity, canalized by a negotiation between self-definition and the array of possibilities offered by the capitalist market" (Friedman, 1994: 104). Market mediated pluralism and market mediated hegemony are intimately infused into the socially possible ways social identities can be composed and narrated by private individuals *vis-à-vis* the social forces of private capital.

The aestheticization and individualization of objects and images – as part of a lifestyle with a focus on enhanced self-image – increasingly mediate people's perception of the social world as a supermarket "within which they are offered a multiplicity of lifestyles and values" (Turner, 1994:174).[76] This creates new challenges and expanding opportunities for commercialists. A Zem manager argued that Zem needs to develop, manufacture and market products that were "... not only useful to people, but also make people feel useful, and make people feel good about themselves. In order to achieve this, our products must become part of our customers' personalities. This is something which the clothing industry comprehended in the 1920s already .... A good product must also be a statement about your personality, or the personality you aspire to" (Zem manager). In Marcuse's words, "[p]eople recognize themselves in their commodities, they find their soul in their automobile..." (Marcuse, 1968:24). The hypervalorization of individualized identities and brand names (e.g., Michael Jordan and Nike),[77] the cultural mediation of identity through objects, and the processes of hermeneutic self consumption are all part and parcel of the contemporary aestheticized commodification of identity.[78] However, the buying of the self is only one side of the commodified identity coin.

The ascendancy of consumable globalism

The ascendancy of consumable globalism (i.e., 'buying the world') is the other important aspect of the contemporary co-mediation of social identities through commodification practices. Generally speaking, consumption practices are today characterized by the proliferation of new patterns of goods acquisition (e.g., electronic and just-in-time home-bound retailing – isolating people socially, whilst integrating them globally at the same time),[79] as well as by access to similar goods, services, objects, artifacts, signs and images through the use of, for example, global generic production and marketing strategies. Albrow (1996) argues that entrepreneurs draw on a common stock of meaning and being global "itself now carries connotations of the commercialization of humanity" (Albrow, 1996:83). This phenomenon is particularly prevalent in service and service-related industries which have a potentially high inherent symbolic content, predisposing them to reflexive and specialized accumulation. In combination, the reality of global production and marketing, and the notions of 'being global,' makes it easier for businesses to use generic strategies. This is especially the case in an era in which the global mass media inculcates local populations with both consumerism and consumable globalism.

The ascendancy of consumable globalism is also apparent in the more direct and immediate global interconnectedness, brought about by advanced telecommunications. The rising mobility of goods via global markets and electronic superhighways, and the growing possibility of traveling through physical, electronic and imaginative spaces, have compacted our sense of the social and natural worlds. The reconstitution of the spatial dynamics of social life via audio and visual consumption allows people to be anywhere and everywhere, without physically leaving their homes. At the same time, these processes have also intensified *and* fragmented people's experience of their connection to the social universe. For example, peoples' experiences of their own participation in globality as active participants, and even constitutive agents of globalization (e.g., global elites, those people who directly or indirectly participate in global financial markets), or as constituted victims of globalization (i.e., disempowered and detached by globalization), or even as an ambiguous mixture of being involved in, as well as detached from, globality, are today continually exacerbated.[80]

The ideas and images portrayed via contemporary communication technologies tend to fragment local identities in terms of their constant exposure to wider and global frames of reference. At the same time, our idea world is also saturated with a proliferation of homogeneous notions of conspicuous consumption drawn from around the globe. Robertson (1992) refers to this fragmentation/homogenization coexisting within the cultural orbits of global capital as the 'global valorization of particular identities,' and the 'universalization of particularism.' This notion can be applied to, and is apparent in, the advertisement campaigns of transnationals. These campaigns often pay more attention to the global consumption of a specific transnational's identity, than to particular products. A typical example is a McDonalds advertising campaign in Australia. In these television advertisements a homogenization of visual images from very diverse and globally dispersed locations (i.e., Perth, Rome, Mexico, New York and Moscow) is achieved through the consumption of MacDonalds food. The visual images are complemented by a subliminal 'all around the world it's Mac time' catch phrase which is repeated several times.[81] Another well-known example of these practices are the advertising campaigns of Benetton, in which globality, as an idea and as an image, engenders a fusion of aestheticization and commodification. These campaigns typically consist of visual images depicting and confronting global issues (e.g., a white and a black woman holding an oriental baby wrapped in a towel, a black woman breastfeeding a white baby, a black child's hand resting on an adult white male's hand, etc.) without textual commentary other than the company logo (i.e., United Colors of Benetton). Through the processes of bricolage, Benetton products became symbols of global integration, to be appropriated by those who wear them.[82]

Conclusion

"In the use of money, everyone is a trader" (Ricardo, 1816).

This chapter highlighted some of the central developments in the interdynamics of the globalization-valorization-marginalization triangle in relation to some of the most important specific modernist identity compositions and narratives at the end of the twentieth century. The influences on contemporary social identities were discussed in terms of three broad categories.

Firstly, the late twentieth century bears witness to the erosion of the national class compromise and the decline of the welfare state. These developments are accompanied by fundamental changes to military technology, decreasing the dependency of the state on mass participation for its functional military operation, and the partial reversal of the 'idea of civil society,' as well as the dismantling of the state as a means of social integration and of institutional barriers which had regulated the commodification of certain social spheres and relations in the past. Consequently, there is an amelioration of the social influences of private capital *vis-à-vis* the social leverage of the state in relation to the management of valorization processes and the composition of social identities. This privatization of social identities, on the one hand, undermines imposed group bonds, frees the individual from the constraints of extended social collectives, and facilitates the emergence of the self-determining individual. On the other hand, it also increases the potential for individual isolation from the reprocipical care of extended social collectives.

Secondly, the primacy of machine technologies – characteristic of industrial social life – is progressively superseded by a range of virtual electrified telecommunications and information technologies. These technologies transcend many of the classical modernist spatial, time and cultural constraints on social exchanges. In the latter part of the twentieth century, new space and time devouring technological advances (e.g., satellites, fiber optic cables, etc.) co-exist with a global media network which enables people to 'witness,' and sometimes participate – physically, virtually or symbolically – in distant events more intensely without necessarily leaving their own locality. This means that social identities and social imaginations are shaped more intimately by real distant events and their symbolic, virtual and reflexive recomposition by culture industries and individuals themselves. As a result of technological developments, social agents have both greater opportunities for *privatized social participation* (e.g., in global financial markets; the virtual media universe; global mass private communications and cyberspace; etc.), and a greater chance for *privatized social isolation* (e.g., through the symbolic distancing of electronic entrepreneurship; the virtualization of class conflict; the emergence of electronically integrated work practices and locations, such as teleworking; the general shift away from mass work mobilization through mass trade unionism, labor centered political parties, etc. towards individualized work mobilization practices, individual work contracts, etc.).

Thirdly, contemporary social stratification and integration processes are increasingly shaped by commodification processes. This contributes to the growing importance of consumption *vis-à-vis* production influences on social identity compositions and narrations. More and more aspects of social interaction are today monetized through the increased acquisition and valorization of physical, symbolic and virtual objects.[83] 'Cultural drenching' (Featherstone, 1991), the enlarged significance and the extent of accumulation as an overtly post-subsistence and post-functional activity, and the increasing aestheticization of valorized social relations are not new modernist tendencies. However, the increased valorization of exchange activities *per se*, as well as the hyperculturalization of reflexive accumulation, are unique and particularly important facets of contemporary social life.

The two aspects of hyperculturalization of reflexive accumulation, namely the aestheticized commodification of identity (i.e., 'buying the self') and the ascendancy of consumable globalism (i.e., 'buying the world'), are central to the contemporary mediation of social identities through commodification practices. In general, these valorization practices have a twofold impact on social identity compositions and narratives. On the one hand, commodified culture and identity can now be appropriated, acquired, bought, worn, used, changed and disposed of more easily and more instantly than before, as the fetishification of objects, images, and ideas continues to accelerate. These phenomena form the basis of a *narcistic aestheticized reflexivity* – the consumption and composition of social identity in the context of the reflexive private self. In other words, buying your identity in order to become yourself. The general expansion of social, private and virtual valorizations creates new opportunities for individuals to free themselves from the constraints of space and time, the state and collective groups. It also creates new opportunities for self development, existentialist liberty, and wealth creation. Contemporary social identities can be self-composed and self-narrated to a much larger extent by individuals applying aestheticized knowledge and converting symbolic goods into cultural cargo.

On the other hand, integrated global markets for physical, symbolic and virtual objects, images, and ideas also add to a global homogenization of the technical artifacts, imagery and signs of global capitalism. At the same time, the spatial spread of this genre contributes to the hegemonization of the structural influences of global capitalism on everyday life. These phenomena constitute the basis of the processes of *global aestheticized reflexivity* – the consumption and composition of the social world in the context of a hegemonic private capitalism. In other words, buying the world in order to become part of it.[84] This obligatory consumption of globality is one of the manifestations of the general expansion of social, private and virtual valorization which increases the potential for social dislocation mediated by valorized activities (e.g., waged labor), valorized spheres (e.g., state of the art technologies) and valorized identities (e.g., buying of life chances).

Conclusion
Globalization, valorization and marginalization:
Some Zeitgeist reflections

"It [the twentieth century] has been a century of emigration and exile, both voluntary and forced. But 'leaving home' is also the dominant metaphor for a time in which all the certainties, social, political and artistic have migrated" (Hall, 1996:1).

Since the 1970s the dominant modernist Zeitgeist, as well as the social and spatial dynamics of modernist marginality have been reconstructed significantly in the context of the contemporary changes in the techniques, forms and patterns of modernist valorization. This has been the central argument throughout this book. Generally speaking, the interplay between globalization, valorization and marginalization is not a new phenomenon. However, the social construction of all three phenomena relative to each other, is changing at a rapid rate. Three of the most important aspects of these interdynamics are highlighted in this conclusion. These developments are: the virtual valorization of time, space and social exchanges; the spatial reorganization of private enterprises and the spatial recasting of marginality; and the growing disequilibrium between private interests and social collectives, including the recasting of the relation between the private self (i.e., the individual) and the collective self (i.e., social collective such as the state).

The virtual valorization of time, space and social exchanges

The conventional boundaries of modernist institutions (e.g., the nation-state), social conglomerates (e.g., space, place and time) and social identities (e.g., class) are today superseded, dissolved or made obsolete in certain areas. This development is one of the consequences of the simultaneous increase in virtual electronic and valorized social exchanges. The global spread of unfettered and digital capitalism also contributes to the replacement of the industrial model (i.e., large groups of workers doing specialized tasks with centralized coordination) with a virtual model of corporate organization. In this model work moves freely between temporary teams of workers who respond to specific market stimuli. The pressure to be virtual – to produce products and deliver services without many fixed assets – is a present day organizational *fait accompli.*

Essentially, the *pari passu* virtualization and valorization of time, space, productive organization, social exchanges and social identities substantially transforms the classical commodification of resources, goods and humans from the concrete to the virtual. This late twentieth century movement towards virtual valorization includes the following. Firstly, there is the emergence of monetization processes as valorizable activities in themselves as one form of money is now sequentially exchanged for other forms of money (e.g., in currency transactions) in global financial markets. Secondly, there is the advent of risk management practices in which risk itself becomes a tradable commodity, as well as a commodification practice (e.g., in derivative transactions). Many of the state-of-the-art spheres of digital capitalism – such as communication, design, software development, on-line shopping, legal- and finance services – are today more and more mediated in cyberspaces, often through instant monetized exchanges.

Thirdly, the movement towards virtual valorization includes the replacement of extractive natural resources (e.g., oil) by time as arguably the most precious contemporary non-

Conclusion

renewable resource, especially in the income-rich, but time-poor industrialized world in which disposable incomes increased dramatically since the 1970s.[1] The effect of the simultaneous emergence of time as a scarce resource and increases in disposable income can, for example, be observed in the growth of the take-away and fast food industry. These replenishment stations do not provide cheap or *haute cuisine*, but the food is provided and consumed within minutes without wasted pockets of time.

Fourthly, there is the incremental displacement of the state-regulated commodification of certain social spheres and relations by the more encompassing monetization of social life through, for example, the mediation of social identities through commodification practices. This phenomenon includes the increased aestheticized commodification of identity – i.e., 'buying the self' – and the ascendancy of consumable globalism – i.e., 'buying the world' as important values and practices of our time and embodies the movement away from socialized and concrete towards individualized and virtual valorizations.

Generally speaking, the ideas and practices of monetary rationalism are embedded in both the view that social interactions and exchanges are transactional relationships, systematically standardized and mediated by money, and in the reality of our time that the market, fueled by high technology, is ever present in more and more social exchanges. The *en masse* virtual valorizations of social exchanges in, for example, the electronic and cyber money markets of the post-1970s, are substantially changing the social character of money in two important ways.

Firstly, virtual valorizations contribute to the transformation of money from *a* social relation (Marx) to *the* social relation of our time. Secondly, virtual valorizations are central to the deconcretization of money. No longer is money merely the *representative of abstract value* (Simmel). Increasingly money is both the *representative* and *abstract value in itself*. The ability of money to exist without been supported by an equivalence in gold as was the case with the Gold Standard is a related occurrence. Articulated differently, the social character of money is changing from a *concrete symbol* for abstract and infinite relative social value of a specific article, experience, idea, etc. *vis-á-vis* all other commodities to a *virtual symbol* of abstract and infinite relative social value. This can be seen, for example, in futures, options and derivatives transactions which are based on the principle of capturing future time in present transactions, increasing the mass of nominal capital *vis-à-vis* bank deposits and assets so dramatically that there appears to be an abstract digression of time and money in which future money is created, realized and generated by time, as well as by the virtual circulation of money.

The ascendancy of virtual electronic and valorized interactions and exchanges as important social influences highlight the complexity of the social construction of contemporary marginalization. It also contributes to the specific social construction of contemporary marginalization. Compared with the pre-1970s, marginalization is today less of a 'material' phenomenon relating predominantly to those people who are impoverished in monetary terms (i.e., the so-called poor). Instead, marginalization and social dislocation now consist of a complex mixture of social and technical influences. Marginalization not only refers to those people who are directly dislocated *from* current valorization activities (e.g., the poor, unemployed, etc.), but reaches substantially beyond 'material deprivation.' As such, it also refers to those people dislocated *by* the current forms of valorization (e.g., people with only limited access to technology; passive recipients of virtual social reality; people, such as teleworkers, suffering intense social isolation and dislocation through advanced technological work practices despite their use of state-of-the-art technologies; etc.).

The specific present day construction of marginalization through new valorization forms is generally under-researched in current sociology. As a result there is a dearth of extensive analyses of the wider social relevance of contemporary valorization techniques, patterns and practices to modernity.[2] In this respect, the renewed interest in Simmel's 'The

Conclusion

Philosophy of Money' (1990), a century after it was written in a very different monetary social environment, is perhaps not only due to its own merits, but also due to the present theoretical and empirical void in this important area of social life.[3]

The spatial reorganization of valorization processes and the spatial recasting of marginalization

The speed and scope of post-1970s technological innovations increased the movement flexibility of transnationals, and have contributed to fundamental changes in the productive processes of global capitalism. In the latter part of the twentieth century the industrial techniques of valorization have been extended and altered through processes such as increased electrification and computerization, as well as through business strategies of so-called non-financial institutions which overtly focused on monetization management as a major area – to complement, or even supersede, the traditional production of goods[4] – in which monetized surplus could be created, realized and generated.

These changes in the techniques of valorization were accompanied with the electrification of work and accumulation processes which instigated rapid changes in the forms, margins and the locational position of surplus. Under the Fordist regime, surplus was mainly produced in the production processes of heavy industries and agriculture. Presently, surplus is also created *en masse* at the intersection of exchange and consumption processes (e.g., through the the electronic techniques of speculative trading, electronic gambling, the valorized manipulation of time and space, and the practices of 'transfer pricing' and tax mobilization). As a result, the importance of financial manipulation and electronic monetization, *vis-à-vis* production processes has increased substantially over the last two decades.[5] These valorization developments contribute to the increased technical and social maneuverability of corporations not only between integrated, yet globally dispersed production sites, but also in complex global financial markets.

The contemporary spatial reorganization of social relations is furthermore influenced by the changes in the global patterns of work and other productive activities. Two of these changes warrent special attention. Firstly, the stability and permanence that characterized labour markets and wage labor in the advanced industrialized world in the post-war 'national-class compromise' era has been replaced by uncertainty and temporality. Selective flexible specialization and flexible labor regimes, including the flexible hours and part-time work, mean that workers experience vastly different levels of work participation during various periods of their working lives, as well as multiple and concurrent careers. The increased segmentation of working lives, with people undertaking numerous time specific 'pieces of work,' contributes to the breakdown of the twentieth century coherent life narratives constructed around relative fixed positions in relatively rigid production hierarchies.

Flexibility no longer refers to the capacity of organizations or individuals to adapt temporarily to changing conditions without losing their original identity, character or form permanently, as it was defined 20 years ago. Today flexibility denotes the capacity to change rapidly from one identity to another, to have no essential identity, character, form or shape at all. The social identities and roles of workers, for instance, are no longer as fixed as before the 1990s. Workers can no longer construct a social identity narrative from an accumulative career and set career path as was the case within the social relations of industrial capitalism. Increased flexibility, efficiency, adaptability, social dislocation, angst and increased prosperity are today intimately interwoven into the emergence of the post-industrialized world.

The degeneration of the idea and reality of stable work and income co-exists with the ascendancy of speculative valorization as a major monetary source. These two developments inadvertently reinforce each other. At the same time as the twentieth century's work ethos (including

Conclusion

transparent career paths and the belief in the value of work as counterweight for a monetary reward) incrementally disintegrates risk, time and space are solidified as valorizable entities in themselves. It is not only the content and ways of work which are fundamentally altered by new valorization techniques, patterns and practices, but also the operation and logic of monetary reward structures as well as the the notion, definition and social construction of work itself. This undermines the modern belief in work as an intervention method through which one can control one's own fate by reducing the influence of chance and luck in life. Modernity gave individuals the opportunity to intervene in their own fate through labor which reduced the influence of chance and luck. This process is, at least, partially reversed today due to the relative ascendancy of chance *vis-à-vis* an intrinsic work ethic.

Secondly, current management-worker relations in advanced industrialized spaces are less overtly polarized and hierarchical, and more vertically integrated than before the 1980s. However, the movement away from the classical caste type of hierarchical Fordist work and class relations co-exists with an increased symbolic spatial distance between those who contribute to the creation, realization and generation of monetized surplus (e.g., workers), and those who appropriate a relative disproportionate quantity of monetized surplus (e.g., owners, management, stockbrokers and shareholders), as well as with a dramatic increase in the relative gap between lower and higher paid workers.[6] This micro level spatial recasting and social reorganization of valorization and work relations is part of the often observed divergence that occurs between the emerging so-called over- and underclasses the world over.

Similar to the micro level spatial recasting of valorization relations, a macro spatial recasting of marginality and social dislocation is also observable today as there is a complex reconfiguration of wealth distribution, accompanied by concomitant shifts in class structures and a partial demobilization of class as a social agent.[7] The ability of labor and other marginal social groups, such as rural African communities, to organize collectively and to act as a counterforce to perceived social inequalities within, or across, national spaces, is progressively eroded through the evolution of ever more complex, more virtual and less face-to-face valorization processes in which these inequalities are embedded. As a result of these developments, the spatial dynamics and individual location of modernist marginality is reconfigured, becoming less nationally encoded and dichotic, and more diasporic, multipolar and multidimensional (i.e., influenced by a range of spatial, social and technological aspects).

The new patterns of geographical peripheralization and social marginalization generally relate to two major macro processes, namely the increased depeasantization of spaces peripheral to the modernist network (e.g., the 'Third World'), and the partial deindustrialization of historical core modernist spaces (e.g., the 'Western World'). The processes which systematically expelled peasants from the land and forced them to migrate to urban centers, have existed for centuries. However, dramatic population increases, and the absorption of more land and forest areas into the global marketplace have accelerated urbanization and depeasantization during the last part of this century. In peripheral modernist spaces the population pressures of rapid urbanization, as well as the population explosion in certain parts (e.g., in Africa)[8] generally exist in isolation from a local production regime seemingly capable of long-term social stability.

In regard to the historical core modernist spaces the scenario appears to be quite different. In the short term, the partial de-industrialization of core spaces is leading to the recomposition of jobs, the reconstruction of the forms of work, and new patterns of marginalization and social dislocation. For example, in advanced industrialized spaces there is a movement away from the relative socialization of production towards the individualization and segmentation (i.e., from full time to part time, from set hours to flexible hours, etc.) of production processes.[9] In the past, the hierarchical divisions of productive practices and relations were central to the formation and maintenance of class-based social and labor movements.

Conclusion

Productive hierarchies also informed the ways in which the twentieth century welfare state forged a coalescence between competing interests in order to stabilize the state.

It stands to reason that the technical and spatial changes to the global social environment raise fundamental questions about the ethos, practices and survival of trade unions in general, and the dominant twentieth century social collectives – such as class-based social movements – in particular. It is unlikely that the post-1970s decline of the state's management of valorization processes and the present demise of the welfare state will lead to the reinvigoration of class struggles as a social force. Present technical, organizational and spatial changes to productive processes – such as the electronic dispersion of workers – fundamentally undermine the social environment in which mass and collective work mobilization (through mass trade unionism, labor centered political parties and class-based social movements), flourished in the past.

Present social turbulence and potential future social chaos are in part the result of late twentieth century global valorization processes. These processes were instrumental to the accelerated polarization of social inequalities – such as the dramatic advancement of income and wealth discrepancies since the 1960s – and are indeed fraught with implications for future global inequalities. They also raise potential difficulties for the management of the social instability which is a likely consequence of large-scale social inequalities which co-exist alongside sophisticated and relatively easy accessible communication and military technologies (which can be used in publicity, propaganda and terrorist campaigns). Presently, the management of the social manifestations of social inequalities seems to be based on policies which aim to contain social instability. This is manifested, for example, in so-called tough policing, crime prevention and punishment regimes on a governmental level.

On an individual domestic level the 'containment of social instability' ideology is often translated into practices which emphasize increased private security and local social insulation, with so-called walled and guarded neighborhoods as an inordinate example. It can be argued that in high security and locally insulated neighborhoods the porous borders of the nation-state, and the ever more fragile social borders of local community networks (essentially due to the escalation of internal wealth descrepancies),[10] are supplemented by more rigid private borders. This links the 'socially connected actors' with each other locally, and globally with the rest of the world via virtual technologies, whilst insulating them at the same time from the rest of their local community.[11]

The practices of private neighborhoods and walled communities, as well as the extensive general privatization of public spaces, constitute a throwback to the practices of social insulation prevalent the Middle Ages. More generally speaking, the daily paths of the socially connected/dynamic (and often rich) social actors and those socially disconnected (and often poor) *from* and *by* current valorization activities are increasingly estranged from each other mainly as a result of either the practices of private exclusivity (e.g., private neighborhoods, social clubs or high participation costs) or through specific policing strategies aimed at controlling the visibility of crime and poverty in specifically targeted public spaces.[12] In cities the world over, the emerging so-called overclass rarely comes into contact with crime, poverty and social dislocation. This selective virtualization of crime and poverty (e.g., existing on television screens) co-exists with increased levels of real wealth and real poverty concentration within local communities. Both virtual insolation and local wealth apartheid are central features of the general disintegration of the collective ethos and local communities.[13]

The incremental, yet progressive demise of the collective ethos is also exacerbated by the commodification of not only goods, labor power and certain social relations – as was the case throughout the modernist epoch – but also of post-industrial goods (e.g., information on a massive scale) and exchange processes (e.g., electronic capital) *per se*. It is becoming progressively easier for transnational corporations, and for 'socially connected actors' (i.e., the emerging so-called overclass, the rich and those people integrated into the

Conclusion

dominant contemporary social spheres by and through state-of-the-art technologies) to locate and relocate production facilities, productive capital and valorized electronic capital around the world. Suitable global productive spaces are sought in regard to optimum skills, work practices, costs, social control, tax mobilization possibilities, and financial deregulation. Access to, and control of, state-of-the-art and virtualizing technologies generally also assist 'socially connected actors' to reflexively co-compose and co-narrate their social identities. These people are most often inclined to view globalization as an inherently positive occurrence resulting in socially advanced developments and challenges which provides progressive opportunities for themselves.

The deterritorialization of monetized opportunities is not an option open to labor, nor to the socially dislocated/ marginalized acted-upon people (i.e., the emerging so-called underclass, the poor and those who have limited access to contemporary technologies, or are socially isolated due to their use of contemporary technologies especially in their work environment). Virtual technologies often impede on the abilities of those with limited or no access and control of these technologies to actively participate in the social world and to co-compose and co-narrate their own social identities. These people are most often inclined to view globalization as an inherently negative occurrence resulting in socially destructive developments and risks which leads to a regression of opportunities for themselves.

The growing disequilibrium between private interests and social collectives

The acceleration of virtual electronics is not only central to the contemporary proliferation of indirect social relationships, but also to the circumvention of collective public institutions by private interests. The general privatization and valorization of the social universe tend to obscure the classical modernist inter-relationships between social decision-making structures, representation, responsibility, accountability, social integration and social control. These changes forces a rethinking of the role and future viability of the central financial artifacts which developed in the era of industrial capitalism, such as central banks, reserves, as well as fiat and national currencies. Extended global technical integration and the general increases in global interdependence, density and awareness furthermore undermine the abilities of governments to manage social valorization processes. The declining influence of social collectives are paralleled by the increased influence of the ideas and practices of monetary rationalism. These two developments tend to reinforce each other in a reflexive way. For example, the failure of social collectives to manage and control contemporary valorization processes, such as the electronic valorization practices of global financial markets, inadvertently becomes part of the social logic which underpins the push for increased monetary rationalism. Articulated simplistically, governments failing to control or manage financial and other markets appears to confirm that governments cannot, *and* should not, interfere in the market. This idea affirms the perception that global forces are inherently voluntaristic, reinforces the social disengaging ideologies of rationalist monetarism and undermines the moral and fiscal space of *inclusive social collectives* (e.g., the general public) *vis-à-vis exclusive individualist collectives* (e.g., individual shareholders).

The decline in the social leverage of social collectives also spawned an evident decline in the language of a nationally defined collective parochialism. Instead, we today encounter an omnipresent globalization lingo in our daily intellectual diet. Globalization is often portrayed in the global media and in academic discourses as a supra-social, metaphysical and voluntaristic force. It is indeed difficult to grasp and concisely articulate the interdynamics and social complexities of the constituent elements of contemporary globalization. This is particulary the case in regard to the forms of virtual valorization and the symbolic distance they have engendered between valorizing processes and people. Virtual valorization processes also contribute to the shift from mass to

Conclusion

individualized work mobilization practices, and accentuate the decline of local social reciprocity (e.g., as money is no longer retained as a productive resource within the social relationships of the nation-state) which has been central to the ethos of the collective self as articulated within the parameters of the welfare state paradigm.

Classical modernist identities (e.g., such as nationality and class) were furthermore entangled with relations embedded in both their geographical location and in local social reciprocity networks. At the end of the twentieth century the spatial dimensions of social distance between the private self – i.e., the individual – and the collective self – i.e., social collectives such as the state – is increasingly attenuated through the decline of real (e.g., via transportation advances and communication technologies) and the escalation of virtual (e.g., via valorization techniques and communication technologies) spaces.[14] This social despatialization contributes to the fragmentation of the modernist notion and practices of the local, and often nationalist, social collective.

The decline in the interrelationship between the private self and the spatially defined collective self is both a manifestation, and an active constituent, of the retrocession of the institutions and ethos of spatially defined public governance. As a result, it could be argued that the contemporary forms of globalization rhetoric in advanced industrialized spaces are symptoms of an intimately interwoven crisis or disequilibrium between the declining social primacy of *local collective power sharing practices* (i.e., so-called national democracy) and the increased social influence of *global individual wealth accumulation practices* (i.e., so-called competitive global capitalism) within advanced industrialized spaces.

The relative ascendancy of the institutions and practices of global capitalism *vis-à-vis* social collective institutions and practices, co-exist with the spatial expansion of global capitalism and the particular amelioration of the social influences of valorization patterns. The privatization of state enterprises, public spaces and social lives means that so-called local or national assets are transferred to global stock markets, and thus come under the control of private global interests. This virtual monetization of local assets has far-reaching implications for privatized social control, exposing people (including those living in the historically core modernist spaces) to the potentially destabilizing consequences of a market-mediated global interconnectedness.[15] It also means that the self-interests, and global interdependencies and networks of those who are directly or indirectly connected to global financial markets, make them less dependent on the extraction of resources and surpluses from a local, or specific, geographical space.

The extent and nature of contemporary global and non-geographical systems of valorization bind together the prosperity and destitution of individuals, groups of individuals, as well as local, global and supra-geographical communities. Consequently, public governance is today haunted by ambiguities in terms of the real, potential and perceived beneficiaries of governmental policies and actions. For example, at the same time as the big 'Australian' corporate icon BHP scales down its Australian operations (e.g., closing its Newcastle operations in 1997), its expansion into China is officially assisted by the Australian government. In other words, the paid Australian representatives of the *vox populi* act on behalf of all Australians, but for the apparent benefit of BHP shareholders, consisting of people who are geographically dispersed around the globe and virtually connected by common global monetary interests. The continued co-existence of national democracy and competitive global capitalism – which tended to stabilize social relationships during the third quarter of the twentieth century – is becoming more and more untenable. This disequilibrium often manifests itself in attempts to consolidate one *vis-à-vis* the other in, for example, nationalist revolts against globalization.

At the end of the eighteenth century, handloom weavers bore the brunt of the Industrial Revolution as they lost their livelihood. Today many millions of people across the world are also suffering an *en masse* redundancy at the hands of an electrificated, informatized and, above all, overtly individualizing commodification genre.[16] The extent the social changes confronting the individual and communities at present is indeed bewildering, and are often referred to as the beginning of universal chaos on an unknown scale, a global Armageddon. However, as illustrated in the Chinese symbol for crisis, each crisis also means opportunity. Perhaps our own difficulties in coming to terms with contemporary changes have resulted in us, similar to the eighteenth century handloom weavers, remaining opaque to the possibility that we are also standing on the brink of a new era of cultural-material and moral growth on a scale beyond our present social imaginations. However, the social influences associated with the escalation of the practices of contemporary valorization – one of the pivotal features of contemporary social life and social identities – cannot be avoided or ignored before we exit from the modernist globalization epoch.

On the one hand, the general expansion of social, private and virtual valorizations creates new opportunities for individuals to free themselves from the constraints of space and time, the state and collective groups. The reflexive immersion of the private self in more temporal, flexible and optional collectives leads to a *narcistic aestheticized reflexivity* in which the sources of the self are amplified and diversified. This is partially achieved through virtual and valorizing technologies, and partially by the application of aestheticized knowledge in the selective conversion of social and private symbolic goods into valorized goods and cultural cargo. At present social agents in advanced industrialized spaces generally have greater opportunities for *privatized social participation* (e.g., in global financial markets; the virtual media universe; global mass private communications and cyberspace; etc.). These processes signal the arrival of the *self-realized individual.*

On the other hand, the consummate infusion of the neo- and post-industrialized valorizations into social interactions and exchanges lead to new patterns of market-mediated hegemony. Within the parameters of this *hegemonic aestheticized reflexivity* regime, social exchanges and identities are more overtly valorized by a global market-mediated pluralism. This private valorization of the social self renders the socially dislocated more vulnerable to structural and virtual marginalization in the long term, and also curtails their ability to convert symbolic goods into valorized goods and cultural cargo. As a result there is a greater change that social agents might suffer *privatized social isolation* (e.g., through the symbolic distancing of electronic valorization; the virtualization of class conflict; the emergence of electronically integrated work practices and locations, such as teleworking; the general shift away from mass work mobilization through mass trade unionism, labor centered political parties, etc. towards individualized work mobilization practices, individual work contracts, etc.).

The electronic globalization of markets and the media undermine the value-adding services of local markets and dissolve the commitments people have to local communities. Present global valorization practices fundamentally alter the relationship between individual and geographical collectives, such as the nation-state, and ferments a new kind of individualism as people experience themselves as having few commitments to geographical collectives, and recasting them as nodes in ever-shifting utilitarian networks (e.g., from members of an enduring nation to a utilitarian network in public social life, and from friends to contacts in private social life). In general, the processes of the hegemonic aestheticized reflexivity regime form the basis of the social construction of the *valorized-self individual.*

The valorization of social exchanges is central to both the *self-realized* and *valorized-self* aspects of the social world and the social identities of contemporary individuals. This duality continues the general pattern of key modernist features, namely that social constructs are characterized by ambivalence and complementary, yet contradictory aspects. However, contemporary valorization processes are leaving no social construct untouched in their wake, signaling the end of the dominant twentieth century patterns of collective social integration, organization and identity construction. The long-term impact of electronic valorization developments largely

Conclusion

depends on whether future valorization practices will foment the emergence of a dramatically different production regime which provides sustainable growth, relatively equitable growth distribution and stable social relations. Whilst this may be difficult to foresee from our present location, historical precedents – such as the developments which followed the social chaos of the Industrial Revolution – suggest it is not far-fetched to speculate that advanced industrialized spaces in particular may indeed be on the brink of a new phase of dramatic growth.

Speculation left aside. Fifty years ago, the atom bomb created the risk and the possibility of instant global chaos and destruction. The atomic weaponry existing today makes this risk a potential reality. However, this is no longer the only possible threat of instant global chaos and destruction. A major crash on the world's central financial markets can today also trigger instant global chaos and destruction in the light of the extensive electronic valorization of social exchanges. There can be little doubt about the central importance that money, global financial markets and the emerging valorization practices and techniques bears on contemporary social life. The *en masse* emergence of fetishized electronic capital, electronic valorization, the amplification of risk, as well as the virtualization of monetary values and social identities are indeed some of the most important, and far-reaching, social changes of our time.

The footprints of the nineteenth century social architecture (e.g., the layout of our cities, railway, electronic and road transportation networks, everyday apparatuses, and artifacts such as department stores and office buildings), ideas and institutional arrangements continue to be ever present at the end of the twentieth century. But for how long? Railroads and coal constituted the primary technological artifact and energy source of the nineteenth century respectively. In the twentieth century it was road/air networks and oil. In the era of digital capitalism digital networks, such as the internet, are emerging as the primary technological artifact of the fore-seeable future. These networks facilitate the digital transfer (via fiber optical cable or satellite) of goods such as software programs, information, music and videos direct from their producers to end users, as well as the direct, instantaneous and digital payment by customers. The slogan 'sell the roads' used to be a joke in right-wing circles during the 1980s. This is no longer far-fetched, or science fiction. Present day digital networks – including specific communication technologies and valorization techniques – make it theoretically possible for car users to automatically pay for their use of some, or all, roads with real-time pricing metods (i.e., rates may increase during peak hours and *visa versa*) in order to increase asset utilization. Whilst technology and electricity are responsible for the functional operation of digital networks, its essential energy source is no longer coal, oil or even electricity. It is money, digital and virtual money.

Money has been central to the daily lives and thinking of traders for centuries. However, it is a new experience for sociologists to think of the social world in terms of the 'bottom line.' However, it seems that the time has come for sociologists to take the *for sale* sign out of the closet. Money is indeed the dominant social mediator of our time. In addition, everything, even globalization, as a conglomerate of social realities, ideas, myths, practices and identities, is now – potentially at least – for sale.

Endnotes: Introduction

1. In this book the concept of modernity is used in particular reference to European (or so-called 'Western') modernity. Culture is used as a theoretical construct referring to the social arrangements for the exchange, production and consumption/accumulation of a conglomeration of physical, intellectual, virtual and symbolic goods.

2. See, for example, Carnoy, Castells, Cohen and Cardoso (1993), Peters (1987) and Porter (1990).

3. See also Offe (1985).

4. The 'origins of globalization' have evoked renewed interest amongst social scientists since the 1960s. Modernist scholars generally argue that whilst some measure of globalization has always occurred, these developments were non-linear until about the middle of this millennium, and that European modernism is the first global social system. In Worsley's (1964) classical formulation: "Until our day, human society has never existed" (Worsley, 1964:1). However, a number of scholars, such as Abu-Lughod (1989), Amin (1989, 1993), Bentley (1993), Bernal (1987), Frank and Gills (1993), Friedman (1994), Mazuri (1980, 1990) and White, Suwa and Asfaw (1994) dispute this assumption on the basis of different propositions. These different approaches range from those which accept the unity of humanity since its origin, as articulated by Mazuri (1980, 1990); Amin's (1993) argument that the itinerary of the earth's population began when the East African hominids ventured down the Nile, crossed the Mediterranean and the Isthmus of Suez to Europe and Asia; Abu-Lughod's (1993) concept of earlier world-systems (such as the thirteenth century world-system which stretched between North-Western Europe and China); Frank and Gills' (1993) world system which extends at least 5,000 years back; and Bernal's (1987) work on the ways in which European modernity was partially informed by earlier social integrations between, for example, Europe, Africa and Asia. Furthermore, there is a growing body of research indicating that homo sapiens have a common, probably African, origin. (See for example, White, Suwa and Asfaw, 1994). Contemporary research by geneticists, such as Jones (1993) and Vigilant (1997), also indicates that there are no separate subgroups within the human population. Whilst the 'origins of globalization' is an interesting and important debate, this book concerns itself with a less contentious issue, namely the valorization and polarization of social exchanges that occurred during the latter part of the modernist globalization epoch. Most scholars tend to agree that, despite the formation of core and peripheral relations and cycles of shifting hegemony in previous epochs or earlier times, the social polarization of this epoch is fundamentally different to that in earlier times. Generally speaking these historical approaches to globalization have little relevance to this study other than highlighting the contestedness of the concept of globalization. For a critique of Bernal's work see Leflkowitz and Rogers (1996).

5. Since the 1970s a number of important changes have occurred in global

social processes. These changes were closely related to a combination of developments (e.g., the internal capitalist accumulation crisis, epitomized by the oil crisis of 1973 to 1974, the debt crisis of the early 1980s, the breakdown of the Bretton Woods regime, the reorganization of transnational production loci, the deregulation of global markets, the emergence of the post-Cold War landscape, as well as new military and trading blocs, etc.). These changes were in part spawned by accelerated technological, and related supra-material cultural, developments (e.g., the increased virtualization of time, space and social identities). For the purposes of analytical clarity, as well as to contextualize modernist marginalization, contemporary social dynamics will be juxtaposed with the dynamics constituting pre-contemporary modernist marginalization in relation to the 'globalization-valorization-marginalization conceptual triangle.' Within the parameters of this study, the post-1970s and pre-1970s are defined as the contemporary and pre-contemporary periods respectively. An alternative typology would be the post-colonial (i.e. post 1960s) versus the colonial era. Nevertheless, the post-1970s changes can be analyzed essentially as part of a presently enduring continuum. For this reason, the post-1970 era is referred to as the contemporary phase of European modernity. The spatial reach of global capitalism has also expanded dramatically since the 1970s. For example, from the 1970s to the present the number of people living in countries with essentially open trade policies doubled from about a quarter to about half of the world's population (Fishermann (1999) in Die Zeit, November 25, 1999). *Time* (1997) articulated this expansion as follows. "Twenty years ago capitalism was largely confined to Western Europe, North America and a handful of developing countries, mostly in East Asia. Together these nations constituted around 20% of the world's population. Another third of the world was under socialist rule while the balance, almost all in developing countries, was governed by various 'third way' systems between capitalism and socialism. All of that has changed suddenly and without time to digest (much less understand) the changes. By the 1980s most of the non-capitalist countries had bankrupted themselves. In response they jettisoned their failed economic strategies and began to emulate the advanced economies. As a result, we are now on the threshold of a new and complex era of global capitalism – one which offers great opportunities for dynamism, but also deep risks of global unrest. In practical terms, capitalism has now spread to nearly 90% of the world's population, since almost all parts of the world are now linked through open trade, convertible currencies, flows of foreign investment, and political commitments to private ownership as the engine of economic growth. This shift is true even in countries such as China which still flies the flag of socialism but where less than 20% of the labor force works within state-owned enterprises. All this casts a new light on the economic summit we have just witnessed in Denver. Twenty years ago, the original G-7 countries accounted for as much as 90% of the output of all capitalist economies (measured by the GDP of each country). Now, with the spread of capitalism and the growth of emerging markets, their share is down to around 50%. So although the G-7 countries now represent the richest part of the capitalist world and are still the largest international traders, they can no longer presume to speak for the world's market economies and will have to think hard about new ways to manage the global capitalist system" (*Time*, July 7, 1997:41).

6. Various authors argue that the so-called economic and cultural spheres are so comprehensively integrated in European modernity that our analytical focus should be on this symbiosis. Examples in this regard include Bell's (1974) notion of 'capitalism as an economic-cultural system,' Lash and Urry's (1994) 'reflexive accumulation,' Lury's (1996) 'material culture,' and Sklair's (1991) concept of the 'culture-ideology of consumerism.' Especially Bell's and Lash and Urry's analytical joiners serve as guiding theorems, and points of departure to this study's conceptual integration of 'cultural' and 'material,' as well as 'cultural' and 'political' spheres. Bell argues that "capitalism is an economic-cultural system, organized economically around the institution of property and the production of commodities and based culturally in the fact that exchange relations, that of buying and selling, have permeated most of the society" (Bell, 1974: 14). Lash and Urry argue that the term 'reflexive accumulation' looks like a contradiction in terms since reflexivity is 'cultural,' accumulation is 'economic.' "However, we use the term to enable us to capture how economic and symbolic processes are more than ever interlaced and interarticulated; that is, that the economy is increasingly culturally inflected and that culture is more and more economically inflected. Thus the boundaries between the two become more and more blurred and the economy and culture no longer function in regard to one another as system and environment" (Lash and Urry, 1994:64). See also Beck (1992).

7. For a brief historical perspective on monetization and marginalization, see Simmel (1990: 221-227). During the 1970s dependency theorists problematized monetized exchanges, particularly in relation to macro geographical social relations. Dependency theorists argue that capitalist development and expansion over time monetized production practices, processes and relations in the core and in the periphery. Amin (1980), for example, argues that this monetization of 'economies' facilitated the immersion of the colonial peasantry into the capitalist system as the market and cash-crop agriculture replaced subsistence agriculture. The monetization of the colonial 'economy' also formed the basis for new exchange and trade relations. In combination with the asymmetrical relationship between the capitalist core and its peripheries, the monetization of the colonial 'economy' inevitably led to an increased valorization of capital and to the expropriation of periphery surplus by the center (Amin, 1980). For example, the colonies' exportation of low-cost raw materials and the importation of high-cost value-added industrial goods from the core led to an unilateral transfer of 'economic' surplus. The asymmetrical flow of capital was accelerated by the increased dependency of the periphery on core technology, capital and loans (e.g., to pay for imported commodities and technologies). Dependency theorists argue that these loans, in turn, contribute to the long-term asymmetrical flow of capital from the periphery to the core.

8. Examples of new valorization developments include: electronic valorization as a valorization technique; the progressive inclusion of large areas and numbers of people, such as China, into the orbits of the capitalist network as a valorization pattern; and the extension of valorization to more

services, ideas and aesthetic artifacts as a valorization practice.

9. The Zem research work formed part of an internal Zem project and included work co-operation, interviews, a number of inhouse workshops and a two day workshop with the twenty of the most senior Zem managers in Australia organized and chaired by the author. In addition, the author engaged in work co-operation and conducted interviews with Zem managers and other employees in Australia, Germany, South Africa, America and Japan, as well as interviews with corporate and business strategists at the company's head office between 1995 and 1998. As the research was conducted at the same time as the author worked on an internal project it is the author's legal and ethical responsibility to protect the identity of the company and the employees involved.

10. See Harris (1990) for a discussion of the 1840-1960 period in particular.

11. See Gareau (1985) for more detail.

12. Anderson's (1983) interpretation of nations as 'imagined communities' rather than 'real communities' of class, has some influence within Marxist theories of the state. Anderson argues that nations are "imagined because the members of even the smallest nation will never know most of their fellow-members, meet them, or even hear of them, yet in the minds of each lives the image of their communion. . . . [A]ll communities larger than primordial villages of face-to-face contact (and perhaps even these) are imagined" (Anderson, 1983:15). Turner (1994) argues that whilst sociology may have been a response to the universalistic implications of both the French and Industrial revolutions, it became institutionalized, "often within the context of the exponential growth of national higher education systems in the post-war period, under the auspices of the state" (Turner, 1994:133). See also Arnason's (1990) notion of the nation as imagined 'cultural totalities.'

13. Albrow (1990) argues that the implicit assumptions sociologists make about the relationships between individuals and societies, between a particular society and other societies, as well as between a particular society and the rest of the world, became strongly encapsulated by the nationalist practices of the nation-state. For a discussion of the dominant features of the various national sociologies, see Robertson (1992).

14. See Bhabha (1994) for a discussion of the of the interrelationships between modernity and the 'ambivalent temporalities of the nation-space.' Bhabha argues that the language of culture and community is poised on "the fissures of the present becoming the rhetorical figures of a national past"(Bhabha, 1994:142).

15. See Shaw (1994).

16. See Chapter 4 for more detail.

17. For a discussion of the general features of European modernity see Sztompka (1993).

Endnotes: Introduction

18. The introduction can present only a partial exploration, explanation and defense of the theoretical assumptions underlying the overall construction, reconstruction and representation of the modernist landscape in relation to the three central sociological questions of this study. The subsequent exploration, explanation and defense of the theoretical assumptions – and their contemporary manifestations – will unfold in more detail in the remaining chapters.

19. In relation to the social world of colonialism, Mudimbe (1988) proposed an alternative, yet somewhat similar scheme to that of Albrow's. Mudimbe argues that it is possible to use three main keys to account for the modulations and methods representative of colonial organization. These areas are: "the procedures of acquiring, distributing, and exploiting lands in colonies; the policies of domesticating natives; and the manner of managing ancient organizations and implementing new modes of production" (Mudimbe, 1988:2). For Mudimbe these areas are related to three complementary hypotheses and actions, namely: the domination of physical space, the reformation of native minds, and the integration of local 'economic histories into the Western perspective.' Mudimbe argues that these complementary projects constitute the 'colonizing structure,' and embrace the physical, human, and spiritual aspects of the colonization experience.

20. See Chapter 4 for more detail.

21. See Burke (1987) for a discussion of the activities of Italian merchants in the thirteenth century. Burke (1987) argues that these activities are an example of the close integration between territorial exploration and material accumulation that characterizes European expansion in general from this period onwards.

22. The new forms and relations that evolved from long-distance sea route trade contributed to the destruction of existing trade routes and relations. Instead of obtaining higher-priced goods transported by caravans and exchanged in the markets of North Africa or South East Asia, European companies were now able to deal directly with African and Asian suppliers. Whilst merchant capital had limited ability to transform local productive processes outside of Europe, it, nevertheless, laid the foundation for the social relations of an industrial capitalist genre, as first traders, then suppliers and then producers – as well as their social networks – came under partial European control. The development of a relatively integrated global commodity market was an essential occurrence in linking the fate of other spaces and peoples to European interests. Merchant capital expansion eroded subsistence networks, established cliental relationships between the core and its peripheries, and layed the foundation of modernist dependency relations. Over time, these processes tended to dissolve the local modes of social and production organization in the peripheries. European merchants progressively extended their activities from trade exchanges to the control of supply, production and resource extraction networks. In combination with the new macro patterns of commodity production, this contributed to the

often unidirectional transfer of extracted surpluses and resources from the peripheries to the core, and to the subjugation of local cultural processes and practices in the peripheries. For more detail in this regard, see Brown (1995), Curtin (1971, 1984), and Freund (1984). Previous epochs were generally also characterized by trade, cultural exchanges and technology transfers. For example, the early spread and establishment of Islam in sub-Saharan Africa was mainly due to the actions of long-distance traders. In East Africa, the Swahili (in Arabic the term means 'coasters,' i.e., those who travel up and down the coast) traded between the villages in the Zanj region in Mogadishu and Sofala. Besides the trade in goods these traders also brought with them the Arabic language, Islamic religion, and cultural practices and institutions which had a profound impact on the areas they visited. Friedman (1994) argues that the trade was a powerful force in earlier forms of globalization. For Friedman the historical trade systems of the Indian Ocean and South-East Asia, for example, produced 'immense institutional and cultural globalization' in what is often referred to as the 'Hinduization of Southeast Asia and Indonesia' and the 'Islamization of the Indian Ocean.'

23. Exceptions to this pattern include the colonial slave plantations of the Spanish and the Portuguese in the so-called Mediterranean Atlantic. These slave plantations actively transformed production processes and relations prior to the advent of industrial capitalism. See Bentley (1993) for a more detailed discussion.

24. The commodities central to early fifteenth and sixteenth century European trade were spices, sugar and gold.

25. See Marx (1977).

26. Commodification, as well as colonialism and global expansion, are not original features of capitalism in particular or modernism in general. For example, attempts to develop large-scale manufacturing industries through industrial production in China and the Soviet Union during the twentieth century were mainly reconstituted industrial production, managed by private capital as industrial production controlled and managed by the state. This fundamentally changed the property relations of industrial capitalism, but it did not essentially alter productive processes, nor the inherent commodification dynamics of industrial production.

27. See note 66 below.

28. See Gray (1993) for a discussion of the effect of market institutions on subsistence communities.

29. See Magdoff (1978). The initial military invasion of colonial Africa by European empires and their private interest collaborators such as the Dutch VOC in Southern Africa, was followed by the mapiological construction of European servitude 'societies.' The late nineteenth and twentieth century scramble for Africa was in part structured by the Berlin conference of 1884-1885. The Berlin Act (signed on the 26th of February 1885) promulgated the

rules for participation in the annexation of various parts of Africa. These rules had little regard for existing and ancient zones of trade, or for social and demographic configurations. European colonialism systematically transformed the local habitat of colonies and other marginal spaces into selective images of Europe. This ecological imperialism involved the total physical environment (i.e., animals, buildings, plants, etc.) and turned the colonies into diasporic European spaces, with European diseases and artificially created environmental imbalances as some of the consequences (Crosby, 1986).

30. The existence of dominant enclaves of settler colonialists in marginal colonial spaces was the major exception to the generally large physical distances which existed between dominant and marginal spaces. The enforced nature of European colonialism is illustrated, for example, by the British occupation of India in the 1930. About 4,000 British civil servants, assisted by 60,0000 soldiers and 90,000 civilians, forced themselves upon a country of 300 million people (Smith, 1981).

31. See Albrow (1990), Bernal (1997), Hall (1992), Nandy (1997), Said (1995), and Waters (1995).

32. Mudimbe (1988) argues that the asymmetrical 'colonizing structure' spawned a dichotomous system of dominant (European) and marginal (colonial) spaces, 'cultures,' and human beings. For Mudimbe this dichotomous system manifests itself in the destabilization of customary organizations by the incoherent establishment of new social arrangements, organizations and institutions. The new social arrangements were controlled hegemonically and unilaterally from the modernist core that diffused cultural modes, discourses, values and attitudes central to the development of core modernist spaces. For Mudimbe (1988), the specific social relations dichotomies of modernist colonialism inevitably reinforced the cultural-material and philosophical foundations of the dichotomous modernist system, as well as its active marginalization of peripheral spaces, and surplus people. For Mudimbe these philosophical foundations are manifested in the modernist epistemological universe, which is characterized by a dichotomizing epistemological system of hierarchical and paradigmatic opposites. They include: primitive/traditional versus modern social constructs, oral versus written and printed communications, agrarian and customary communities versus urban and industrialized 'civilization,' subsistence 'economies' versus highly productive 'economies', black versus white, 'Third World' versus 'First World', etc. As a result, Mudimbe argues that social life is articulated by modernist theorists as an evolutionary process moving from 'underdevelopment' to 'development' within the parameters of European modernity. In addition, positive and negative values are most often attached to these oppositional dichotomies in everyday life. For Mudimbe concepts such as, 'development, modern, white, etc.' consequently became innately positive attributes, whilst their opposites are viewed as naturally negative and evolutionary backward. Mudimbe concludes that modernist dichotomous epistemological postulates and conjectures not only represent, but generally also contribute to reificate the secondary ontological status of marginal and other (than European) spaces and

peoples. Quite literally, the life of 'the poor, the underdeveloped, the black,' is worth less than that of 'the rich, the developed, the white.'

33. See Bernal (1987).

34. LeBon's (1912, 1947) 'primitive, inferior, intermediate and superior race' classification typology is another explicit example of this form of sophisticated scientific racism. See Serequeberhan (1994) for a discussion of the Marx and Engels in regard to Eurocentrism and racism.

35. Various analysts (i.e., Mulgan, 1991 and Sassen, 1991) argue that the most important social changes in the periphery (including cultural-material and cultural-political re-organization) are today largely caused by developments in the core.

36. See Sassen (1991).

37. See Mazrui (1980, 1990, 1995) and Mudimbe (1988, 1994).

38. For more detail see Davis (1990), Lee and Townsend (1993), Sugihara (1988) and Wilson (1987).

39. With an analysis based on the UNHDP statistics, Thirwall (1994) concluded that approximately 60 percent of the world's population receive only 6 percent of the world's income.

40. See Kennedy (1993) and UNHDP (1996).

41. See the United Nations' Human Development Report' (1998). According to this report less than 4 percent of the wealth of the richest 225 individuals would be sufficient to meet the additional cost of basic food, safe water, sanitation, education and sanitation for all.

42. "If we add to the OECD the four newly industrialized countries of Asia, in 1988 the three major economic regions represented 72.8% of world's manufacturing production, and in 2000 their share should still amount to 69.5%, while the population of these three regions in 2000 would only be 15.7% of world population. The concentration of resources is even greater at the core of the system, in the G-7 countries, particularly in terms of technology, skills, and informational infrastructure, key determinants of competitiveness. Thus, in 1990 the G-7 countries accounted for 90.5% of high-technology manufacturing in the world, and were holding 80.4% of global computing power"(Castells, 1996:108).

43. See UNDP (1992).

44. UNHDP (1999).

45. In the period from 1977 to 1992, the real wages of the lowest paid 10 percent of the British population declined by 17 percent, median wages grew by 35 percent, and high wages rose by 50 percent, with the real wages of the

Endnotes: Introduction

highest paid 10 percent increasing by 60 percent (The Joseph Rowntree Foundation Report, 1995).

46. See Lee and Townsend (1993) for more detail.

47. See Head (1996).

48. See the United Nations' Human Development Report (1998).

49. See Thurow (1996) and Trent (1994). A similar tendency towards growing inequality can be observed in Australia. In 1983 the top 1 percent of income earners received as much as the bottom 11 percent, by 1989 they received as much as the bottom 21 percent (Lombard, 1991). Based on 1986 statistics, it is estimated that the top 1% of wealth holders owned 19.7 percent of total wealth, the top 10 percent 55.2 percent, the top 20 percent 72 percent, while the top 50 percent owned 98.4% of the total wealth. The bottom 50 percent thus owned only 1.6 percent of total wealth. "Indeed, members of the latter group as often as not had negative wealth, because indebtedness ... outweighed the value of assets owned"(Stillwell, 1993:22). According to research undertaken by Access Economics' Hans Baekgaard the number of millionaires in Australia increased from around 25,000 to 71,700 from the mid-1980s to 1993, and to 188,200 in 1998. "In absolute terms the wealth of millionaires [in Australia] rose almost as much as the rest of the population [in the 1993 to 1998 period]" (Baekgaard, quoted in The Australian Financial Review, January 9-10, 1999:22).

50. See Rifkin (1996), Thurow (1996) and Wasserman (1983). The 1870-1920 period was also characterized by many of the central features of the 1980s, such as low protectionist taxation, minimal public cultural-material control, few governmental constraints on cross-border capital movement, and a lack of restrictions on the allocation of foreign resources and the transfer of profits.

51. See the report of 'The Centre for Budget and Policy Priorities' (1999), quoted in the AZ, September 9, 1999.

52. See Davis (1990).

53. For a detailed analysis of the emergence and characteristics of the new 'underclass,' see Wilson (1987). Wilson defines the underclass in terms of six central characteristics: living in isolation from other 'social classes'; long term joblessness; female-headed households; absence of training and skills; long-term welfare dependency; and high levels of street crime.

54. See Bhuta (1996). Sklair (1996) argues that the 'transnational capitalist class' has played a critical role in transforming Australia from an inward-looking and protectionist country, to an outward-looking globally oriented one. For Sklair the transnational capitalist class can be divided into four fractions, namely; transnational corporation executives and their local affiliates; globalizing bureaucrats; capitalist-inspired politicians and professionals; and consumerist elites. See also Marceau (1989) for a

discussion of the transnational capitalist class. Various authors (Stopford and Strange, 1991; Thrift, 1994; Held, 1995; Featherstone, 1990) also pay attention to what Ohmae (1990) refers to as the emergence of a new 'global class' of transnational business managers, and the impact of this social class, not only on business, but also on social values in general.

55. See Kothari (1995).

56. Similar wealth disparities can also be found in South Africa where the richest 5 percent of the population owns 88 percent of all personal wealth (Chetty, 1994).

57. The author conducted some fieldwork in the African village of Spoegrivier, a rural community 700 km north-west of Cape Town. In 1993/1994 Spoegrivier had a population of 611, of which 72 percent were unemployed. Some of this research was compiled in a report for the Land Development Unit, De Swardt (1994).

58. See the World Bank (1990) and the United Nations Human Development Report (1998). Furthermore, the African continent has presently a population of about 650 million people which is increasing at a dramatic rate. For example, in 1950 Africa's population was half that of Europe's; by 2025 it is expected to be three times that of Europe, namely 1.58 billion compared to 512 million (Kennedy, 1993).

59. See World Bank (1990).

60. See Ayittey (1992).

61. See the World Bank Report (1994) and Speth (1992) for more detail. See also Davidson (1992) in regard to net transfers from Africa in particular.

62. See Beck (1992).

63. See Sztompka (1993) for more detail in this regard.

64. Whilst wealth and poverty is only one manifestation of social differences, it is nevertheless an important one.

65. See Barraclough (1978) and Focus (December 6, 1999). For more detail of wealth polarization around the world, see Brar (1997), Davis (1990), The Economist (October 12, 1996), Head (1996), The Joseph Rowntree Foundation Report (1995), Kothari (1995), Lee and Townsend (1993), McMicheal (1996), Rifkin (1996), The Star and SA Times (January 8, 1997), Thirwall (1994) and Waters (1995).

66. In the realm of globalization the tension between freedom and commodification is illuminated, for example, by the large-scale migrations within and across core and peripheral spaces. These migrations were initiated by the evolving modernist commodity networks and commodification practices. Historically a threefold movement of people

took place in and between core European and disempowered colonial spaces, namely within core and marginal spaces (e.g., the displacement of peasants from the land into centralized urban labor forces), from core to marginal spaces (e.g., settler colonialism) and from marginal to core spaces (e.g., slaves which were dispatched from the other (than European) spaces, such as Africa, over a period of almost four centuries, especially between 1750 and 1850). An estimated ten to thirteen million African slaves were sent to the Americas alone. The trade in human beings dramatically increased the significance of colonial spaces as a source of labor. The slave trade, of course, did not exist in a social vacuum. In Africa the export of human beings went hand in hand with the import of new commodities, such as European metalware and Indian textiles which replaced domestically produced goods and undermined the trade of these goods. Displaced peasantries and slaves provided cheap labor, food and other goods for European consumers. The patterns of European trade also enhanced the evolution of dependency and disempowerment relations between the core and its periphery. In general the trade in humans not only increased the significance of colonial spaces as a source of labor, but the commodification of people as private property also became a central historical feature of the modernist phenomenon of valorized subjugation, as well as its most visual articulation. As such, slavery is an important moral and theoretical aspect of modernist globalization, despite its total absence from the nexus of modernist globalization discourses.

67. The twin policies of the extermination of the indigenous Americans, and the importation of enslaved Africans within the American colonies are extreme examples of valorized subjugation.

68. Consequently, the historic development of the macro patterns of modernist social marginalization became characterized by a strong macro-geographical apartheid between core and peripheral and colonial spaces and peoples.

69. See Bhabha (1994), Malik (1996), Van Horne (1997). Malik (1996) argues that the narrative of race is 'the story' of how social inequalities became regarded as being natural ones. For Malik it is through "... the conflation of social and natural inequality that the contradiction between the universalist ideology of capitalist society and the particularist reality of capitalist social relations becomes grasped in the discourse of race" (Malik, 1996:71). See also Gould (1981) for a detailed description and analysis of the history of scientific measures, the ways in which the dominant ideas of the time were reflected and represented, and the ways in which they were used to scientifically justify racism.

70. See Amin (1989) for more detail.

71. The complementary, yet contradictory dependencies and ambivalences existing between these two aspects of modernist monetization is addressed in more detail in Chapter 4.

72. There is some similarity between these two categories of intellectual genres and the distinction made by Jessop (1990), who argues that social

Endnotes: Globalization for Sale

discourses are divided by the either 'discursive construction of social reality' or 'material deterministic' perspectives.

73. I once asked a student in South Africa about his thoughts on the reading material for sociology. Did he enjoy sociology? Did he understand the social world around him better? He replied that he always feels "painted" when he leaves the library. Painted? [I asked, getting excited, thinking that this was new student lingo for being stoned – was he intellectually stoned by sociology?] Did he mean painted like on a high after sniffing paint residues? "No, [he replied] I feel really painted, like painted white. A black with a white skin, and that's great, [he said with a huge smile], because in a white world even when you're black you have to be white... But sociology does not really help me to understand the social world around me. Mr Giddens does not write about us... Mr Giddens writes about the world, but the white man's world – and black spots like me, he paints them white. [He laughed] Maybe one day I will be white enough to be a sociologist."

74. Mandel's 'Late Capitalism' (1976) applied the Marxist concept of valorization in its orthodox form to twentieth century capitalist developments up to the 1970s.

75. See Beilharz (1996), Deutschmann (1996), Roberts (1996) and Poggi (1993).

76. See Chapter 1 for more detail.

77. These issues are addressed in more detail in Chapter 4.

78. For example, on a given day 10 apples might cost US$1, the same as 1 kilogram of potatoes in a specific town. If the town is then hit with gale-force winds and the unharvested apples (above the ground) suffer substantial damage, but the unharvested potatoes (below the ground) suffer no damage the price of apples might increase to 5 for a dollar whilst the price of potatoes stay consistent.

Endnotes: Chapter 1

1. See Barraclough (1978), Hoogvelt (1997), Krasner (1976) and Morgenstern (1959).

2. See Magdoff (1978).

3. See also Bergesen and Schoenberg (1980), Bloomfield (1968), Keynes (1971), Kondratieff (1979) and Krasner (1976). Approximately twenty million Europeans crossed the Atlantic to settle 'voluntarily' in the so-called New World within a single generation before the First World War. The labor migrations of settler colonialism were central to the appropriation of land, surplus production and raw materials via settler occupied and ruled territorial spaces. Settler colonialism also enhanced the institutionalized control exercised by the distant core over colonial spaces. The mixture of the social, cultural-political and cultural-material rationales behind modernist colonialism is illustrated in the social programs employed in settler colonies. For example, in Kenya large tracts of vacant arable land inhabited by Maasai pastoralists were handed over to settlers. These settlers also received huge grants, competition was nullified through the 'white highland' policy which reserved large sections of central Kenya for whites only, legislation allowed only whites to grow coffee, and any African enterprises or uprisings that might have endangered the steady supply of cheap labor, were stifled and suppressed by colonial sanctioned violence (Freund, 1984). Settler colonialism also provided a solution to some of the 'internal' social problems of certain European spaces as European countries could now export their own surplus population. This development was aptly formulated by one of the most famous European explorers – and the only person who had a modern state named after him – Cecil John Rhodes. "I was in the East End of London yesterday and attended a meeting of the unemployed. I listened to the wild speeches, which were just a cry for 'bread, bread, bread,' and on my way home I pondered over the scene and I became more than ever convinced of the importance of imperialism.... My cherished idea is a solution for the social problem, i.e. in order to save the 40,000,000 inhabitants of the United Kingdom from a bloody civil war, we colonial statesmen must acquire new lands to settle the surplus population, to provide new markets for the goods produced in the factories and the mines. The Empire, as I have always said, is a bread and butter question. If you want to avoid civil war, you must become imperialists" (Rhodes, quoted by Lenin, 1936:72).

4. 'National Sozialismus' was an extreme case of the national-capital project, in which, for example, the development of a motor vehicle for the nation 'Volkswagen' (people's car) by a private enterprise became part of the processes and articulations of nation building.

5. See Willetts (1995).

6. The Economist (December 11-17, 1999).

Endnotes: Globalization for Sale

7. See Brett (1985).

8. For example, in 1955, America insisted that the trade in agricultural goods be excluded from GATT considerations. At that time, the American government wanted to protect its farm supply policies, which used subsidies and production controls to establish a floor for farm prices, as well as the structure of its aids programs. At the height of the Cold War during the mid-1960s, 80 percent of American wheat exports were in the form of food aid (Raikes, 1988). During the 1980s changing domestic and foreign interests meant that the American government included the trade in agricultural goods in the Uruguay Round because it was now in its interest to extend GATT liberalization measures to agricultural goods.

9. See Mulhearn (1996).

10. See Capling and Crozier (1996).

11. The international flow of technology has been governed mainly by general financial and trade agreements and regulatory structures. With the deregulation of the flow of money and goods, the international transfer of technology was, consequently, also 'liberalized.' The international flow of social technology (especially the flow of proprietary knowledge) has, however, evolved separately from those governing other flows. Lesser (1990) argues that many of the international regulations and agreements on intellectual property rights date back to the previous century. In 1967 the formation of the World Intellectual Property Organization, as well as a number of regional initiatives in Africa and Europe, increased the regulation of proprietary knowledge. Intellectual property rights were also included in the Uruguay Round of GATT negotiations.

12. Both of these processes were to a large extent relative to the specific cultural-material interests and the cultural-political strength of America.

13. Keynes's proposed Development Fund was aimed at providing assistance to countries suffering from long-term disequilibrium. In order to achieve this, the Development Fund was to draw upon both taxes and borrowing in order to maintain full employment and reduce inequalities between so-called 'national economies.'

14. See Mulhearn (1996) for more detail.

15. The general agreements which underpin these principles included the following: that the lowering of tariffs by one member against another's exports, will be matched by reductions from the other member; that any protectionist measure should be in the form of tariffs, rather than import quotas; and that no member should grant preferential treatment to another country, but that the most favorable terms negotiated with any one trading partner should be extended to all trading partners.

16. At that time, the industrial tariffs of its major trading partners averaged 2.9 percent (Japan) and 4.7 percent (the EU) respectively (Walters and Blake

1992).

17. See McMichael (1996).

18. See the discussion of the Uruguay Round of GATT later in this chapter in this regard.

19. The organization of the liberalization of trade has been absorbed into the new World Trade Organization (WTO) after the final GATT round.

20. A series of regional initiatives during the 1980s, such as the European Community's directives on capital movements, has also contributed to the liberalization of financial markets.

21. A more detailed analysis of the influences of private enterprises follows later in this chapter, as well as in the remaining chapters.

22. See the discussion of the 1980s monetary crises later in this chapter.

23. The 1970s OPEC 'petrodollors' were largely recycled through investments in Treasury bills.

24. See Harvey (1989) and Mulhearn (1996).

25. In order to stabilize the global flow of money and to provide currency stability, the IMF introduced so-called Special Drawing Rights (SDRs), a weighted mix of five currencies ($US, £Stg, DM, FFr, and the Yen).

26. See the section on 'The *pari passu* globalization of money and the valorization of speculation' later in this chapter for more detail in this regard.

27. See Hallwood and MacDonald (1994) for more detail.

28. See Bhagwati (1989), Hoogvelt (1997) and McMichael (1996) for more detail.

29. See Anderson and Cavanagh (1996).

30. See the section 'the decline of absolute location in relation to relative location' in Chapter 2 for more detail.

31. See Leys (1994).

32. See McMichael (1996).

33. These loans dropped to $50 billion in 1985 as a result of the debt crisis that followed the period of overextended loans (Strange, 1994).

34. See Adepoju (1993).

35. See McMichael (1996).

36. See Lissakers (1993).

37. See Begg (1999).

38. See GATT (1987).

39. See George (1997).

40. See Clairmont and Cavanagh (1987), George (1997) and the OECD (1990, 1991) for more details.

41. See Toussaint (1999).

42. The downsizing of the public and civil service occurred *en masse* during the 1980s, either through the intervention of 'structural adjustment' programs or 'internal' governments. For example, between 1986 and 1992 30,000 public sector workers lost their jobs in Uganda (Khadiagala, 1995). In general, more than 6,800 previously state-owned enterprises were privatized in 80 different countries during the 1980s. These enterprises were mainly monopoly suppliers of essential public services like water, electricity, post, telecommunications, public transport, etc. (Sandberg, 1994). The official aims and objectives of these reform measures were the short-term 'stabilization of the economy,' and the long-term market oriented restructuring. The quintessential intentions of the restructuring measures also included the facilitation of the transfer of foreign investment, goods, money and production loci around the world with minimal public control or interference.

43. See the discussion earlier in this chapter for more detail.

44. See the 'Historical Tables, Fiscal Year 1995' (1994).

45. See Teweles and Bradley (1998) for more detail.

46. Changes in the financial and social restrictions on debt continue to make credit and loans more readily available. Lury (1996) argues that the social restrictions on borrowing money has changed with the destigmatization of 'being in debt.' "During this century, for example, there has been a shift from the dubious respectability of the 'never-never,' through the anxieties of hire purchase, to the competitive display of credit cards – to a situation now in which an Access card is your 'flexible friend' and a gold American Express card is a symbol of elite exclusivity" (Lury, 1996:31).

47. See Clairmont (1996). In South Africa the gross interest on household debt alone now amounts to 12 percent of the yearly income of households (Star and SA Times, January 8, 1997).

48. In the words of the billionaire financier George Soros "This is a

Endnotes: Global Exchange Processes

wonderful world, but it cannot last forever" (Soros, quoted in the Australian Financial Review, January 23-24, 1999:48).

49. The Uruguay Round of GATT generally accelerated the influence of private global enterprises on the new global financial environment. The initial failure to conclude the agreements related to the transnational trade in services and the partial impasse in transnational trade agreements, somewhat inadvertently, contributed to the increased influence of transnational corporations relative to public instruments.

50. See Madden and Madeley (1993) for more detail in this regard.

51. The Lome Convention is an European aid and trade agreement with approximately 70 African, Caribbean and Pacific countries.

52. See Bhagwati (1989) for more detail.

53. Castells (1996) argues that the dynamics of trade and foreign investment between countries and macro-regions decisively affect the performance and profits of firms. The ideal competitive position for firms is a combination of an unchallenged monopoly within at least one of the large affluent markets, with as much as possible unrestricted access to some of the other important markets. Firms consequently attempt to protect their dominance in certain markets by seeking governmental regulation of these markets. At the same time, they often aim to increase their market share in those markets in which they are minor competitors, by seeking governmental deregulation of those markets.

54. An example in this regard is the Namibian attempts to gain access to European markets for Namibian produced grapes. Namibia is one of the poorer countries of the world and due to various environmental and historical factors, Namibia has few opportunities for generating foreign exchange. Its climate, however, is suitable for the production of grapes, and being in the Southern Hemisphere, it can produce fresh grapes when Europe cannot do so *en masse*. For these reasons, the Namibian government in 1994 tried to gain duty-free access for 5,000 tonnes of Namibian produced grapes under the preferential access granted to some 70 poor countries under the Lome Convention. However, they were only granted 500 tonnes. The recently signed GATT agreement will make things even more difficult for them as tariff barriers are reduced for everyone. They will, consequently, lose the comparative advantage they enjoyed under the Lome Convention of preferential access to the European market. See Atkinson (1994) and Castells (1996) for more detail.

55. In the post-1980s period, these multilateral cultural-material agreements and institutions are having a major impact on the organization of world trade. World trade is increasingly organized by these competing trade blocs, such as APEC, that seek to remove trade barriers between members but are protectionist relative to the rest of the world.

56. The integration of public and private interests in this public/private

Endnotes: Globalization for Sale

hybrid financial establishment is formulated in, for example, the World Bank Annual Report of 1992. It proposed that a stronger relationship between the World Bank, the International Monetary Fund and private corporations will achieve greater cohesiveness in global cultural-material policy making (World Bank, 1992).

57. The influence of private corporations on cultural-political affairs is, for example, illustrated by the following account of developments in Zaire in 1997. "The De Beers diamond cartel has secretly bowed to rebel demands that it sever ties to President Mobutu Sese Seko's regime after decades of colluding in the regime's plunder of Zaire. De Beers jumped ship amid a new scramble by multinationals from the Americas, Europe and South Africa to curry favor with the rebels and divide up Zaire's vast mineral riches. An American company yesterday signed a $US1 billion deal – the largest so far – to mine copper, cobalt and zinc. It includes a large down payment that will go to fund the rebel's war effort to take over the rest of the country. Zaire's diamond industry is theoretically worth about $US480 million a year, although massive illicit mining makes a nonsense of official figures. De Beers had a monopoly over the output from the largest legal operations, which brought in more than $US160 million a year. Mr Laurent Kabila's Alliance for the Liberation of Congo-Zaire has laid out its conditions for De Beers even to negotiate continuing to do business in Zaire" (The Melbourne Age, April 18, 1997:B8). This was one month before Kabila took control of the government of the country.

58. See The World Investment Report (1994) for a detailed discussion.

59. See Brar (1997) and The World Investment Report (1997).

60. See Dunning (1993).

61. See Hoogvelt (1997).

62. See UNCTC (1993).

63. See Hirst and Thompson (1995).

64. See Köhler (1998) and Martin and Schumann (1997). In regard to the governmental subsidies for a microchip factory in Dresden. Martin and Schumann (1997) write that the federal government and the state of Saxony are providing loan security "to the tune of a full billion marks, and a banking consortium of which the state government is part has contributed a further 500 million marks. At the final count, then, the corporation does not have to put up even a fifth of the total outlay; almost the entire market risk falls on the taxpayer's shoulders" (Martin and Schumann, 1997:202).

65. See Stopford and Strange (1991) for more detail.

66. See Thrift (1994).

67. See The Economist (22/9/1990).

Endnotes: Global Exchange Processes

68. See Chapter 2 for more detail.

69. The impact of currency speculation on so-called 'national economies,' was demonstrated, for example, in 1997 by the currency instability of South-East Asian currencies (especially the Malaysian ringit). See Soros (1998) for more detail. Strange (1986) refers to these developments in speculative trading as 'Casino Capitalism.' See also Davidson (1997).

70. See Chapter 2.

71. See Blumenthal (1987/8) and Ohmae (1990).

72. See Crook (1992).

73. See Akyuz (1994).

74. See Beeson (1997), Brand (1996), Chesnais (1994), Crook (1992), and Kothari (1995) for more detail.

75. See Brar (1997).

76. See Hallwood and MacDonald (1994).

77. Transnationals also increased their 'currency neutrality,' through the fragmentation of production and distribution networks across national boundaries.

78. With my students in Australia I discussed hedging using a simple example from Australian Rules Football (Footy). Footy is composed of a mixture of football, rugby, basketball and general athletic abilities. On a Thursday before a game between Geelong and Carlton the internet odds were 1,8:1 for Carlton and 2,8:1 for Geelong. With a bet of A$1,000 on Carlton we would win A$800, if Carlton loses we make a loss of A$1,000. During the game on Saturday Carlton were leading 40 to 9 after 20 minutes. For most of the students that meant that we had a good chance of winning A$800. In live trade the internet betting odds for Carlton were now 1,4:1, whilst the odds for Geelong were now up to 4:1. This was the ideal opportunity to hedge our bet. For this reason we then bet A$500 on Geelong. If Carlton wins we make a profit of A$300 (with A$1,000 at the original odds of 1,8:1 and a total expenditure of A$1,500), if wins Geelong we make A$500 (with A$500 at the live trade odds of 4:1, thus A$2,000 minus A$1,500). This is an example of the principles of hedging.

79. Disintermediation refers to the commercial financial activities of 'non-financial' institutions.

80. Direct and digital producer-end user supply and payment processes also reduces the need for the so-called middle-man in the supply network.

81. See Martin and Schumann (1997).

Endnotes: Globalization for Sale

82. Teweles and Bradley (1998:22).

83. See Capling and Crozier (1996) Speculative behavior often feeds into a cycle of risks. The element of risk and volatility which corporations seek to avoid, is sometimes exacerbated by these risk management strategies since they often fuel more speculation, create more and new risks, and fuel more speculation. In addition, risk management strategies inadvertently increase pressure from the greater deregulation of international controls on capital movements, whilst at the same time increasing the importance of electronic valorization.

84. See Bishop (1996).

85. The Economist (11-17 December, 1999).

86. See Hallwood and MacDonald (1994). In 1989, open positions in three month Eurodollar futures amounted to US$670 billion, by 1991 this had increased to US$1.1 trillion amounting to 40 percent of interbank redepositing, up from 14 percent in 1987.

87. See The Bulletin (June 8, 1999).

88. Teweles and Bradley (1998:12).

89. See Martin and Schumann (1997).

90. See Ohmae (1990).

91. See Harvey (1993) and Ohmae (1990).

92. In other words, when an individual employee chooses a new investment option for his/her pension scheme, the fund managers of the particular scheme is given the authority to exert pressure for wage cuts, downsizing, etc. as long as maximum benefits can be delivered to the particular pension fund. The current movement of a sizable share of world savings and pension funds into speculative financial spheres, has a potentially dramatic impact on a broad spectrum of the population in numerous parts of the world. The immediate repercussions are demonstrated, for example, by the turmoil caused in financial markets during the fall of the American dollar in 1986-1987, the collapse of the European Monetary System in 1992, and the events in Mexico in 1994. In the late 1980s and early 1990s there was massive speculation in the Mexican peso, as investors expected NAFTA to strengthen the so-called 'Mexican economy.' This did not happen and the peso was finally devalued in December 1994. The huge flight of capital that followed, severely destabilized the 'Mexican economy.' In the light of Mexico's connection with America through NAFTA, the fall of the peso sent shudders through global financial markets. In order to prevent a potentially serious crisis in global financial markets, America stepped in to support the Mexican currency with billions of dollars of new loans. The bailout deal came at a very high cost, not only to 'Western public' funds, but also to

Mexico, as they were required to deposit their oil revenues in the American Federal Reserve System. If Mexico defaulted on its loans, America would then have access to those funds. Martin and Schumann (1997) argue that the Mexico deal of December 1994 was both a disaster-aversion exercise and a brazen plundering of the tax coffers of contributor nations for the benefit of a wealthy minority. "As never before, the main actors demonstrated the force with which global economic integration has changed the structures of power in the world. The government of the American superpower, the once omnipotent IMF and all the European central banks seemed guided by an unseen hand as they bowed to the dictates of a higher power whose destructive capacity they were no longer able to evaluate: namely, the international money market" (Martin and Schumann, 1997:45-46). In Albania in January 1997, huge losses, including the selling of homes and land in order to buy shares, were incurred by as many as half of all Albanian families as a result of collapsing pyramid schemes. This resulted in violent demonstrations against the government for failing to control these financial schemes, and for allowing people with direct links to the government to profit from the collapse (The Australian, January 28, 1997). In regard to the global interconnectedness of contemporary electronic valorization processes, Hoogvelt writes that "[t]he world is now like this: if our pension fund works well for us, the peasants in northern China will just have to go a bit more hungry. If we, as we did during the consumer boom of the 1980s, push up interest rates through our incautious use of credit cards, it has knock-on effects for the interest rates that Brazil pays on its loans, and this in turn prejudices the livelihood of peasants in Brazil" (Hoogvelt, 1997:130).

93. See The Australian (April 30, 1997).

94. The argument is not that the denationalization and globalization of money is solely a result of the self interests of those who participate in the global financial markets. The declining national governmental control of financial markets (as, for example, facilitated by new technologies) is a major factor in the specific composition of financial globalization. The fall of the dollar in 1986-1987 is an example of the decline in governmental control of global financial markets. In 1985, the seven 'largest national economies' affected a controlled devaluation of the dollar. However, the dollar remained unstable, and in 1986 the Bank of Japan injected about $7 billion into the currency markets to arrest the dollar's fall. In the first two and one-half weeks of 1987 the Bank of Japan added more than $8 billion. In 1987, more than 90 billion dollars were bought. However, even this large amount had very little effect on the value of the dollar and failed to protect the currency's value. It became clear that governments have lost much of their control (and arguably their understanding) of financial markets.

95. The role of those with global financial interests is, for example, demonstrated by the events in Mexico in 1994. On the twentieth of December 1994 a private gathering of Mexican 'financial, political and labor leaders' decided to allow a 15 percent devaluation of the Mexican peso in order to deal with a spiralling current account deficit. The meeting adjourned at 4 am with European and Asian financial markets still open. "Sensing that the government may not have the funds to support the peso

should it slide further, some left the meeting and made frantic international phone calls, requesting their brokers to buy dollars. By the start of the business day on December 20, before any official announcement had been made, US$3 billion had already fled the country" (Bhuta, 1996:54).

96. See Chapter 3 for more detail. This capital flight from 'Third World' spaces is a contributing factor to the reorganization of global spatial relations between the already rich and the already poor spaces and people around the world.

97. McDonalds Annual Report (1995:12).

98. See The Australian Financial Review (January 9-10, 1999).

99. Wolff, quoted in Die Zeit (September 30, 1999).

100. See Teweles and Bradley (1998).

101. Castells (1996) reasons that process of marketing future development leads to a constant dissolution of the time frame of capital "into its present manipulation after being given a fictitious value for the purpose of monetizing it. Thus capital not only compresses time: it absorbs it, and lives out of (that is, generates rent) its digested seconds and years" (Castells, 1996:437).

102. One proposal for the partial control (at least in terms of taxation) of global financial flows, was made as far back as the 1970s by Tobin. Tobin proposed that a small tax be placed on all international financial transactions. For a discussion see Wiseman (1997). Another idea would be to move towards a single global currency.

103. However, it is clear that the implications stretch far beyond the transformation of use values into exchange values as postulated, for example, by Marxists. Kahn (1995) argues that the formation of exchange value as opposed to use value, is at the heart of the destructive tendencies of modernity. "According to this view we moderns apprehend a world in which distinctive objects and particular human beings are evaluated not for the practical uses to which we may put them or the individual ways in which we may relate to them, but also for a value which differs only quantitatively from the value of quite different objects and human beings" (Kahn, 1995:60).

Endnotes: Chapter 2

1. See Braverman (1974) for a detailed discussion of scientific management.

2. In 1923 Henry Ford argued that producing a Model T Ford required 7,882 distinct tasks of which only 949 needed 'strong able bodied, and practically physically perfect men.' Ford argued that, "[t]he lightest jobs were again classified to discover how many of them required the use of full faculties, and we found that 670 could be filled by legless men, 2,637 by one-legged men, two by armless men, 715 by one-armed men, and ten by blind men" (Ford, 1923:108).

3. Once electricity was effectively harnessed as a source of power it contributed to a new proliferation of valorized opportunities as oil and coal could now be used to run motors for transport and production. In combination, electric power machinery and the industrial division of labor dramatically augmented the productive capacity of enterprises, ushering in the era of large-scale mass manufacturing industries. Together, the specific global production and property relations, and systematically standardized mass production initiated new forms of human relations, new patterns of human movements (e.g., mass urban migrations) and new forms of labor and human commodification.

4. See Gramsci (1971) and Aglietta (1979) for more detailed discussions.

5. See Business Week (May 1, 1995).

6. See De Swardt (1994).

7. See Chapter 3 for a more detailed discussion.

8. See Aglietta (1979) for a discussion of this phenomenon.

9. Brown (1995) argues that most of the strengths of pre-colonial Africa, such as skillful small-scale farming, the central role of women in the village ecology, mixed cropping, urban crafts, a balance between urban and rural life and co-operation between agriculturalists and pastoralists, have been undermined by large-scale mechanized projects, stock ranching, gigantic and ecologically unsound hydroelectric and irrigation projects, deforestation, waged work for men and the marginalization of women, new industries dependent on imported machines, etc. "On this reckoning, the outbreaks of civil violence and internecine wars in Africa seemed to be more the result of the impasse of accumulating debt and the destruction of old forms of community action than of any irreconcilable differences between ethnic groups" (Brown, 1995:6).

10. Increased urbanization is one of the consequences of the impact of global capitalism on rural communities. For example, mass migration from rural Central American and African communities to urban areas is not an endogenous process, triggered by internal developments. On the contrary,

these communities, seemingly untouched by global developments, can no longer sustain themselves as their remaining life-support networks are integrated into the global commodification network. For example, the deforestation of Central America is linked to the global market by an expanding fast food industry in America. Presently, more than half of Central American land is being used for cattle grazing, displacing peasants and forest dwellers from their land and ushering them into the urban reserve army of labor (McMicheal, 1996 and Myers, 1981). This means that less land is available for subsistence farming and for the production of traditional staple foods. Therefore, countries such as Costa Rica have to use beef export earnings to purchase basic grains on the world market since there is no longer enough land available for subsistence farming and the production of traditional staple foods. See McMicheal (1996) and Myers (1981). McMichael argues that the 'Hamburger Connection' is part of the global production processes, responsible for major social and other changes in North and Central America, as forests were converted to pastures for cattle (especially between 1960 and 1990), that were in turn converted into hamburgers. "About one-tenth of American burgers use imported beef, much of it produced under contract for transnational food companies by Central American meat-packing plants. The Central American beef industry has had powerful institutional support through government loans assisted by the World Bank, the Agency for International Development (AID), and the Inter-American Development Bank (IADB). The plan was to tie the development of Central American societies to this valuable export earner. Few people realized that consuming a hamburger might also involve consuming forest resources or that Central America's new beef industry would have vast environmental and social consequences" (McMichael,1996:7).

11. See Simai (1995) and ILO (1994) for more detailed discussions on global unemployment trends.

12. Rifkin (1996) argues that whilst certain countries, such as America, might continue to have low levels of unemployment despite dramatic increases in automation, the same does not apply to poorer countries.

13. See Rifkin (1996).

14. See Rifkin (1996).

15. In 1993 1.4 billion people were living in the urban areas of so-called developing countries. According to projections made by Kennedy (1993), this number will increase to around 4.1 billion by the year 2025. In 1985, about 32 percent of the population of the so-called developing world lived in urban areas. It is estimated that this figure will increase to about 40 percent by 2000, and to about 57 percent by 2025. By that time, 85 percent of the population of Latin America and 58 percent of the African population are likely to be urbanized (Kennedy, 1993).

16. This data was collected by the author (De Swardt, 1994). The precarious employment situation and the desperation of the extremely large number of

Endnotes: The Organization of Production Processes

South Africa's unemployed to find work is chillingly formulated in the following news extract. "Dawn, outside a Johannesburg metal-casting factory in January. Two thousand black South Africans are queuing in the street outside, drawn by rumors that the factory has 200 job vacancies. In the scuffle for a place in line, gunshots are fired. Eight people are shot dead" (The Economist, October 12, 1996:22).

17. See Chapter 3 for more detail.

18. See Rifkin (1996) for more detail in this regard.

19. See The Wall Street Journal (March 16, 1993).

20. However, the influence of technological advancement on levels of unemployment is not altogether clearcut. For example, Clegg and Redding (1990) argue that it is those organizations which did not develop more advanced technologies, rather than those which did, who contributed disproportionately to unemployment.

21. The fact that marginalized groups usually bear the brunt of major changes, such as brought about through automation, is discussed in more detail by Rifkin (1996). "The arrival of the mechanical cotton picker in the South was timely. Many black servicemen, recently back from the war, were beginning to challenge Jim Crow laws and segregation statutes that had kept them in virtual servitude since Reconstruction. Having fought for their country and been exposed to places in the United States and overseas where segregation laws did not exist, many veterans were no longer willing to accept the status quo. Some began to question their circumstances; others began to act. ... Whites in Mississippi, and elsewhere in the South, were worried. The rumblings of change were getting louder and threatened to undermine the precarious arrangement that had maintained the plantation economy for so long. A prominent planter in the Delta wrote to the local Cotton Association with a suggestion that was to be taken up, in short order, by white landowners all over the South. His name was Richard Hopson, the brother of Howard Hopson, whose land was used to demonstrate the marvels of the new mechanical cotton picker. In his letter, Hopson reflected on the growing racial tension in the Delta and wrote, 'I am confident that you are aware of the serious racial problem which confronts us at this time and which may become more serious as time passes.... I strongly advocate the farmers of Mississippi Delta changing as rapidly as possible from the old tenant or sharecropper system of farming, to complete mechanized farming . . . Mechanized farming will require only a fraction of the amount of labor which is required by the sharecropper system thereby tending to equalize the white and negro population which would automatically make our racial problem easier to handle' (Lemann, 1992). In 1949 only 6 percent of the cotton in the South was harvested mechanically; by 1964, it was 78 percent. Eight years later, 100 percent of the cotton was picked by machines. For the first time since they had been brought over as slaves to work the agricultural fields in the South, black hands and backs were no longer needed. Overnight, the sharecropper system was made obsolete by technology. Planters evicted millions of tenants from the land, leaving them homeless and jobless"

Endnotes: Globalization for Sale

(Rifkin, 1996:71).

22. See Mulgan (1994) for more detail.

23. See Alasdair Munn, regional director for the Australian and New Zealand operations of Astea International, cited in The Australian (May 27, 1999).

24. See Castells (1996) for more detail in this regard.

25. Hamelink (1983) argues that the global use of data flows, especially through transnational corporations, is having an impact on the synchronization of techniques (i.e., via the standardization of equipment), symbols (i.e., through the use of an universal computer language and computerized environment) and social relations (i.e., through the organization of industrial production and job patterns).

26. See also Chapter 3 for a discussion of the impact of information technologies on production relations.

27. In general, these statistics exclude certain activities (e.g., assets and trade from non-equity contractual agreements and strategic alliances) and certain areas (e.g., the activities of transnationals in Eastern Europe). These statistics come from a variety of sources, namely Barnet and Cavanagh (1994), Brecher and Costello, (1994), Dunning (1993), Giddens (1990), Kothari (1995), Neville (1997), Robock and Simmonds (1989), The Economist (27/3/97), Thrift (1994), and UNCTC (1992a).

28. The changes in the self-perceived identities of corporations and the re-articulation of their relationships and moral responsibilities co-exist with a range of governmental policies and regulations (e.g., New Right monetarism, deregulation, privatization, etc.) and with the general de-socialization and individualization of social life (see Chapter 4 for more detail).

29. See Ohmae (1990) for a discussion, and a different interpretation, of this and other similar media stories.

30. See Chapters 1, 3 and 4 for more detailed discussions in regard to the state as an operational agent and structure.

31. These five trends largely exist within the school of thought that emphasizes the impact of private enterprises on the production influence triad.

32. Similarly, Reich (1992) analyzed the 'national' division of US$ 10,000 received by General Motors for an 'American' car. Of the total amount, US$6,000 was transferred to other countries for a variety of inputs, such as assembly in Korea, marketing in the United Kingdom, data processing in Barbados, etc.

33. See Dunning (1993). In the period from 1986 to 1990 so-called

American companies increased their overseas research and development (R&D) spending fivefold compared to their spending in the United States (Dunning, 1993).

34. See Ohmae (1990).

35. Examples of electronic, social and legal valorization networks include financial markets, the increased monetization of services, and areas of copyright respectively.

36. See Köhler (1998).

37. See 'The Asian Wall Street Journal' (February 21, 1997). "Our [Germany] biggest export is jobs"(Hans-Olaf Henkel of the Federation of German Industry, quoted in The Asian Wall Street Journal, February 21, 1997:24).

38. See Dunning (1993).

39. See Bainbridge (1997) for more detail in this regard. However, in regard to the decline in manufacturing *vis-à-vis* service industries, Cohen and Zysman (1987) argue that the development of many services depend heavily on direct linkage to the manufacturing industry. In the case of America, about 24 percent of GNP originates directly from the manufacturing industry. About 25 percent of GNP stems from services that are totally dependent on direct links with the manufacturing industry. For Cohen and Zysman the so-called postindustrial economy does not exist, not even in the so-called advanced industrial economies.

40. In the Pearl River Delta alone, for example, at least six million new manufacturing jobs were created in the last decade. See Castells (1996) for more detail.

41. See Dunning (1993) and Ernst (1994) for more detail.

42. See Stopford and Strange (1991) for more detail.

43. See Stopford and Strange (1991).

44. See The World Investment Report (1994) for more detail. The World Investment Report (1994) argues that the dramatic reductions in, for example, the cost of an Intelsat telephone circuit, "have enabled companies to bypass national telecommunication systems and assimilate rapidly these technologies for their own use. Similarly, the speed, cost and capacity of computers has changed at a dramatic pace and there is little indication of this slowing down. ... Although reinforcing the international production of a number of activities that have traditionally contained a large information or knowledge component (such as financial activities), these technologies are transforming the nature and organization of activities which have traditionally given less weight to these components" (World Investment Report, 1994:125-126).

Endnotes: Globalization for Sale

45. For example, in the period between 1976 and 1987, the total number of joint ventures in research and development increased sixfold (Steidlmeier, 1992).

46. See Porter (1990) for more detail.

47. According to Ohmae diversification strategies have opened new areas of competitive advantage (i.e., *vis-à-vis* beating the competition) for some Japanese companies, such as Yamaha and Kao. "It means working hard to understand a customer's inherent needs and then rethinking what a category of product is all about. The goal is to develop the right product to serve those needs – not just a better version of competitors' products. In fact, Kao pays far less attention to other toiletry companies than it does to improving skin condition, circulation, or caring for hair. It now understands hair and skin so well that its newest men's product, called Success, and women's product, called Sofina, fall somewhere between cosmetics and medicine. In that arena, there is no competition" (Ohmae, 1990:42).

48. "A new product a day, keeps the bank manager away!" (Slogan at the work desk of a Zem software engineer).

49. Major car manufacturers now have extensive alliances with, and cross-ownerships of, their competitors. For example, Ford owns 25 percent of Mazda; Chrysler owns 24 percent of Mitsubishi; and General Motors owns 37.5 percent of Isuzu and has joint ventures with Toyota (Brar, 1997).

50. This typology is based on the work of Ernst (1994).

51. In the past, one of the subsidiaries of Zem measured, and rewarded, the performance of its employees, using only financial, i.e. return on investment, criteria. Within the context of contemporary global capitalism, and the evolution of a new organizational format of the 'networked corporation,' this approach was no longer considered appropriate. As a result, management is encouraged to set financial and non-financial performance indicators in a combination of areas, such as shareholders, employees, customers and suppliers.

52. See The Economist (June 3, 1995) and McMichael (1996).

53. See The World Investment Report (1994).

54. 'Rule Britannia' was used as background music for the television commercial made to celebrate Nissan's achievement of becoming the largest exporter of motor vehicles from the United Kingdom. A friend's father was injured by the Japanese during the Second World War and continued to be very resentful towards Japanese (and Asian) people and businesses in the UK. However, after seeing this advertisement (and later believing its content to be indeed true), he dramatically changed his opinion of Japanese and Asian people and businesses. For him they were now providing 'us' with work and opportunities, and they were thus no longer Japanese (i.e 'bad'), but British

(i.e. 'good').

55. See Naisbitt (1994).

56. For example, during a visit to Mazda's head office in Hiroshima in 1996, the author asked the public relations person and some of the staff about the future of the firm. At the time, Mazda experienced considerable difficulties in the local Japanese and global markets. "The future of Mazda lies in globalization" remarked one of the staff members. When asked to elaborate on this answer, the global production of a Mazda sports car was given as an example of the 'globalization future of Mazda.' This car was designed in California, financed mostly from Tokyo, some parts were developed in New Jersey and manufactured in Hiroshima, whilst the car itself was assembled in Mexico and in Michigan. This example is itself inconsequential, however, it highlights the possibilities open to corporations to string single or multiple products together globally.

57. See Die Woche (November 3, 1995).

Endnotes: Globalization for Sale

Endnotes: Chapter 3

1. See Barber (1987) for more detail.

2. See Curtin (1971, 1984), Frank and Gills (1993), Freund (1984), Magdoff (1978), McMichael (1996) and Rahnema and Bawtree (1997) for more detail.

3. See Chapter 1 for more detail.

4. See Schultz (1995) and Terpstra and David (1991) for more detail.

5. See the section on 'The relative decline in bureaucratic hierarchies' later in this chapter for more detail.

6. According to Hoogvelt (1997) Toyota made the most of domestic market segmentation by producing a wide variety of the same generic product (i.e., vehicles of all kinds), and by making a whole variety of products with the same general tool. "For example, in Fordist automobile plants 'dedicated' machines were used to produce each one of the 300 sheet steel parts that go into a motor car. Mass producers used automated blanking presses and, next, stamping presses containing matched upper and lower dies. The same parts were stamped for months or even years without changing the dies. Toyota developed a simple technique for quickly changing dies so that a variety of parts could be stamped with the same machine without significant 'downtime.' Moreover, the changing of the dies could be done by the production workers themselves"(Hoogvelt, 1997:95).

7. See Chapter 4 for more detail.

8. See Chapter 2, Kotthoff (1998) and Rawlence (1985) for more detail.

9. The integration of cultural intervention strategies and TPPI contributes to the earlier mentioned labor practices labeled as 'self-directed Taylorism' by Kotthoff (1998).

10. See Köhler (1998).

11. For a critique of the flexible specialization thesis see Amin and Robins (1990).

12. See Clairmont (1996). On the Fortune magazine cover of December 1993 were the four CEOs of General Electric, Allied Signal, Ameritech and Tenneco. "The four companies whose CEOs who are on the cover of this magazine have shed upwards of 250,000 jobs under these present leaders while creating $104 billion of new wealth, in the form of increased shared values. General Electric alone has shed over 200,000 employees since 1981, while its net income nearly tripled and its market value increased by $67 billion" (Schrecker, 1994:1).

13. Business Week, April 26, 1993. Thurow (1996) argues that 1980s and

Endnotes: The Recomposition of Production Relations

1990s downsizing have eliminated about 2.5 million 'good' jobs in America. The figure for 1995 was about 600,000. At this very same time, "corporations were making the highest profits they had made in more than twenty-five years"(Thurow, 1996:26).

14. Clegg (1991) found that in the Japanese automobile industry approximately 75 percent of work was sourced out from the big companies to primary subcontracting firms, which in turn subcontracted to tertiary outworkers. According to Clegg, these Japanese automobile outworkers were often paid at a fifth of the rate of workers in the larger firms.

15. The CCR 1999 Asia Pacific Call Centre Report, reported in The Australian (May 27, 1999).

16. See Geoff Pountney, marketing director of Schiavello Commercial Interiors, cited in The Australian (May 27, 1999).

17. The figures come from Paul Smith, managing director of Telcus Pty Ltd, cited in The Autralian (May 27, 1999).

18. See The Autralian (May 27, 1999) for more detail.

19. The Melbourne Age, April 10, 1999.

20. See for example Clegg (1991), Dunning (1993), Hammer and Champy (1994), Naisbitt (1994, 1995), and Rifkin (1996) for more detail.

21. Reorganizing the integration of work processes has also led to a reduction in job categories in many corporations. Kennedy and Florida (1993) argue that so-called Japanese corporations in particular have reduced their job categories dramatically in the 1990s. At the LTV-Sumitomo plant, for example, the job categories have been reduced from 100 to only 3, namely: entry-level, intermediate, and advanced. During a Zem workshop a corporate strategist explained 'the reversal of Taylorism and Fordism' as follows. "The reversal of Taylorism and Fordism is not a step backwards. For example, during the development of Hi-fi sound many years ago manufacturers separated the different components. For this reason you ended up with separate amplifiers, record players, tape decks, and later separate CD players. All of these components had a separate specialized function and this was a major part of the success of Hi-fi sound. Presently a number of companies, such as Bose, are reversing this process. They are recombining all the components into a single system, not because its cheaper, or smaller, but because new technologies enable them to improve on the sound quality by recombining the separate parts in a single unit. Similarly, our new system of integrating all the different stages into a single process with only three levels represent a major step forward in which we use the available technology to our advantage" (Zem corporate strategist).

22. See also Crook, Pakulski and Waters (1992) for a discussion of these developments.

Endnotes: Globalization for Sale

23. See Chapters 1, 2 and 4 for more detail.

24. See Wouters (1989) for a detailed discussion of this phenomenon.

25. See Chapters 2 and 4 for more detail.

26. For these middle-level managers the prospects of retraining or redeployment within Zem is further reduced due to a company policy that employees will not be redeployed at a lower level than before, even if they themselves were willing to accept this demotion.

27. It is only the very small percentage of knowledge workers that fall in the category of workers where skill increases occurred. See also Aglietta (1979).

28. See Thurow (1996), Marceau (1989) and Stopford and Strange (1991) for more detail.

29. See Rifkin (1996).

30. See 'The Centre for Budget and Policy Priorities' (1999), quoted in AZ, September 9, 1999.

31. In other words, flexible both in terms of the total length of employment and the division of time during the working week. For a more detailed discussion of the 'new international division of labor,' see Carnoy, Castells, Cohen and Cardoso (1993).

32. See Cox, Clegg and Ietto-Gillies (1993) for more detail.

33. For example, the number of part-time workers increased by 42 percent for men and by 253 percent for women in Japan from the mid-1970s to the 1990s (Castells, 1996). In Japan, two-thirds of part-time workers are women. "Women are the skilled, adaptable workers that provide flexibility to Japanese labor management practices"(Castells, 1996:269). The position of women as an easy disposable and highly flexible reserve army of labor is being exploited by transnationals on a grand scale. "Women have provided TNCs in some industries with the flexibility they seek: cost-cutting initiatives, undertaken by TNCs, such as part-time work or adaptable working hours, have evoked favorable responses among female workers. For example, the introduction of part-time jobs at Philips Electronics (the Netherlands), favored because of its positive effect on labor costs, has dramatically increased the number of women employed. However, the proportion of women in the five highest layers of that company's management remained very low" (World Investment Report, 1994:202). In America up to two-thirds of the new jobs created in the mid 1990s are in the bottom of the wage pyramid (Rifkin, 1996).

34. The Australian Center for Industrial Relations Research and Training, cited by Bagnall (1999).

Endnotes: The Recomposition of Production Relations

35. According to the Australian Bureau of Statistics the percentage of casual workers has doubled since 1982. (ABS, cited in Bagnall, 1999). In its attempts to increase flexibility and reduce overhead costs, Bank America Corporation, one of the largest American banks, estimated that less than 19 percent of its employees will be full-time workers in the near future, whilst nearly 60 percent will be working for fewer than twenty hours a week. See Rifkin (1996) for more detail.

36. See Chapter 1 for a brief discussion of the period up to the 1920s.

37. Whilst labor cost savings are important, they are part of a much more complex organizational structure. Nevertheless, in the early 1990s workers in the footwear industry in Indonesia earned around US $1 per day. This was approximately one-sixth of the comparable (i.e., so-called country adjusted) average hourly wage in the American footwear industry at the time. The data regarding Nike comes from a variety of sources, namely Business Week, April 18, 1994; Donaghu and Bariff (1990); Green Left Review, August 13, 1997; Lang and Hines (1993); The Melbourne Age, April 15, 1997; McMichael (1996); and World Investment Report (1994).

38. According to Barnet and Cavanagh (1994), Michael Jordan was reportedly paid US$20 million by Nike in 1992. This sum exceeded the annual earnings of the thousands of workers in the Indonesian factories that made Nike shoes. This type of personal valorization (i.e., of Michael Jordan) constitutes a kind of contemporary slavery by self choice.

39. See Chapter 4 for a more detailed discussion of consumption practices.

40. See Chapter 4 for more detail.

41. See Fröbel, Hendricks and Kreye (1980).

42. See Castells (1996) for more detail.

43. See Thurow (1996).

44. See The Australian Financial Review, January 16-17, 1999.

45. See also the section on 'the redefinition of the social organization of labor processes by organizations' above.

46. See Dunning (1993).

47. See Appadurai (1990).

48. This historical comparison is not without problems. For example, in 1913 Japan was part of the 'Third World.' However, the relative and absolute decline of the role played by poorer countries and regions in global trade is a general trend.

49. See Hoogvelt (1997).

50. See Woodall (1994).

51. Competitive cost advantages are central to the development of new production loci in spaces outside of the advanced industrialized core. However, the increased globalization – or to be more specific in this regard, the despatialization of production loci – infuses this issue into the realm of social morality. For example, labor theorists sometimes argue that uniform labor reward structures may be disadvantageous to workers outside of the advanced industrialized world, since their global competitive advantages often reside in factors such as cheaper labor and less regulated working conditions. Within Zem, the moral aspect of peripheral industrialization was often highlighted by corporate strategists and managers.

52. According to Bond and Hofstede (1990), there is another very important reason for the success of the Asian countries over the last decades. They argue that there is a correlation between certain Confucian values and cultural-material growth, and that certain cultural values can hold a strategic advantage and form the basis for prosperity. This view is typical of the infusion of culture into the organizational sphere by management theorists.

53. See Davidson (1992) and Fadayomi (1993).

54. See Castells (1996).

55. See Durufle (1988).

56. See Fashoyin (1993).

57. See Borenstein (1994).

58. Africa's population explosion has been very dramatic, even compared to Europe's nineteenth century demographic explosion. In the early 1990s Africa had a population of about 650 million people. In 1950 Africa's population was half of Europe's; by 2025 it is expected to be three times that of Europe, namely 1.58 billion compared to 512 million (Kennedy, 1993).

59. See Chapter 1.

60. See Darnton (1994).

61. See Attali (1991). According to Hallwood and MacDonald (1994), the foreign indebtedness of developing countries was almost $1.5 trillion in 1993 – most of this amount was owed to private creditors.

62. See the World Bank Report (1994).

63. See Ihonvbere (1994). For a discussion of the debt crises, see Chapter 1.

64. See Hallwood and MacDonald (1994) for more detail.

Endnotes: The Recomposition of Production Relations

65. For example, in the period from 1961 to 1978, Africa's measured self-sufficiency was reduced from 98 percent to 79 percent (McMichael, 1996).

66. See Chapter 2.

67. See Shaw (1994).

68. The one exception to the inability of labor to organize globally, is the growing category of a post-national business elite that is very mobile indeed (Thrift, 1994). Corporations solicit the required highly skilled labor from around the globe for specific tasks and projects. The globe-trotting consultant with his international accent and mannerisms, Apple Macintosh notebook computer, gold frequent flyer card, and rational interest in ecological issues and in the latest stockfigures, is indeed one of the icons of the late twentieth century – and unlike James Dean he does not smoke.

69. See Habermas (1981).

70. See the Zem examples in the section on 'vertical organizational disintegration and work polarization' earlier in this chapter.

Endnotes: Globalization for Sale

Endnotes: Chapter 4

1. See Kunda (1992).

2. The classification of categories such as gender and race as 'supra-modernist' does not mean that these categories exist in a space of a-historical retroversion which can be grasped outside of its modernist rearticulation, but only that they are not unique to this epoch.

3. See Habermas (1981).

4. See Chapter 1 for more detail.

5. See Swatuk and Shaw (1994) for a discussion of the effects of the end of the Cold War on the South, and Pizzorno (1991) in regard to the importance of the determination of difference in the maintenance of macro identities.

6. See Chapter 2 for more detail.

7. The development of new technologies, such as remote sensing which scientifically monitors global environmental changes, have also made a substantial contribution to the emerging global ecological consciousness.

8. See Axford (1995) and Held (1995).

9. The national state project is today under increasing pressure from internal social disintegration. One of the indications of this development is the marked change in the occurrence of armed conflict. The most common source of armed conflict no longer consists of disputes between states, but of armed conflict within states. For example, between 1989 and 1992, no less than 79 of the 82 major worldwide armed conflicts were confined within states (Evans, 1995). Raeschemeyer and Evans (1985) argue that it is the capacity of the state to intervene in different social spheres which activates sectional interests to invade and to colonize the state. Alternatively, one could argue that within the parameters of the welfare state the coalescence of competing interests by and large prevented sectoral interest groups from seeking to invade the state, since their own interests were dependent on the endurance of the national class compromise.

10. See Held (1995), Keohane (1984), Lash and Urry (1994a), Shaw (1994) and Thrift (1994).

11. The interconnectedness between 'political' developments and globalization was historically the theoretical domain of 'international relations.' Until today this area is dominated by the theoretical perspective labeled Realism, with Liberalism the less influential historical alternative. Dunne (1997) argues that Realism consists of three core elements. Firstly, realists argue that the state is the pre-eminent social actor and the legitimate representative of the collective will of its citizens. For realists, the meaning of the sovereign state is, on the one hand, defined by the existence of an

Endnotes: Social Identity Compositions and Narratives

independent 'political' community. On the other hand, it is also inextricably bound up with the use of force in order to organize power domestically and to accumulate it internationally. Within the realist framework power was historically (e.g., by Machiavelli, 1532/1988) defined exclusively in military strategic terms. Contemporary realists, such as Waltz (1979) have augmented the notion of power to include the capabilities of the state (e.g., size of population and territory, resource endowment, 'economic' capability, military strength and 'political' competence and stability) as key elements in external state relations. For Dunne the realist notion of statism is today challenged on both empirical (due to challenges to state power from 'above' and 'below') and normative grounds (due to the inability of states to respond to collective global problems such as famine, environmental degradation, and human rights abuses). Secondly, realists argue that the survival of the state in its current form is the prime objective of those in government. For Dunne this principle leads to a specific "ethic of responsibility: the careful weighing up of consequences; the realization that individual acts of an immoral kind might have to be taken for the greater good" (Dunne, 1997:116). In other words, those in government adopt an ethical code which judges not the individual act (e.g., was it right or wrong to drop the nuclear bombs on Hiroshima and Nagasaki in 1945), but the outcome of the action. The notion that moral judgements can, and should, be suspended until the final goal is achieved clearly continues to permeate the current global 'political' landscape, with the 1999 Nato intervention in Yugoslavia an recent example. However, the intensification of global connectedness, as well as the growing consciousness of this intensification inevitably raises increasingly pertinent questions about social actions which value parochial prudence over a more universal global morality. Thirdly, realists argue that the coexistence of a particular state is achieved through the maintenance of 'the balance of power' and some co-operation between states. However, in an anarchical state system without a global government no state can rely on other states for their own survival. As such, the security, juridical authority over its territory and the maintenance of a state in its current form are, in the final instance, based on the self-reliance or self-help. The theoretical viability of 'self-help,' as well as the general realist view of states as the only social 'actors which really count' (Dunne, 1997) have been progressively undermined by the incremental pluralization of sovereignty during the latter part of the twentieth century.

12. See also Thrift (1994) for a discussion on the new patterns of global governance. During the 1970s, the populations, as well as the elites of so-called First World spaces became increasingly vulnerable to globalization. This was due to events and developments such as, the recession, the 1970s oil crises, the emergence of new competitive and innovative centers of in parts of the old periphery, the dramatic increase in the conventional and unconventional military power of countries, such as Libya, Iraq, etc. The unease of the dominant post-Second World War hegemon, America, with the unfolding changes in global social organization, has been articulated with a growing intensity from the late 1980s. For example, the former American assistant secretary of state for African affairs, Chester Crocker, wrote in 1992 that: "[h]istoric changes since 1989 have profoundly destabilized the previously existing order without replacing it with any recognizable or

legitimate system. New vacuums are setting off new conflicts. Old problems are being solved, begetting new ones. The result of this process is a global law-and-order deficit that is straining the capacity of existing and emerging security institutions" (Crocker, quoted by Deng, 1995:209). Some commentators (e.g., Deng, 1995) argue that the Gulf War, and the American insistence of keeping a low-intensity war going in the Gulf, goes beyond the direct interests (i.e. in oil) of America, to the shaping of the post-Cold War 'world order' itself.

13. The Treaty of Westphalia of was signed in 1648. This Treaty consolidated the then existing European state system and for the first time 'entrenched' the principle of territorial sovereignty in interstate affairs and relations. The essential features of the Westphalian model is summarized by Held. "(i) The world consists of, and is divided by, sovereign states which recognize no superior authority. (ii) The processes of law-making, the settlement of disputes and law enforcement are largely in the hands of individual states. (iii) International law is orientated to the establishment of minimal rules of co-existence; the creation of enduring relationships among states and peoples is an aim, but only through the extent that it allows national political objectives to be met. (iv) Responsibility for cross-border wrongful acts is a private matter concerning only those affected. (v) All states are regarded as equal before the law: legal rules do not take account of asymmetries of power. (vi) Differences among states are ultimately settled by force; the principle of effective death power holds sway. Virtually no legal fetters exist to curb the resort to force; international legal standards afford minimal protection. (vii) The minimization of impediments to state freedom is the collective priority" (Held, 1995:78). By the end of the Second World War the Westphalian model of democracy clearly no longer reflected the political realities and needs of the new United Nations period. The United Nations period has, nevertheless, not totaly displaced the Westphalian logic of international governance. At present the reminisces of the Westphalian logic and the realities of the specific globalness of the contemporary political arena are often incompatible. Ascending universalistic pressures are exerted on global interdependence and supra-national issues. Moreover, national sovereignty and particularistic political pressures (as structured by modernist institutions), continue to be dominant forces and a major threat to global stability and, indeed, to the planet's survival. For example, the Commission on Global Governance argues that whilst governments have suffered an erosion in their authority, they have retained enough sovereignty to ensure a potential invasion of the state by various interest groups. Governments today face the pressures of globalization at one level, and those of grassroots movements (e.g., making demands for devolution, if not succession) at another. In some extreme cases, such as in Liberia, Somalia, etc., this has led to the disintegration of public order, rampant violence and the collapse of civil institutions (Commission on Global Governance, 1995:11). The invasion of the state is often a direct consequence of the role of state institutions as intermediaries between foreign resources (including so-called foreign aid programs) and local populations. This is clearly illustrated in many African countries such as Angola, Ethiopia, Somalia and Mozambique. Arbitrary colonial national borders; military empowerment of the state and opposition groups (e.g.,

Endnotes: Social Identity Compositions and Narratives

Savimbi in Angola) induced in the Cold War era; and the 1980s debt and famine crises elevated the importance and potential for the military control of state institutions.

14. See Chapter 1 for more detail.

15. See also Chapters 1, 2, and 3 for more detail.

16. See Thurow (1996) for more detail.

17. The so-called informal economic activities and the global crime industry are further areas in which global developments have undermined state control. See Martin and Schumann (1997) for more detail.

18. See Der Spiegel (no.12, 1996). Owens (1993) argues that "[t]axes on interest payments made to wealthy individuals are now almost a voluntary tax. Most of the major financial centers have abolished withholding taxes on interest payments to non-residents and, in practice – with the exception of scrupulously honest investors – interest receipts from abroad are increasingly not taxed in the home country of the investor" (Owens, 1993:31).

19. See Martin and Schumann (1997).

20. See Brar (1997).

21. This is another example of the contemporary interdynamics of risk, time and valorization. See Chapter 1 for more detail.

22. See Chapter 1.

23. See, for example, Carnoy, Castells, Cohen and Cardoso(1993), Peters (1987) and Porter (1990).

24. For more detail in this regard see Bainbridge (1997), Clairmont (1996), Heelas (1991), Hoogvelt (1997), Hutton (1995), James (1996), Thurow (1996), Stillwell (1993) and Yahaya (1993).

25. See Kurer (1998).

26. The magical figure of budget deficit seems to be the Maastricht target of three percent. Even the ANC government of South Africa has set itself the target of reducing the budget deficit from six to three percent of GDP. Johnson argues that if "that is difficult for G7 states it is going to be tough indeed for South Africa, where there is less fat to cut. The European Union states typically have large welfare budgets and no foreign debt. They can trim welfare and devalue their currency without inflating the value of their debt. South Africa can do neither. Politically, the macro-economic strategy is gravity-defying. A glance at the 1994 election results shows that the ANC is, above all, the party of the African rural poor. ... The National Institute for Economic Policy (NIEP) argues that the macro-economic strategy is too

conservative, pointing out, quite correctly, that not only has it killed off the RDP but that, in effect, the Government has accepted the IMF's structural adjustment program without the formal involvement of the IMF. But the contradiction goes deeper. The savings rate is so low that it cannot possibly provide the investment necessary to prevent unemployment from climbing uncontrollably" (Johnson, 1996:21). The overall logic of reductions in government spending are also questioned by a number of economists. Alperovitz, for example, notes that "there have been no extended periods of rapid economic growth in this century without rapid growth in government purchases"(Alperovitz, 1993:18). Alperovitz's compares the current American deficit (around 5 percent) to that during the two world wars (27.7 percent of GNP in 1919 and 39.0 percent of GNP by the end of the Second World War). Alperovitz argues that budget deficits are not the 'demon' it is made out to be as near-term deficits have, in the past, stimulated strong growth and were thus often recouped during growth phases by, for example, increased taxes.

27. Clegg and Redding (1990) argue that the response of Australia and New Zealand Labor governments to global financial markets in the mid-1980s took place within a rationalist monetary framework which ensured rapid deregulation. This facilitated the greater availability of capital for the restructuring of the manufacturing industry in particular. According to Australian Reserve Bank figures (cited in Hayward, 1998), Australian governments have sold public assets worth AUS$61 billion during the 1990s. Hayward (1998) highlights two aspects of Australian privatization. First, another AUS $ 69 billion of public assets is the target of privatization by the turn of the century, bringing the total amount of public assets privatized to around AUS$130 billion. According to Hayward this total of AUS$130 billion represents a little less than "the value of the Victorian economy, and a little more than the values of the economies of Western Australia, South Australia, The Australian Capital Territory, the Northern Territory and Tasmania" (Hayward, 1998:8). Second, a large quantity of money (AUS$3.5 billion – or the equivalent of the entire sale proceeds from Qantas, Australian Airlines and Melbourne Airport) has been paid so far to private enterprises, such as financial advisers and advertisers, which helped to facilitate the sales.

28. See Chapter 3 for more detail.

29. See Chapters 1, 2 and 3 as well as the latter part of this chapter for more detail.

30. For the purpose of this book social technology does not refer to the instrumental reorganization of social arrangements via, for example, Taylorism as a social technology. Instead, the concept is used here to refer to technologies which overtly influence everyday social exchanges in an ongoing and substantial manner.

31. For more details see Chapter 4.

32. See Science (1987).

33. See Dunning (1993).

34. It is important to note that Harvey (1989) does not argue that this 'time-space compression' undermines localization. On the contrary, Harvey argues that globalization indeed generates localization. The collapse of spatial barriers does not mean that the significance of space is decreasing. Rather, people become much more aware of the specificity of local spaces in relation to global spaces. "As spatial barriers diminish so we become much more sensitized to what the world's spaces contain" (Harvey 1989:294). Waters (1995) argues that most significant event in nineteenth-century globalization perhaps occurred during the Crimean War of the 1850s when the war correspondent of The Times was able to telegraph his reports instantly back to London. For the first time, descriptions of the events were available a mere day or two after they happened. "The rest, as they say, is history – by about the turn of the century communication could be achieved by telephone, by wireless, by cinematography, and even by television. Distant events could be known about, even 'witnessed' without leaving one's own locality" (Waters, 1995:146).

35. See Chapter 3 for a discussion of the decline of the classical cast type of structured hierarchical Fordist work and class relations which contribute to less structured and less overtly polarized management-worker relations. See also Chapter 2 for a discussion of the impact of the contemporary global financial markets on forging new kinds alliances between those who directly or indirectly participate in these global financial markets.

36. Previous chapters have dealt with the general technological developments which contribute to the re-ordering of the specific relationship between capital and labor. This section only deals with an additional aspect of the technologically induced capital/labor environment.

37. See Chapters 1, 2 and 3 for more detail.

38. See the section on production *vis-à-vis* consumption influences later in this chapter.

39. See Reeves (1993).

40. A rather extreme, but not isolated, example of the fusion of reality and fiction is the highly popular and influential Brazilian telly-novelle in which fiction, imagination and reality become indistinguishable from one another. The synchronization and fusion of news, advertising and entertainment takes place either indirectly through the 'hidden' cultural messages expressed and portrayed during standard programs, or directly in so-called infotainment programs.

41. See Castells (1996).

42. See Hannerz (1992b) for a discussion of the spatial ordering of culture.

Endnotes: Globalization for Sale

43. "Last Friday Ten [a TV station] debuted its new interactive music program, 'Ground Zero,' and within minutes of the show being beamed live in Melbourne and Sydney, the first of viewer messages, were being sent to Jade Gatt and his 'Ground Zero' team. By the end of the night, 1,000 e-mail messages had been sent, with viewers requesting music videos, sending greetings or making comments on the show. At last count, the number of hits had risen to 18,000" (The Melbourne Age, 13 November 1997).

44. The emergence of cyberspace as a social medium is well documented. An internet user articulated this as follows."I regularly communicate with people I do not know. Sometimes I do not even know in which country they live. I don't care. ... I have made a lot of friends this way. ... I mean, if I don't like somebody I just ignore them. I choose only to communicate with people I find interesting and stimulating. ... I have very few friends here in New York, especially were I live I know nobody. But maybe I will one day meet some of my neighbors on the net! But then again, if I do not like them I have to move. The net is better" (Internet conversation, 10/4/97).

45. See Held (1995) for more detail.

46. For more detail in regard to the role of technology in the construction of 'imagined communities,' see Calhoun (1991). One of the most publicized symptoms of the 'crises of identity' and its mediation through technology, is the Aum Shinrikyo in Japan. The Aum draws its members mainly from young, highly educated segments of the population. Furthermore, it constructs a new collective self by mixing spirituality, advanced technologies (such as in chemistry), global business operations, and notions of general social destruction and doom.

47. Thompson (1995) argues that the upheavals in Eastern Europe in 1989 provide another example of the ways in which the media can stimulate distant collective action. Whilst many factors contributed to the events, it, nevertheless, seems unlikely that the unrest "would have occurred as they did – with breathtaking speed and with similar results in different countries – in the absence of extensive and continuous media coverage. Not only did television provide individuals in Eastern Europe with a flow of images of the West, portraying life conditions which contrasted sharply with their own, but it also provided Eastern Europeans with a virtually instantaneous account of what was happening in neighbouring countries, as well as in neighbouring cities or locales in their own countries"(Thompson, 1995:115-116).

48. See Baudrillard's 'The Reality Gulf' in 'The Guardian' (1991), cited in Mestrovic (1993).

49. See Mestrovic (1993).

50. See Thompson (1995).

51. See Lury (1996).

Endnotes: Social Identity Compositions and Narratives

52. See Bell (1980), Dittmar (1992), Hall (1991a), Kuper (1992), Lury (1996) and Thompson (1990). The dramatic impact of the production practices of industrialism on social life seemed to have led sociologists to 'believe' that these practices were the sole 'creator' of modernist social life. Consequently, sociologists tended to focus almost exclusively on the directly commodified 'supply side' of social life. Three of the major exceptions to the intellectual practice focusing on the directly commodified 'supply side' of social life, can be found in the work of Simmel (1990), who addressed the intimate relationship between money and modernity, Marx's (1970, 1973) work on 'commodity fetishism,' and Veblen's (1967) writings on 'conspicuous consumption' in 'The Theory of the Leisure Class' (1967).

53. See Sklair (1991).

54. See Brand (1996).

55. See The Economist 'World in Figures' (1996).

56. See Williams (1974) in regard to the notion of 'mobile privatization.' In the dominant spaces of the commodification genre, media consumption is the second largest category of activity of the present day. Work being the largest, and shopping the third largest. See Goss (1993) for more detail. The average American adult, for example, engages approximately seven hours a day in media consumption. In contrast, only about fourteen minutes per day are spent in interpersonal interaction within the household (Sabbah, 1985).

57. Data collected by the author, De Swardt (1994).

58. The global ecological implications of consumption behavior and patterns are also important. In this regard the advanced industrial world is contributing considerably to the ecological genocide of the planet. For example, according to Kennedy (1993) "... the average American baby represents twice the environmental damage of a Swedish child, three times that of an Italian, thirteen times that of a Brazilian, thirty-five times that of an Indian, and 280 (!) times that of a Chadian or Haitian because its level of consumption throughout its life will be so much greater. That is not a comfortable statistic for anyone with a conscience" (Kennedy, 1993:32). Only about 1 percent of all materials mobilized to serve the needs of American consumers is turned into products which are still in use 6 months after their sale (Lovins, A., Lovins L., and Hawken, 1999).

59. See, for example, the credit requirements of the ANZ bank (Australia) available from local bank branches on the request of a loan.

60. See Handelsblatt (January 25, 1996).

61. At present the system of 'user pays' education is rationalized further through the introduction of non-merit access to university education. For example, under legislation passed in 1996 Australian universities can now sell up to 25 percent of the places in their courses to full fee-paying students.

Endnotes: Globalization for Sale

62. See, for example, Gramsci (1971).

63. See Lash and Urry (1994a) for a more detailed discussion.

64. See Appadurai (1986) for more detail.

65. See Lury (1996).

66. See Adorno (1974) for more detail.

67. See Dittmar (1992) for more detail in this regard. Durning (1991) discusses some of the general aspects of expansion of consumption. According to Durning the world's people have consumed as many goods and services during the second part of the twentieth century as all previous generations together.

68. See Lury (1996).

69. See Lash and Urry (1994a) for more detail.

70. See Chapter 3 for more detail.

71. See Abercrombie (1994) for a discussion of the commodification of images and signs.

72. Myers (1986) refers to these consumption of self-identity processes as a form of 'consumption cannibalism.' In relation to this phenomenon, Berger 1972 writes that "[t]he spectator-buyer is meant to envy herself as she will become if she buys the product. She is meant to imagine herself transformed by the product into an object of envy for others, an envy which will then justify her loving herself. One could put this another way: the publicity image steals her love of herself as she is, and offers it back to her for the price of the product" (Berger, 1972:134).

73. Bricolage is a concept used by Levi-Strauss (1964) to describe the process in which objects acquire new meaning through recontextualization. An example of bricolage is the redefinition of the unremarkable, mundane and inappropriate items, such as safety pins, razor blades, nails, etc. to a coherent cultural ensemble in punk. In this study the concept of bricolage is used within a broader context as the process in which both objects and subjects acquire new meanings and identities through the recontextualization of objects.

74. Albrow (1996) argues that the relativization of identity has important implications for both individuals and social theory in general. Albrow argues that the multiplication of worlds means that individuals can inhabit several simultaneously, but that they can only make a relative limited and small selection. For Albrow the result of a plurality of individuals making their own selections is that each individual builds a different repertoire. "This has major consequences in every sphere of social life, in particular for

Endnotes: Social Identity Compositions and Narratives

the state, which has to accept the competing and cross-cutting allegiances of its citizens, up to and even including the point where they are committed to other states. But it has had equally direct consequences for individuals and the theorization of their relations to society. The problem of individual and society has moved away from what used to be the central issue, agency and structure, to the problem of identity, and this has increasingly been made the focus of contemporary controversy as so-called identity politics has detracted from old-style class politics. Identity politics has centered on the relative positions of groups whose very existence is problematized by processes of global social change. Where the identity of the group is problematical, this translates into difficulty in assigning membership of the group to individuals. The result is that identity politics becomes a matter of identity for groups and individuals equally. This development is difficult for much of older modern theory to handle. In particular, both political theory, with its emphasis on citizenship as the route to social recognition, and sociological theory, which stresses the construction of individual identity through social interaction, tend to postulate unambiguous, defined social formations as a precondition for the emergence of clear personal identity" (Albrow, 1996:150). The changes in the dissemination of the modernist cultural épistémé and cultural praxis, and in the dominant influences on social identities, more and more originate outside the traditional domains of sociology and orthodox modernist social networks. This docs seem to require a Kuhnian scientific revolution in social theory in order for it to coherently conceptualize the complex interrelatedness of the modernist cultural épistémé and the modernist cultural praxis. Interestingly, early modernist philosophers, such as Bacon (1906, 1972) and Spinoza (1910), did highlight the centrality of collective symbolic accumulation (e.g., knowledge) to the expansion and development of the modernist cultural genre. In the wake of the industrialization euphoria this insight somehow receded as symbolic systems became intellectualized as 'non-material cultural artifacts,' whilst production was transposed into a 'non-cultural material constructive force.'

75. Without making reference to the Sydney Gay and Lesbian Mardi Grass (although it would have been very much appropriate to it), Kahn argues that, "We live in a world characterized not just by difference, but by a consuming and erotic passion for it" (Kahn, 1995:125).

76. I once saw a person in a Melbourne (Australia) street wearing a hat decorated with Australian Aboriginal art, a shirt with the Australian Aboriginal flag on it, whilst the Rheebok insignia on his shorts, socks and shoes made it clear that he was also a 'Rheebok-man.' What made this person stand out, was the fact that he was clearly from Chinese descent. The 'Australian Aboriginal Chinese Rheebok,' despite being an inconsequential example, is, nevertheless, indicative of the commodification of symbolic identity compositions. The significance of the Australian Aboriginal flag was highlighted by the publicity, both positive and negative, given to Cathy Freeman carrying both the Australian and Australian Aboriginal flags on a victory lap during the Commonwealth games in 1994. Despite the possibility that the symbols displaced by the 'Australian Aboriginal Chinese Rheebok' might have been a non-statement, coincidental

phenomenon, this is not the most likely explanation. Brandname clothes are expensive and are most often bought exactly because of their status and identity narration qualities. See also Appadurai (1986).

77. See Chapter 3 for more detail.

78. The contemporary processes of hermeneutic self consumption exist in contrast to the period of Fordist growth, when national production relations dominated both social stratification and people's sense of their relationship to, and integration into, the social world. "After the war ... my father was a German worker. All his friends were German workers. They talked about their work all the time. Even I knew what kind of work my father's friends did. ... I am still German, but I am not a German manager. I am a global entrepreneur! ... With some of my friends I share certain interests, such as sailing. We go sailing together, talk about a lot of things, but hardly talk about work related issues. With some of my friends I do not really know what kind of work they do. It does not worry me. As long as they have money – sailing is an expensive hobby. ... By the way, I do not think my own children really know what kind of work I do. They just know that it is important since I drive a good car" (Zem manager).

79. For example, the greatest threat to the spatially dominating shopping mall in many advanced industrialized spaces, is the emergence of home-shopping via telephone, television, and the internet (Business Week, July 26, 1993). Research in certain parts of the advanced industrial world indicates that the patterns of shopping times and venues are changing. The single most important shift is a move towards the privatization of the social activity of shopping, whereby the home is becoming an important shopping location (Forbes, May 24, 1993). There are some indications that just-in-time home-bound retailing is increasing in certain parts of the advanced industrial world (The Australian Financial Review, April 1-5, 1999). For example, about half of American book sales are now conducted via the internet (The Melbourne Age, September 16, 1997). See also Rifkin (1996) for more detail.

80. A similar idea is expressed by Featherstone (1991) in relation to the relative micro processes of contemporary consumption practices. Featherstone (1991) writes that the widespread availability of images has provided a context for the development of mass consumer dream-worlds within which individuals increasingly swing between the pleasures of immersion in objects and detachment from them. For Featherstone the contemporary techniques of the self "permit the development of sensibilities which can allow us to enjoy the swing between the extremes of aesthetic involvement and detachment so that the pleasures of immersion and detached distantiation can both be enjoyed" (Featherstone,1991:81).

81. See Domatob (1987) for a discussion of the impact of advertising on Africa in particular. In reference to India, Vilanilam (1989) notes that in a country where there is an acute shortage of safe drinking water, low nutritional aerated soft drinks are extensively advertised. Most often the consumption of these soft drinks is directly linked to 'international' [global

Endnotes: Social Identity Compositions and Narratives

capital's] values.

82. The phenomenal growth in the tourist and leisure industries, and the evolution of tourism and leisure as aesthetic cultural activities, are further examples of the extension of aesthetic cultural services in contemporary social life. Miller argues that "The building of social networks and leisure activities around ... highly particular pursuits is one of the strangest and most exotic features of contemporary industrial society, and one which is forever increasing. There is no more eloquent confrontation with the abstraction of money, the state and modernity than a life devoted to racing pigeons, or medieval fantasies played out on a microcomputer" (Miller, 1987: 210).

83. Continued capital appropriation and accumulation is dependent on the continuous expansion of the processes of capital commodification and social valorization. After the Second World War the symbiotic relation between 'supply' and 'demand' was articulated by the American retailing analyst Victor Lebow. Lebow argued that, "[o]ur enormously productive economy . . . demands that we make consumption our way of life, that we convert the buying and use of goods into rituals, that we seek our spiritual satisfaction, our ego satisfaction, in consumption.... We need things consumed, burned up, worn out, replaced, and discarded at an ever increasing rate" (Lebow, quoted by Durning, 1991:57).

84. It is not surprising that the mobile telephone is presently one of the dominant icons representing the hypervalorized modernist individual, since it combines narcissistic aestheticized reflexivity and global aestheticized reflexivity into a single, highly visible sign. The 'I' is directly and consistently connected to, and integrated into, 'the world.' On my first visit to Hong Kong in 1994, I arrived at the airport in the early hours of the morning. When I entered the toilets, I saw four men urinating. In their right hands they held the ascribed icon of Freudian modernism, while their left hands clutched the acquired icon of late twentieth century modernism. Standing next to these four people was indeed a surreal experience. With quasi relaxing new age 'waterfall music' in the background, the person next to me was talking to a business associate in New York. Coming from Africa, mobile telephones were a novelty to me, and I impulsively asked one of my four urinating companions (when he was drying his hands and before he could make his next call) the rather stupideous question, whether mobile phones had changed his business life. He nodded, looked around, smiled at his mobile phone, and replied: "Now I can even work when I make love, ... and women love that. It turns them on like a red Ferrari." Later that day I listened to Dvorak's ninth symphony and wondered what he would have made of this 'new world' of the hyperculturalization of reflexive accumulation.

Endnotes: Globalization for Sale

Endnotes: Conclusion

1. For example, in the United Kingdom, the average disposable income have more than doubled over the last 20 years.

2. During the 1960s in particular critical theorists from the Frankfurt School, as well as other streams of social analysis – such as dependency theorists – did focus on the interdynamics of commodification and modernity. During the 1990s these research traditions were, however, neither updated to take account of contemporary valorization techniques, patterns and practices, nor were they infused into a theoretical narrative that specifically problematized the interdynamics of globalization, valorization and marginalization.

3. See Beilharz (1996), Deutschmann (1996), Roberts (1996) and Poggi (1993).

4. See the example, used in Chapter 1, of the transnational corporation Siemens who now earns more from its financial transactions than from its acclaimed products.

5. See Chapter 1 for more detail.

6. See Chapter 3 for more detail.

7. See the Introduction and Chapter 4 for more detail.

8. See Chapter 3 for more detail.

9. See Chapter 3.

10. See the Introduction for examples in this regard.

11. According to Egan (1995), around twenty-eight million Americans lived in so-called walled and guarded properties in 1995, with this figure set to double within a decade.

12. On May 28, 1994 the British Prime Minister John Major reiterated an earlier statement on the damage done by the poor to the tourist industry. Major recommended that people report beggars to the police, under laws that provide for a fine of a up to £1,000 pounds. Major argued that people sleep rough not out of necessity, but out of choice it had, he believed, become a lifestyle. George (1997) argues that attitudes such as these epitomize the essence of the various programs for 'the eradication of poverty.' They also inform the contemporary focus on policing strategies aimed at controlling the visibility of crime and poverty in specifically targeted public spaces.

13. For more detail see Davis (1990), Lee and Townsend (1993), Sugihara (1988) and Wilson (1987).

Endnotes: Conclusion

14. The notion of the 'spatial dimension of distance' originates from the work of Bhabha (1994).

15. Wilkinson (1993) argues that the Western 'civilization' is now global in scope, without a periphery for further expansion. This view parallels Gramsci's (1957) classical argument about the dependency of core profit monopolies on the incomplete diffusion of production methods and technologies from the core to the periphery. However, both Wilkinson and Gramsci conflate the capital and national projects. Consequently, they assume that core capital would not peripheralize and marginalize sections of 'its own' national population *en masse*, for example, by means of the systemic destruction of welfare safety nets. In the light of the post-1970s monetary rationalist policies, these assumptions seem to have been unfounded. However, it is clear that people living in historically core modernist spaces are today increasingly co-vulnerable to global market interconnectedness. In the wake of the 1960s decolonialization struggles, the 1970s oil crises, the Vietnam war, the increased media circulation of global images, and a growing vulnerability to, and awareness of, global interdependency, modernist discourses began to focus more overtly on global sociality and the interrelationship between core/so-called advanced industrial and marginal/so-called developing spaces. In the last part of the twentieth century there are trends towards the increased professionalization of intellectual life, as well as a general shift towards more policy-oriented sociological genres. (See Turner, 1994) In addition to the shift away from the vocational intellectual genre, the subject orientation of sociology also seems to be changing. For decades, mastery of the discourse of 'national industrialism' was thé *rite de passage* for sociologists. At the end of the twentieth century, fluency in 'globalization discourse' appears to be a prerequisite for sociological conformism as global analyses permeate more and more social research and writing. In combination, the increased policy-orientated focus on the one hand, and the shift in the subject orientation of sociology towards globalization on the other hand, have spawned a greater issue-related and a less macro theoretical-orientated contemporary sociological genre.

16. The post-1970s, in particular, have been characterized by: the erosion of the national class compromise; the decline of social Keynesianism, which infused social production and private accumulation into the realm of centralized state power in advanced industrialized spaces; increases in the state-sanctioned commercialization of life opportunities; new technologies which enlarge the options open to corporations *vis-à-vis* collectively organized labor, and collectively organized modernist collective institutions, such as the state; new techniques, patterns and practices of valorization which augment the social influences of the dominant commodification genre on the social world; an escalation in both absolute and relative wealth and poverty across the world; and new technologies which form a virtual *and* active ingredient of contemporary social identity compositions and narrations.

References

Abercrombie, N. 1994. "Authority and Consumer Society," in *The Authority of the Consumer*, edited by R. Keat, N. Whiteley and N. Abercrombie. London: Routledge.

Abercrombie, N., S. Hill, and B. Turner. 1980. *The Dominant Ideology Thesis*. London: Allen and Unwin.

Abercrombie, N., R. Keat, and N. Whiteley, eds. 1994. *The Authority of the Consumer*. London: Routledge.

Abou-El-Haj, B. 1991. "Language and Models for Cultural Exchange," in *Culture, Globalization and the World System: Contemporary Conditions for the Representation of Identity*, edited by A. King. London: Macmillan.

Abu-Lughod, J. 1989. *Before European Hegemony: The World System A.D. 1250-1350*. New York: Oxford University Press.

Abu-Lughod, J. 1993. "Discontinuities and Persistence: One World System or a Succession of Systems?" in *The World System: Five Hundred Years or Five Thousand?*, edited by A. Frank and B. Gills. London: Routledge.

Adepoju, A., ed. 1993. *The Impact of Structural Adjustment on the Population of Africa: The Implications for Education, Health and Employment*. London: James Currey.

Adorno, T. 1974. *Minima Moralia: Reflections on a Damaged Life*. London: New Left Books.

Aglietta, M. 1979. *A Theory of Capitalist Regulation: The US Experience*. London: Verso.

Aké, C. 1979. *Social Science as Imperialism: The Theory of Political Development*. Lagos: University of Abadan Press.

Aké, C. 1994. "The Marginalization of Africa: Notes on a Productive Confusion," in *Council on Foreign Relations African Studies Seminar*. New York.

Akyuz, Y. 1994. *Taming International Finance: Controls, Policy Coordination or Convergence?* Geneva: UNCTAD.

Albrow, M. 1990. *Max Weber's Construction of Social Theory*. Houndmills: Macmillan Education.

Albrow, M. 1996. *The Global Age*. Cambridge: Polity Press.

Alexander, J., and S. Seidman, eds. 1990. *Culture and Society: Contemporary Debates*. Cambridge: Cambridge University Press.

Alperovitz, G. 1993. "The Clintonomics Trap," in *The Progressive*, June 18.

Amin, S. 1974. *Accumulation on a World Scale*. New York: Monthly Review Press.

Amin, S. 1980. *Class and Nation*. New York: Monthly Review Press.

Amin, S. 1989. *Eurocentrism*. New York: Monthly Review Press.

References

Amin, S. 1993. "The Ancient World-System versus the Modern Capitalist World System," in *The World System: Five Hundred Years or Five Thousand?*, edited by A. Frank and B. Gills. London: Routledge.

Amin, A., and K. Robins. 1990. "The Re-emergence of Regional Economies? The Mythical Geography of Flexible Accumulation." *Environment and Planning* 8: 7-34.

Anderson, B. 1983. *Imagined Communities*. London: Verso.

Anderson, S., and J. Cavanagh. 1996. *The Top 200 - the Rise of Global Corporate Power*. Washington, D.C.: Institute for Policy Studies.

Appadurai, A., ed. 1986. *The Social Life of Things: Commodities in Cultural Perspective*. Cambridge: Cambridge University Press.

Appadurai, A. 1990. "Disjunction and Difference in the Global Cultural Economy," in *Global Culture, Nationalism, Globalization and Modernity*, edited by M. Featherstone. London: Sage Publications.

Appiah, K. 1992. *In my Father's House: Africa in the Philosophy Culture*. New York: Oxford University Press.

Appiah, K. 1995. "Why Africa? Why Art?" *The Royal Academy Magazine* 48: 40-41.

Appignanesi, R., and C. Garratt. 1995. *Postmodernism for Beginners*. Cambridge: Icon Books.

Archer, M. S. 1988. *Culture and Agency: The Place of Culture in Social Theory*. Cambridge: Cambridge University Press.

Archer, M. 1990. "Theory, Culture and Post-Industiral Society," in *Global Culture, Nationalism, Globalization and Modernity*, edited by M. Featherstone. London: Sage Publications.

Arnason, J. 1990. "Nationalism, Globalization and Modernity," in *Global Culture, Nationalism, Globalization and Modernity*, edited by M. Featherstone. London: Sage Publications.

The Asian Wall Street Journal. 1997. February 21.

Atal, Y. 1981. "The Call for Indigenization." *International Social Science Journal*, 189-197.

Atkinson, J. 1994. GATT: *What Do the Poor Get?* Melbourne: Community Aid Abroad.

Attali, J. 1991. *Winners and Losers in the Coming World Order*. New York: Times Books.

The Australian Financial Review. 1999. January 9-10, 16-17, 23-24; April 1-5.

The Australian. 1997. January 8, January 28, April 30.

The Australian. 1999. May 27.

Axford, B. 1995. *The Global System: Economics, Politics and Culture*. Cambridge: Polity Press.

Ayittey, George B. N. 1992. *Africa Betrayed*. London: Macmillan.

AZ München. 1999. February 21.

Bachelard, G. 1964. *The Poetics of Space*. New York: Orion Press.

Bacon, F. 1906. *The New Atlantis.* London: Oxford University Press.
Bacon, F. 1972. *Essays.* London: J. M. Dent & Sons.
Bagnall, D. 1999. "All Work, No Jobs." *The Bulletin,* 12-15.
Bainbridge, B. 1997. "A Nation-Building State Loses its Mind." *Arena.* No. 31.
Baker, P., A. Boraine, and W. Krafchik, eds. 1993. *South Africa and the World Economy in the 1990s.* Cape Town: David Philip.
Bangura, Y., and B. Beckman. 1993. "African Workers and Structural Adjustment: A Nigerian Case-study," in *The Politics of Structural Adjustment in Nigeria,* edited by A. O. Olukoshi. London: James Currey.
Baran, P. 1957. *The Political Economy of Growth.* New York: Monthly Review Press.
Barber, K. 1987. "Popular Arts in Africa." *African Studies Review,* 30: 1-18.
Barnet, R. 1994. "Lords of the Global Economy," in *The Nation,* December 19.
Barnet, R., and J. Cavanagh. 1994. *Global Dreams: Imperial Corporations and the New World Order.* New York: Simon and Schuster.
Barraclough, G. 1978. *The Times Atlas of World History.* London: Times.
Barten, P. 1999. "Your Next Job," *The Bulletin,* 47-55.
Barth, F. 1992. "Towards Greater Naturalism in Conceptualizing Societies," in *Conceptualising Society,* edited by A. Kuper. London: Routledge.
Baudrillard, J. 1983. *Simulations.* New York: Semiotext.
Baudrillard, J. 1986. *America.* London: Verso.
Baudrillard, J. 1988. *Selected Writings.* Stanford: Stanford University Press.
Bauman, Z. 1989. *Modernity and the Holocaust.* Cambridge: Polity Press.
Bauman, Z. 1990. "Modernity and Ambivalence," in *Global Culture, Nationalism, Globalization and Modernity,* edited by M. Featherstone. London: Sage Publications.
Bauman, Z. 1992. *Intimations of Postmodernity.* London: Routledge.
Baylis, J., and S. Smith, eds. 1997. *The Globalization of World Politics: An Introduction to International Relations.* Oxford: Oxford University Press.
Beck, U. 1992. *Risk Society.* London: Sage Publications.
Beeson, M. 1997. "In the Grip of Global Finance," in *The Melbourne Age,* August 7.
Begg, Z. 1999. "Debt," in *Resistance,* July 7.
Beilharz, P. 1996. "Negation and Ambivilence: Marx, Simmel and Bolshevism on Money," *Thesis Eleven,* 47: 21-32.
Bell, D. 1974. *The Coming of Post-Industrial Society.* New York: Basic Books.
Bell, D. 1980. *Sociological Journeys: Essays 1960-1980.* Cambridge: ABT Books.
Benson, J. 1995. "Firm Performance: Unions and Management in Japanese Manufacturing Enterprises," *Hiroshima Journal of International Studies,* 1.
Bentley, J. 1993. *Old World Encounters.* New York: Oxford University Press.

References

Berger, J. 1972. *Ways of Seeing*. London: BBC Books.
Berger, P., and T. Luckmann. 1966. *The Social Construction of Reality*. New York: Basic Books.
Bergesen, A., ed. 1980. *Studies of the Modern World System*. New York: Academic Press.
Bergesen, A. 1990. "Turning World-System Theory on its Head," in *Global Culture, Nationalism, Globalization and Modernity*, edited by M. Featherstone. London: Sage Publications.
Bergesen, A., and R. Schoenberg. 1980. "Long Waves of Colonial Expansion and Contraction, 1415-1969," in *Studies of the Modern World System*, edited by A. Bergesen. New York: Academic Press.
Bernal, M. 1987. *Black Athena* (Vol 1). New Brunswick: Rutgers University Press.
Bernal, M. 1997. "Race in History," in *Global Convulsions: Race, Ethnicity, and Nationalism at the End of the Twentieth Century*, edited by W. A. van Horne. New York: State University of New York Press.
Bhabha, H. 1994. *The Location of Culture*. London: Routledge.
Bhagwati, J. 1989. *Protectionism*. Cambridge: The MIT Press.
Bhaskar, R. 1989. *Reclaiming Reality: A Critical Introduction to Contemporary Philosophy*. London: Verso.
Bhuta, N. 1996. "Mexico and Free Trade." *Rabelais*, La Trobe University Student Magazine Publication March: 54-55.
Bird, J., B. Curtis, T. Putnam, and L. Ticker, eds. 1993. *Mapping the Futures: Local Cultures, Global Change*. London: Routledge.
Bishop, M. 1996. "A Brief History of Derivatives. It is not the Idea that is New, it is the Volume." *The Economist*, February 10.
Blackburn, R. 1988. *The Overthrow of Colonial Slavery, 1776-1848*. London: Verso.
Bloch, E., ed. 1977. *Aesthetics and Politics*. London: New Left Books.
Bloomfield, A. 1963. *Short-term Capital Movements under the Pre-1914 Gold Standard*. Princeton: Princeton University Press.
Bloomfield, A. 1968. *Patterns of Fluctuation in International Investment Before 1914*. Princeton: Princeton University Press.
Blumenbach, J. 1865. *The Anthropological Treatises of Johann Friedrich Blumenbach*. London: Anthropological Society.
Blumenthal, W. 1987/8. "The World Economy and Technological Change." *Foreign Affairs* 66.
Bond, M., and G. Hofstede. 1990. "The Cash Value of Confucian Values," in *Modern Organizations: Organizational Studies in the Post-Modern World*, edited by S. Clegg and S. Redding. London: Sage Publications.
Bone, P. 1997. "Intervening in the Global Myth of Wealth," in *The Melbourne Age*, December 11.
Borenstein, E. 1990. *Primary Commodities: Market Development and Outlook*. Washington, D.C.: International Monetary Fund.

Borenstein, E. 1994. *The Behaviour of Non-Oil Commodity Prices.* Washington, D.C.: International Monetary Fund.

Bortfeld, B., and I. Thiede, eds. 1995. *Globale Trends 1996: Fakten, Analysen, Prognosen.* Bonn: Fischer Tagebuch Verlag.

Bourdieu, P. 1984. *Distinction: A Social Critique of the Judgement of Taste.* London: Routledge and Kegan Paul.

Bourdieu, P. 1994. "The Field of Cultural Production," in *The Polity Reader in Cultural Theory,* edited by Polity. Cambridge: Polity Press.

Bourdieu, P. and J. Coleman, eds. 1991. *Social Theory for a Changing Society.* Boulder: Westview Press.

Boyne, R. 1990. "Culture and the World-System," in *Global, Culture, Nationalism, Globalization and Modernity,* edited by M. Featherstone. London: Sage Publications.

Brand, D. 1996. "Along came the Transnationals." *Nexus,* 4: 13-17.

Brar, H. 1997. *Imperialism: Decadent, Parasitic, Moribund Capitalism.* Delhi: Harpal Brar.

Braverman, H. 1974. *Labor and Monopoly Capital: The Degradation of Work in the 20th Century.* New York: Monthly Review Press.

Brecher, J., and T. Costello. 1994. *Global Village or Global Pillage.* Boston: South End Press.

Bretherton, C. 1996. "Global Politics in the 1990s," in *Global Politics: An Introduction,* edited by C. Bretherton and G. Ponton. Oxford: Blackwell.

Brett, E. 1985. *The World Economy since the War: The Politics of Uneven Development.* New York: Praeger.

Brooks, C., and J. Manza. 1994. "Do Changing Values Explain the New Politics? A Critical Assessment of the Postmaterialist Thesis." *The Sociological Quarterly,* 35 (4): 541-570.

Brown, B., and P. Tiffen. 1992. *Short Changed: Africa and the World Trade.* London: Pluto Press.

Brown, M. 1995. *Africa's Choices: After Thirty Years of the World Bank.* London: Penguin Books.

Brunn, S., and T. Leinbach. 1991. *Collapsing Space and Time: Geographic Aspects of Communications and Information.* London: Harper Collins Academic.

Bull, H. 1977. *The Anarchical Society.* New York: Columbia University Press.

The Bulletin. 1999. June 8.

Burke, P. 1987. *The Italian Renaissance: Culture and Society in Italy.* Cambridge: Polity Press.

Burrell, G., and G. Morgan. 1979. *Sociological Paradigms and Organizational Analysis.* London: Routledge.

Business Week. 1993. April 4, April 26, July 26.

Business Week. 1994. April 18, April 25.

Business Week. 1995. May 1.

Business Week. 1996. April 25.

References

Byrne, J. 1994. "The Pain of Downsizing," in *Business Week*. May 9.
Calhoun, Craig. 1991. "Indirect Relationships and Imagined Communities: Large-scale Social Integration and the Transformation of Everyday Life," in *Social Theory for a Changing Society*, edited by Pierre Bourdieu and James S. Coleman. Boulder: Westview Press.
Camilleri, J. 1995. "Conceptualizing the UN's Place in the Post-Cold War Era," in *The United Nations: Between Sovereignty and Global Governance*. La Trobe University, Melbourne.
Capling, A., and M. Crozier. 1996. *"Broken on the (Roulette) Wheel."* Arena. No. 25.
Carew, Edna. 1996. *The Language of Money*. St Leonards, NSW Australia: Allen & Unwin.
Carnoy, M., M. Castells, S. Cohen, and F. Cardoso, eds. 1993. *The New Global Economy in the Information Age*. Basingstoke: Penn State Press.
Castells, M., ed. 1985. *High Technology, Space and Society*. Beverley Hills: Sage Publications.
Castells, M. 1996. *The Information Age: Economy, Society and Culture*. Cambridge: Blackwell.
CGG. 1995. *Our Global Neighbourhood: Report of The Commission on Global Governance*. Oxford: Oxford University Press.
Chase-Dunn, C. 1989. *Global Formation: Structures of the World Economy*. Oxford: Basil Blackwell.
Chesnais, F. 1994. *La Mondialisation du Capital*. Paris: Syros.
Chetty, T. 1994. "The Market Economy and Social Justice: The Case of South Africa." Tokyo: Institute of Social Sciences, Chuo University.
Churchland, P. M., and A. H. Clifford, eds. 1985. *Images of Science: Essays on Realism and Empiricism*. Chicago: University of Chicago Press.
Clairmont, F. 1996. *The Rise and Fall of Economic Liberalism*. Penang: Southbound Third World Network.
Clairmont, F., and J. Cavanagh. 1987. *The Guardian*. January 9.
Clegg, S. 1991. "Postmodern Organizations in Management Vol.16." Bond University School of Business Discussion Papers.
Clegg, S. 1992. "French Bread, Italian Fashions, and Asian Enterprises: Modern Passions and Postmodern Prognoses," in *Reworking the World*, edited by J. Marceau. Berlin: Walter de Gruyter.
Clegg, S., and S. Redding, eds. 1990. *Modern Organizations: Organization Studies in the Post-Modern World*. London: Sage Publications.
Cline, W. 1984. "International Debt: Systemic Risk and Policy Response." Washington, D.C.: Institute for International Economics.
Coates, J., J. Jarratt, and J. Mahaffie. 1991. "Future Work." *Futurist*, 25: 9-19.
Cohen, S., and J. Zysman. 1987. *Manufacturing Matters: The Myth of Postindustrial Economy*. New York: Basic Books.
Colchester, N., and D. Buchan. 1990. *Europe Relaunched*. London: Hutchinson.

Cole, R. 1971. *Japanese Blue Collar: The Changing Tradition*. Berkeley: University of California Press.
Cope, N. 1990. "Walkmen's Global Stride." *Business*. March.
Cox, H., J. Clegg, and G. Ietto-Gillies. 1993. *The Growth of Global Business*. London: Routledge.
Crawford, Tad. 1994. *The Secret Life of Money: Teaching Tales of Spending, Receiving, Saving and Owing*. Sydney: Harper Perennial.
Creech, B. 1994. *The Five Pillars of TQM: How to Make Total Quality Management Work for You*. New York: Truman Talley Books.
Cribb, Joe, ed. 1986. *Money: From Cowrie Shells to Credit Cards*. London: The British Museum Publications.
Crook, S., J. Pakulski, and M. Waters. 1992. *Postmodernization: Changes in Advanced Society*. London: Sage Publications.
Crook, C. 1992. "Fear of Finance." *The Economist*. September 19.
Crosby, A. 1986. *Ecological Imperialism: The Biological Expansion of Europe 900-1900*. Cambridge: Cambridge University Press.
Curtin, P. 1971. *Imperialism*. NewYork: Walker.
Curtin, P. 1984. *Cross-cultural Trade in World History*. Cambridge: Cambridge University Press.
Darnton, J. 1994. "In Poor, Decolonized Africa Bankers are New Overlords." *The New York Times*. June 20.
Davidson, B. 1978. *Africa in Modern History: The Search for a New Society*. London: Allen Lane.
Davidson, B. 1992. *The Black Man's Burden: Africa and the Curse of the Nation-State*. London: Fountain Publishers.
Davidson, K. 1997. "A Game of Roulette with the Dollar." *The Melbourne Age*. September 18.
Davis, M. 1990. *City of Quartz*. London: Verso.
De Swardt, C. 1994. "Spoegrivier Report." Cape Town: Land Development Unit, University of the Western Cape.
De Swardt-Kraus, C. 1998. "Contemporary Marginalization," in *Globalization: Restructuring Capital-Labour Relations*. URCOT, Melbourne.
De Swardt-Kraus, C. 1999. "A Snapshot at the Modernist Globalization Epoch and Marginality," in *Sonderheft Soziale Welt zum Thema Globalisering*, edited by G. Schmidt, R. Trinczek and U. Beck. Baden-Baden: Nomos Verlag.
De Swardt, C., M. Simons, and A. Charman. 1991. "The Politics of Gender: Negotiating Liberation." *Transformation*.
Deng, F. 1995. "State Collapse: The Humanitarian Challenge to the United Nations," in *Collapsed States: The Disintegration and Restoration of Legitimate Authority*, edited by I. Zartman. London: Lynne Rienner Publishers.
Dent, G., ed. 1992. *Black Popular Culture*. Seattle: Bay Press.
Descartes, R. 1912. *A Discourse on Method*. London: Dent.
Desola, P. 1992. "Societies of Nature and the Nature of Society," in

Conceptualizing Society, edited by A. Kuper. London: Routledge.
Deutschmann, C. 1996. "Money as a Social Construction: On the Actuality of Marx and Simmel." *Thesis Eleven*, 47.
DiMaggio, P. 1991. "Social Structure, Institutions, and Cultural Goods: The Case of the United States," in *Social Theory for a Changing Society*, edited by P. Bourdieu and J. Coleman. Boulder: Westview Press.
Dittmar, H. 1992. *The Social Psychology of Material Possessions*. Hemel Hempstead: Harvester Wheatsheaf.
Domatob, J. 1987. "Ethical Implications of Transnational Corporation Advertising in Sub-Saharan Africa," in *Mass Media and the African Society*, edited by J. Domatob, A. Jika and I. Nwosu. Nairobi: The African Council on Communication Education.
Donaghu, M., and R. Bariff. 1990. "Nike just did it: International Subcontracting and Flexibility in Athletic Footwear Production." *Regional Studies*, 24.
DosSantos, T. 1970. "The Structure of Dependence." *American Economic Review*.
Douglas, M., and B. Isherwood. 1979. *The World of Goods: Towards an Anthropology of Consumption*. London: Allen Lane.
Du Gay, P., S. Hall, L. Janes, H. Mackay, and K. Negus. 1997. *Doing Cultural Studies: The Story of the Sony Walkman*. London: Sage Publications.
Dubois, P., M. Heidenreich, M. La Rosa, and G. Schmidt. 1995. "New Technologies and Post-Taylorist Regulation Models: The Introduction and Use of Production Systems in French, Italian and German Enterprises," in *The New Division of Labour: Emerging Forms of Work Organisation in International Perspective*, edited by W. Littek and T. Charles. Berlin: Walter de Gruyter.
Dunne, T. 1997. "Realism," and "Liberalism," in *The Globalization of World Politics: An Introduction to International Relations*, edited by J. Baylis and S. Smith. Oxford: Oxford University Press.
Dunning, J. 1993. *Multinational Enterprises and the Global Economy*. Workingham: Addison-Wesley Publishing Company.
Durning, A. 1991. "How Much is Enough?" Washington D.C.: Worldwatch Institute.
Durufle, G. 1988. *L'Ajustement Structurel en Afrique*. Paris: Karthala.
Eagleton, Terry. 1990. *The Ideology of the Aesthetic*. Oxford: Basil Blackwell.
The Economist. 1990. September 22.
The Economist. 1992. September 19.
The Economist. 1993. March 27.
The Economist. 1995. June 3.
The Economist. 1996. *World in Figures*. London: Penguin Books.
The Economist. 1996. October 12.
The Economist. 1997. March 27.

The Economist. 1999. December 11.
Egan, T. 1995. "Many Seek Security in Private Communities." New York Times. September 3.
Ekholm, K., and J. Friedman. 1993. "Capital Imperialism and Exploitation in the Ancient World Systems," in *The World System: Five Hundred Years or Five Thousand?*, edited by A. Frank and B. Gills. London: Routledge.
Engels. 1946. *Socialism, Utopian and Scientific*. New York: International Publishers.
England, G., and I. Harpaz. 1990. "How Working is Defined: National Contexts and Demographic and Organizational Role Influences." *Journal of Organizational Behaviour*, 11.
Ernst, D. 1994. "Inter-Firms Networks and Market Structure: Driving Forces, Barriers and Patterns of Control." Berkeley: University of California, BRIE Research Paper.
Estel, B. 1988. "Gesellschaft ohne Nation?" *Sociolgia Interntaionalis*, 26.
Esteva, G., and M. S. Prakash. 1997. "From Global Thinking to Local Thinking," in *The Post-Development Reader*, edited by M. Rahnema and V. Bawtree. London: Zed Books.
Evans, G. 1995. "Australia's Commitment to Global Multilateralism and its Implications for the Asia Pacific Region," in *The United Nations: Between Sovereignty and Global Governance*. La Trobe University, Melbourne.
Eyres, H. D. 1994. "The Impact of Globalisation and Modernity." *International Sociology*, 9.
Fabian, J. 1983. *Time and the Other: How Anthropology Makes its Object*. New York: Columbia University Press.
Fabian, J. 1986. *Language and Colonial Power: The Appropriation of Swahili in the Former Belgian Congo, 1880-1938*. Cambridge: Cambridge University Press.
Fadayomi, T. 1993. "Nigeria: Consequences for Education," in *The Impact of Structural Adjustment on the Population of Africa: The Implications for Education, Health and Employment*, edited by A. Adepoju. London: James Currey.
Fage, J. D. 1981. "The Development of African Historiography," in *General History of Africa, Vol. 1: Methodology and African Prehistory*, edited by J. Ki-Zerbo. London: Heinemann.
Fanon, F. 1961. *The Wretched of the Earth*. New York: Grove Press.
Fanon, F. 1967. *Black Skin, White Masks*. New York: Grove Press.
Fanon, F. 1988. *Towards the African Revolution*. New York: Grove Press.
Fashoyin, T. 1993. "Nigeria: The Consequences for Employment," in *The Impact of Structural Adjustment on the Population of Africa: The Implications for Education, Health and Employment*, edited by A. Adepoju. London: James Currey.
Featherstone, M., ed. 1990. *Global Culture, Nationalism, Globalization and Modernity*. London: Sage Publications.

References

Featherstone, M. 1991. *Consumer Culture and Postmodernism*. London: Sage Publications.
Ferguson, M. 1992. "The Mythology about Globalization." *European Journal of Communication*, 7.
Fieldhouse, D. 1986. *Black Africa, 1945-1980: Economic Decolonization and Arrested Development*. London: Allen & Unwin.
Fields, A. 1994. "Can there be Political Democracy without a Democratic Economy?" XVI World Congress of IPSA. Berlin.
Focus. 1999. December 6.
Fontaine, J., ed. 1992. *Foreign Trade Reforms and Development Strategy*. London: Routledge.
Forbes. 1993. May 24.
Ford, H. 1923. *My Life and Work*. Sydney: Angus & Robertson.
Fortune. 1993. December.
Foucault, M. 1979. *Discipline and Punish: The Birth of the Prison*. Harmondsworth: Penguin Books.
Frank, A. 1969. *Capitalism and Underdevelopment in Latin America*. New York: Monthly Review Press.
Frank, A. 1971. *Capitalism and Underdevelopment in Latin America*. Harmondsworth: Penguin Books.
Frank, A. 1993. "Bronze Age World System Cycles." *Current Anthropology*, 34.
Frank, A., and B. Gills, eds. 1993. *The World System: Five Hundred Years or Five Thousand?* London: Routledge.
Frank, R., and P. Cook. 1995. *Winner-Take-All Society*. New York: The Free Press.
Franke, R., G. Hofstede, and M. Bond. 1991. "Cultural Roots of Economic Performance: A Research Note." *Strategic Management Journal*, 12.
Freund, B. 1984. *The Making of Contemporary Africa: The Development of African Society since 1800*. Bloomington: Indiana University Press.
Friedman, J. 1990. "Being the World: Globalization and Localization," in *Global Culture, Nationalism, Globalization and Modernity*, edited by M. Featherstone. London: Sage Publications.
Friedman, J. 1991. "Further Notes on the Adventures of Phallus in Blunderland," in *Constructing Knowledge: Authority and Critique in Social Science*, edited by L. Nencel and P. Pels. London: Sage.
Friedman, J. 1994. *Cultural Identity and Global Processes*. London: Sage Publications.
Fröbel, F., J. Hendricks, and O. Kreye. 1980. *The New International Division of Labor*. Cambridge: Cambridge University Press.
Furnham, A., B. D. Kirkcaldy, and R. Lynn. 1994. "National Attitudes to Competitiveness, Money and Work among Young People: First, Second and Third World Differences." *Human Relations*, 47.
Gallie, D. 1978. *In Search of the New Working Class: Automation and Social*

Integration within the Capital Enterprise. Cambridge: Cambridge University Press.
Gareau, F. 1985. "The Multinational Version of Social Science with Emphasis upon the Discipline of Sociology." *Current Sociology,* 33.
GATT. 1987. International Trade, 1986-1987. Geneva: GATT.
Geertz, C. 1986. "The Uses of Diversity." *Michigan Quarterly,* 25.
Gellner, E. 1983. *Nations and Nationalism.* Oxford: Basil Blackwell.
George, S. 1988. *A Fate Worse than Debt: The World Financial Crises and the Poor.* New York: Grove Press.
George, S. 1997. "How the Poor Develop the Rich," in *The Post-Development Reader,* edited by M. Rahnema and V. Bawtree. London: Zed Books.
Giddens, A. 1976. *New Rules of Sociological Method.* London: Hutchinson.
Giddens, A. 1985. *The Nation-State and Violence.* Cambridge: Polity Press.
Giddens, A. 1990. *The Consequences of Modernity.* Cambridge: Polity Press.
Giddens, A., ed. 1992. *Human Societies: An Introductory Reader in Sociology.* Cambridge: Polity Press.
Giddens, A. 1995. *A Contemporary Critique of Historical Materialism.* Houndsmill: Macmillan Press Ltd.
Green Left Review. 1997. August 13
Goldsmith, J. 1994. *The Trap.* New York: Carroll & Graf.
Goldthrope, J., D. Lockwood, R. Bechnofer, and J. Platt. 1968. *The Affluent Worker.* Cambridge: Cambridge University Press.
Gomes, A. 1996. "Development," in *Social Self, Global Culture,* edited by A. Kellehear. Melbourne: Oxford University Press.
Gong, Y. 1995. "Beyond Ethnocentrism: Globalization and Korean Culture," in *The United Nations: Between Sovereignty and Global Governance.* La Trobe University, Melbourne.
Goss, J. 1993. "The Magic of the Mall: An Analysis of the Form, Function and Meaning in the Contemporary Retail Built Environment." *Annals of the Association of American Geographers.*
Gould, S. 1981. *The Mismeasure of Man.* New York: W. W. Norton.
Gourevitch, P. 1978. "The Second Image Reversed: The International Sources of Domestic Politics." *International Organization,* 32.
Gramsci, A. 1957. *The Modern Prince and Other Writings.* New York: International Publishers.
Gramsci, A. 1971. *Selections from the Prison Notebooks.* London: New Left Books.
Gray, P. 1993. *Transnational Corporations and International Trade and Payments.* London: Routledge.
Greenberg, J., and W. Kistler, eds. 1992. *Buying America Back.* Oklahoma: Council Oak Books.
The Guardian. 1987. August 13.
Guile, B., ed. 1985. *Information Technologies and Social Transformation.* Washington D.C.: National Academy of Engineering.

References

Habermas, J. 1963. *Theorie und Praxis*. Neuwied: Luchterhand.
Habermas, J. 1970. *Towards a Rational Society*. London: Heinemann.
Habermas, J. 1981. *The Theory of Communicative Action*. Boston: Beacon Press.
Habermas, J. 1987. *The Philosophical Discourse of Modernity*. Cambridge: Polity Press.
Hahn, C. 1995. "The Clash of Civilisations Revisited: A Confucian Perspective," in *The United Nations: Between Sovereignty and Global Governance*. La Trobe University, Melbourne.
Hall, E. 1984. *The Dance of Life: The Other Dimension of Time*. Garden City, New York: Anchor.
Hall, M. 1996. *Leaving Home*. London: Faber and Faber.
Hall, S. 1991a. "The Local and the Global: Globalization and Ethnicity," in *Culture, Globalization and the World System: Contemporary Conditions for the Representation of Identity*, edited by A. King. London: Macmillan.
Hall, S. 1991b. "Old and New Identities, Old and New Ethnicities," in *Culture, Globalization and the World System: Contemporary Conditions for the Representation of Identity*, edited by A. King. London: Macmillan.
Hall, S. 1992. "What is this 'Black' in Black Popular Culture?" in *Black Popular Culture*, edited by G. Dent. Seattle: Bay Press.
Hall, S. 1996. "On Postmodernism and Articulation," in *Stuart Hall: Critical Dialogues in Critical Studies*, edited by D. Morley and K. Chen. London: Routledge.
Hallwood, C., and R. MacDonald. 1994. *International Money and Finance*. New York: Basil Blackwell.
Hamelink, C. 1983. *Cultural Autonomy in Global Communications*. New York: Longman.
Hammer, and Champy. 1994. *Re-engineering the Corporation: A Manifesto for a Business Revolution*. St Leonards: Allen & Unwin.
Hampden-Turner, C., and F. Trompenaars. 1993. *The Seven Cultures of Capitalism: Value Systems for Creating Wealth in the United States, Britain, Japan, Germany, France, Sweden, and the Netherlands*. London: Judy Piatkus Publishers.
Handelsblatt. 1996. January 25
Hannerz, U. 1990. "Cosmopolitans and Locals in World Culture." *Theory, Culture and Society*, 7.
Hannerz, U. 1991. "Scenarios for Peripheral Cultures," in *Culture, Globalization and the World System: Contemporary Conditions for the Representation of Identity*, edited by A. King. London: Macmillan.
Hannerz, U. 1992a. "The Global Ecumene as a Network of Networks," in *Conceptualising Society*, edited by A. Kuper. London: Routledge.
Hannerz, U. 1992b. *Cultural Complexity: Studies in the Social Organization of Meaning*. New York: Columbia University Press.
Hardcourt, W., ed. 1994. *Feminist Perspectives on Sustainable Development*.

London: Zed Books.
Harris, N. 1990. *National Liberation*. London: Tauris.
Harvey, D. 1989. *The Condition of Postmodernity*. Oxford: Basil Blackwell.
Harvey, D. 1993. "From Space to Place and Back Again: Reflections on the Condition of Postmodernity," in *Mapping the Futures: Local Cultures, Global Change*, edited by J. Bird, B. Curtis, T. Putnam and L. Ticker. London: Routledge.
Hauchler, I., ed. 1995. *Globale Trends 1996: Fakten, Analysen, Prognosen*. Frankfurt: Fischer Taschenbuch Verlag.
Hayward, D. 1998. "Voters Don't Buy the $61 billion Sell-Off." *The Melbourne Age*. June 14.
Head, S. 1996. "Das Ende der Mittelklasse." *Die Zeit*. April 26.
Heelas, P. 1991. "Reforming the Self: Enterprise and the Characters of Thatcherism," in *Enterprise Culture*, edited by R. Keat and N. Abercrombie. London: Routledge.
Held, D. 1980. *Introduction to Critical Theory: Horkheimer to Habermas*. London: Hutchinson.
Held, D. 1995. *Democracy and the Global Order: From the Modern State to Cosmopolitan Government*. Cambridge: Polity Press.
Heller, A. 1990. "Sociology as the Defetishisation of Modernity," in *Globalization, Knowledge and Society: Readings from International Sociology*, edited by M. Albrow and E. King. London: Sage Publications.
Henige, D. 1970. *Colonial Governors from the 15th Century to the Present*. Madison: University of Wisconsin Press.
Hing, A., P. Wong, and G. Schmidt, eds. 1995. *Cross Cultural Perspectives of Automation: The Impact on Organizational and Workforce Management Practices*. Berlin: Edition Sigma.
Hirsch, F. 1977. *The Social Limits of Growth*. London: Routledge.
Hirst, P., and G. Thompson. 1992. "The Problem of 'Globalisation': International Economic Relations, National Economic Management and the Formation of Trading Blocks." *Economy and Society*.
Hirst, P., and G. Thompson. 1995. *Globalization in Question: The International Economy and the Possibilities of Governance*. London: Polity Press.
Hobsbawm, E. 1992. *Nations and Nationalism since 1780*. Cambridge: Cambridge University Press.
Hofstede, G. 1980. *Cultural Consequences: International Differences in Work-related Values*. Beverly Hills: Sage Publications.
Hofstede, G. 1983. "The Cultural Relativity of Organizational Practices and Theories." *Journal of International Business Studies*, 14.
Hofstede, G. 1991. *Cultures and Organizations: Software of the Mind*. Berkshire: McGraw-Hill Book Company.
Hofstede, G. 1994. "Images of Europe." *The Netherlands' Journal of Social Sciences*, 30.

References

Hogan, T. 1996. "Globalization: Experiences and Explanations," in *Social Self, Global Culture*, edited by A. Kellehear. Melbourne: Oxford University Press.

Holzner, B., and R. Roberston, eds. 1980. *Identity and Authority: Explorations in the Theory of Society.* Oxford: Blackwell.

Hoogvelt, A. 1997. *Globalisation and the Postcolonial World: The New Political Economy of Development.* London: Macmillan Press Ltd.

Hughes, S. 1997. "Father and the Holy Swoosh." *The Melbourne Age.* January 27.

Hugill, B. 1994. "A Civil Service on its Last Legs." *The Observer.* May 29.

Hume, D. 1903. *Essays: Moral, Political and Literary.* London: Grant Richards.

Hutton, W. 1995. *The State We're In.* London: Jonathan Cape.

Ihonvbere, J. 1994. "Political Conditionality and Prospects for Recovery in Sub-Saharan Africa," in *The South at the End of the Twentieth Century: Rethinking the Political Economy of Foreign Policy in Africa, Asia, the Caribbean and Latin America*, edited by A. Swatuk and T. Shaw. New York: St. Martin's Press.

ILO. 1994. "The World Employment Situation: Trends and Prospects." Geneva: International Labor Organization.

Im, H. 1995. "Globalization and Democratization: Born Companions or Strange Bedfellows?" in *The United Nations: Between Sovereignty and Global Governance.* La Trobe University, Melbourne.

IMF. 1991. "IMF Occasional Paper 7: Determinants and Systematic Consequences of International Capital Flows." Washington, D. C.: International Monetary Fund.

Inkeles, A. 1983. *Exploring Individual Modernity.* New York: Columbia University Press.

James, P., ed. 1996. *The State in Question: Transformations of the Australian State.* St Leonards: Allen & Unwin.

Jessop, B. 1990. *State Theory: Putting the Capitalist State in its Place.* Cambridge: Polity Press.

Johnson, P. 1993. "How to Restore the Good Name of Colonialism." *Spectator.* January 9.

Johnson, R. 1996. "On the Way to First Base: R. W. Johnson Reports from Southern Africa." *London Review of Books.* October 1.

Johnston, P. 1989. *The Sea-craft of Prehistory.* Cambridge: Havard University Press.

Jones, S. 1993. *The Language of the Genes: Biology, History and the Evolutionary Future.* London: Harper Collins.

JRFR. 1995. "The Joseph Rowntree Foundation Report: Inquiry into Income and Wealth." Joseph Rowntree Foundation.

Kahn, J. S. 1995. *Culture, Multiculture, Postculture.* London: Sage Publications.

Kalberg, S. 1992. "The German Sonderweg Demystified: A Sociological Biography of a Nation." *Theory, Culture and Society*, 9.

Kamulu, C. 1990. *Foundations of African Thought: A World View Grounded in the African Heritage of Religion, Philosophy, Science and Art.* London: Karnak House.

Kao, H., D. Sinha, and N. Sek-Hong, eds. 1995. *Effective Organisations and Social Values.* New Delhi: Sage Publications.

Keat, R., and N. Abercrombie, eds. 1991. *Enterprise Culture.* London: Routledge.

Kegley, C., and E. Wittkopf. 1989. *World Politics.* London: Macmilian.

Kellehear, A., ed. 1996. *Social Self, Global Culture.* Melbourne: Oxford University Press.

Kennedy, P. 1993. *Preparing for the 21st Century.* London: Harper Collins Publishers.

Kennedy, M., and R. Florida. 1993. *Beyond Mass Production: The Japanese System and Its Transfer to the United States.* New York: Oxford University Press.

Keohane, R. 1984. *After Hegemony.* Princeton: Princeton University Press.

Keohane, R., and J. Nye. 1972. *Power and Independence.* Boston: Brown.

Kerr, C., J. Dunlop, F. Harbison, and C. Myers. 1973. *Industrialism and Industrial Man.* Harmondsworth: Penguin Books.

Keynes, J. M. 1971. *The Economic Consequences of Peace.* London: Macmillan.

Khadiagala, Gilbert M. 1995. "State Collapse and Reconstruction in Uganda," in *Collapsed States: The Disintegration and Restoration of Legitimate Authority*, edited by I. Zartman. London: Lynne Rienner Publishers.

Ki-Zerbo, J., ed. 1981. *General History of Africa, Vol. 1: Methodology and African Prehistory.* London: Heinemann.

Kindleberger, C. P. 1986. *The World in Depression 1929-1939.* Berkeley: University of California Press.

King, A., ed. 1991. *Culture, Globalization and the World System: Contemporary Conditions for the Representation of Identity.* London: Macmillan.

Köhler, D. 1998. "Concession Bargaining and Globalisation in the German Automobile Industry," in *Globalisation: Restructuring Capital-Labour Relations.* URCOT, Melbourne.

Kondratieff, N. 1979. "The Long Waves of Economic Life." *Review*, 2.

Kothari, S. 1995. "Where are the People? The United Nations, Global Economic Institutions and Governance," in *The United Nations: Between Sovereignty and Global Governance.* La Trobe University, Melbourne.

Kotthoff, H. 1998. "Mitbestimmung in Zeiten Intressenpolitischer Rückschritte." *Industrielle Beziehungen*, 5.

Kranzberg, M. 1985. "The Information Age: Evolution or Revolution?" in *Information Technologies and Social Transformation*, edited by B. Guile.

References

Washington D.C.: National Academy of Engineering.
Krasner, D. 1976. "State Power and the Structure of International Trade." *World Politics*, 28.
Kreinin, M., ed. 1993. *International Commercial Policy: Issues for the 1990s*. Washington: Taylor & Francis.
Kunda, G. 1992. *Engineering Culture: Control and Commitment in a High-Tech Corporation*. Philadelphia: Temple University Press.
Kuper, A., ed. 1992. *Conceptualising Society*. London: Routledge.
Kurer, O. 1998. "Globalisation and the Welfare State," in *Globalisation: Restructuring Capital-Labour Relations*. URCOT, Melbourne.
Laclau, E. 1977. *Politics and Ideology in Marxist Theory: Capitalism, Fascism, Populism*. London: New Left Books.
Lal, M. 1984. *Settlement History and the Rise of Civilization in Ganga-Yamuna Doab, from 1500 BC to AD 300*. New Delhi: B. R. Publishers.
Lang, T., and C. Hines. 1993. *The New Protectionism. Protecting the Future Against Free Trade*. New York: The New Press.
Lash, S., and J. Urry. 1987. *The End of Organized Capitalism*. Cambridge: Polity Press.
Lash, S., and J. Urry. 1994a. *Economies of Signs and Space*. London: Sage Publications.
Lash, S., and J. Urry. 1994b. "Postmodernist Sensibility," in *The Polity Reader in Cultural Theory*, edited by Polity Press. Cambridge: Polity Press.
LeBon, G. 1912. *The Psychology of Peoples*. New York: Stechert.
LeBon, G. 1947. *The Crowd*. New York: Macmillan.
Lee, P., and P. Townsend. 1993. "Trends in Deprivation in the London Labour Market: A Study of Low-Incomes and Unemployment in London between 1985 and 1992." *International Institute of Labour Studies*, Discussion paper 59/1993.
Leflkowitz, M., and G. Rogers, eds. 1996. *Black Athena Revisited*. London: University of North Carolina Press.
Lehman, C., and R. Moore, eds. 1992. *Multinational Culture: Social Impacts of a Global Economy*. London: Greenwood Press.
Lenin, V. 1936. *Imperialism, the Highest Stage of Capitalism*. London: Lawrence and Wishart.
Lesser, W. 1990. "An Overview of the Intellectual Property System," in *Strengthening Frotection of Intellectual Property in Developing Countries: A Survey of the Literature*, edited by W. Siebeck. Washhington D.C.: World Bank.
Levi-Strauss, C. 1964. *Totemism*. London: Merlin Press.
Levi-Strauss, C. 1973. *Structural Anthropology*. London: Allen Lane.
Levitt, T. 1983. "The Globalization of Markets." *Harvard Business Review*. May-June.
Leys, C. 1994. "Confronting the African Tragedy." *New Left Review*.
Lipietz, A. 1988. "New Tendencies in the International Division of Labour:

Regimes of Accumulation and Modes of Regulation," in *Production, Work, Territory: The Geographical Anatomy of Industrial Capitalism*, edited by A. Scott and M. Storpor. Winchester: Unwin Hyman.

Lissakers, K. 1993. *Banks, Borrowers, and the Establishment: A Revisionist Account of the International Debt Crises*. New York: Basic Books.

Littek, W., and T. Charles, eds. 1995. *The New Division of Labour: Emerging Forms of Work Organisation in International Perspective*. Berlin: Walter de Gruyter.

Lloyd, C. 1986. *Explanation in Social History*. Oxford: Basil Blackwell.

Lombard, M. 1975. *The Golden Age of Islam*. Rotterdam: North Holland.

Lombard, M. 1991. "Income Distribution in Australia 1983-1989." *Economic Papers*, 10.

Lovins, A., L. Lovins, and P. Hawken. 1999. "A Road Map for Natural Capitalism." *Harvard Business Review*. May - June.

Lury, C. 1996. *Consumer Culture*. Cambridge: Polity Press.

Machiavelli, N. 1988. *The Prince*. Cambridge: Cambridge University Press.

Madden, P., and J. Madeley. 1993. "Winners and Losers: The Impact of the GATT Uruguay Round on Developing Countries." Christian Aid.

Magdoff, H. 1978. *Imperialism: From the Colonial Age to the Present*. NewYork: Monthly Review Press.

Maitland, J. 1998. "Core Labour Standards and Beyond: Reigning in the Multinationals," in *Globalisation: Restructuring Capital-Labour Relations*. URCOT, Melbourne.

Malik, K. 1996. *The Meaning of Race*. London: Macmillan Press.

Mandel, E. 1976. *Late Capitalism*. London: New Left Books.

Marceau, J. 1989. *A Family Business*. Cambridge: Cambridge University Press.

Marceau, J., ed. 1992. *Reworking the World*. Berlin: Walter de Gruyter.

Marcuse, H. 1968. *One Dimensional Man*. London: Sphere.

Marcuse, H. 1972. *Eros and Civilisation*. London: Baacus.

Martin, H., and H. Schumann. 1997. *The Global Trap: Globalization and the Assault on Democracy and Prosperity*. New York: Zed Books.

Marx, K. 1970. *Capital, Vol. 1*. London: Lawrence & Wishart.

Marx, K. 1972. *Capital, Vol. 3*. London: Lawrence & Wishart.

Marx, K. 1973. *Gundrisse*. Harmondsworth: Penguin Books.

Marx, K. 1977. *Selected Writings*. Oxford: Oxford University Press.

Marx, K., and F. Engels. 1972. *The Basic Writings on Politics and Philosophy*. London: Collins.

Marx, K., and F. Engels. 1983. *The Communist Manifesto*. New York: International Publishers.

Mattelart, A. 1978. "The Nature of Communications Practice in a Dependent Society." *Latin American Perspectives*, 5.

Mattelart, A. 1980. *Mass Media, Ideologies and the Revolutionary Movement*. Sussex: Harvester Press.

References

Mazrui, A. 1980. *A World Federation of Cultures: An African Perspective.* New York: Free Press.
Mazrui, A. 1990. *Cultural Forces in World Politics.* London: James Currey.
Mazrui, A. 1995. "The United Nations and Four Ethical Revolutions of the Twentieth Century," in *The United Nations: Between Sovereignty and Global Governance.* La Trobe University, Melbourne.
McDonalds. 1995. "Annual Report."
McGrane, B. 1989. *Beyond Anthropology: Society and the Other.* New York: Columbia University Press.
McLuhan, M. 1964. *Understanding Media: The Extensions of Man.* New York: Macmillan.
McMichael, P. 1996. *Development and Social Change: A Global Perspective.* Thousand Oaks, California: Pine Forge Press.
McNeill, W. H. 1983. *The Pursuit of Power: Technology, Armed Forces and Society since A D. 1000.* Chicago: University of Chicago Press.
McNeill, W. H. 1985. *Polyethnicity and National Unity in World History.* Toronto: University of Toronto Press.
The Melbourne Age. 1997. April 1, April 15, April 18, September 16, September 23, October 10, November 13.
The Melbourne Age. 1998. September 10.
The Melbourne Age. 1999. April 10.
Mestrovic, S. 1993. *The Barbarian Temperament: Toward a Postmodern Critical Theory.* London: Routledge.
Miller, D. 1987. *Material Culture and Mass Consumption.* Oxford: Blackwell.
Modelski, G. 1987. *Long Cycles in World Politics.* London: Macmillan.
Morgan, G. 1986. *Images of Organization.* London: Sage Publications.
Morgenstern, O. 1959. *International Financial Transactions and Business Cycles.* Princeton: Princeton University Press.
Mort, F. 1989. "The Writing On the Wall." *New Statesman and Society,* May 12.
Mudimbe, V. 1988. *The Invention of Africa.* Bloomington: Indiana University Press.
Mudimbe, V. 1994. *The Idea of Africa.* Bloomington: Indiana University Press.
Mulgan, G. J. 1994. "The Dynamics of Electronic Networks," in *The Polity Reader in Cultural Theory,* edited by Polity Press. Cambridge: Polity Press.
Mulhearn, C. 1996. "Changes and Development in the Global Economy," in *Global Politics: An Introduction,* edited by C. Bretherton and G. Ponton. Oxford: Blackwell.
Munck, R. 1990. *The Difficult Dialogue: Marxism and Nationalism.* London: Zed Books.
Myers, N. 1981. "The Hamburger Connection: How Central America's forests became North America's hamburgers." *Ambio,* 1.
Myers, K. 1986. *Understains: The Sense and Seduction of Advertising.*

London: Pandora.
Naisbitt, J. 1994. *Global Paradox: The Bigger the World Economy, the More Powerful its Smallest Players.* St Leonards: Allen & Unwin.
Naisbitt, J. 1995. *Megatrends Asia: The Eight Asian Megatrends that are Changing the World.* London: Nicholas Brealey.
Nandy, A. 1997. "Colonization of the Mind," in *The Post-development Reader*, edited by M. Rahnema and V. Bawtree. London: Zed Books.
Nankervis, A., R. Compton, and T. McCarthy. 1993. *Strategic Human Resource Management.* Melbourne: Nelson.
Nencel, L., and P. Pels, eds. 1991. *Constructing Knowledge: Authority and Critique in Social Science.* London: Sage Publications.
Neville, R. 1997. "The Business of Being Human." *The Melbourne Age.* August 23.
Nicholson-Lord, D. 1993. *The Independent on Sunday.* December 12
Norris, C. 1993. *The Truth about Postmodernism.* Oxford: Blackwell.
Norwine, Jim, and Alfonso Gonzalez, eds. 1988. *The Third World: States of Mind and Being.* Boston: Unwin Hyman.
O'Connor, N. G. 1995. "The Influence of Organizational Culture on the Usefulness of Budget Participation by Singaporean-Chinese Managers." *Accounting, Organizations and Society*, 20.
OECD. 1985. "Structural Adjustment and Multinational Enterprises." Paris: Organisation for Economic Co-operation and Development.
OECD. 1987. "Interdependence and Co-operation in Tomorrow's World." Paris: Organisation for Economic Co-operation and Development.
OECD. 1990. "Financing and External Debt of Developing Countries." Paris: Organisation for Economic Co-operation and Development.
OECD. 1991. "Financing and External Debt of Developing Countries." Paris: Organisation for Economic Co-operation and Development.
OECD. 1992. "Globalization of Industrial Activities." Paris: Organisation for Economic Co-operation and Development.
OECD. 1994a. "Main Economic Indicators." Paris: Organisation for Economic Co-operation and Development.
OECD. 1994b. "Employment/Unemployment Study." Paris: Organisation for Economic Co-operation and Development.
OECD. 1994c. "Economic Surveys: Korea." Paris: Organisation for Economic Co-operation and Development.
Offe, C. 1985. *Disorganized Capitalism.* Cambridge: Cambridge University Press.
Ohmae, K. 1990. *The Borderless World: Power and Strategy in the Interlinked Economy.* London: Collins.
Olukoshi, A. O., ed. 1993. *The Politics of Structural Adjustment in Nigeria.* London: James Currey.
OMB. 1994. "Historical Tables, Fiscal Year 1995." Washington, D.C.: Office of Management and Budget.

References

Ottaway, Marina. 1995. "Democratization in Collapsed States," in *Collapsed States: The Disintegration and Restoration of Legitimate Authority*, edited by I. Zartman. London: Lynne Rienner Publishers.
Owen, R. 1996. *The Times World Organisations: Their Role and Reach in the New World Order*. London: Times Books.
Owens, J. 1993. "Globalisation: The Implications for Tax Policies." *Fiscal Studies*, 14.
Pawson, R. 1989. *A Measure for Measures: A Manifesto for Empirical Sociology*. London: Routledge.
Pels, P., and L. Nencel. 1991. "Critique and the Deconstruction of Anthropological Authority," in *Constructing Knowledge: Authority and Critique in Social Science*, edited by L. Nencel and P. Pels. London: Sage Publications.
Peters, T., and R. Waterman. 1982. *In Search of Excellence*. New York: Harper & Row.
Peters, T. 1987. *Thriving on Chaos: Handbook for a Management Revolution*. London: Pan Books.
Petras, J. 1997. "The New Cultural Domination by the Media," in *The Post-Development Reader*, edited by M. Rahnema and V. Bawtree. London: Zed Books.
Pieterse, J. 1994. "Globalisation as Hybridisation." *International Sociology*, 9.
Pizzorno, A. 1991. "On the Individualistic Theory of Social Order," in *Social Theory for a Changing Society*, edited by P. Bourdieu and J. Coleman. Boulder: Westview Press.
Poggi, G. 1993. *Money and the Modern Mind: Georg Simmel's Philosophy of Money*. Berkeley: University of California Press.
Porter, M. E. 1990. *The Competitive Advantage of Nations*. London: Macmillan Press.
Prebisch, K. 1950. *The Economic Development of Latin America and Its Problems*. New York: UN Publications.
Raeschemeyer, D., and P. Evans. 1985. "The State and Economic Transformation: Towards an Analysis of the Conditions Underlying Effective Intervention," in *Bringing the State Back In*, edited by P. Evans, D. Raeschemeyer and T. Skocpol. Cambridge: Cambridge University Press.
Rahnema, M., and V. Bawtree, eds. 1997. *The Post-Development Reader*. London: Zed Books.
Raikes, P. 1988. *Modernising Hunger: Famine, Food Surplus and Farm Policy in the EEC and Africa*. London: Catholic Institute for International Affairs.
Ranald, P. 1988. "Disciplining Governments: What the Multilateral Agreement on Investment would mean for Australia." Sydney, Evatt Foundation.
Rawlence, C. 1985. *About Time*. London: Jonathan Cape.
Reeves, G. 1993. *Communications and the 'Third World'*. London: Routledge.

Reich, R. 1992. *The Work of Nations: Preparing Ourselves for 21st Century Capitalism.* New York: Random House.
Riccardo, D. 1816. *Proposals for an Economic and Secure Currency.* Unpublished Paper.
Richie, M. 1994. "GATT Facts: Africa Loses under GATT Working Paper." Institute for Agriculture and Trade Policy, Minneapolis.
Rifkin, J. 1996. *The End of Work: The Decline of the Global Labor Force and the Dawn of the Post-Market Era.* New York: G. P. Putnam's Sons.
Ritchie, M. 1993. "Breaking the Deadlock: The United States and Agriculture Policy in the Uruguay Round." Institute for Agriculture and Trade Policy, Minneapolis.
Ritzer, G. 1993. *The McDonaldization of Society.* Thousand Oaks: Pine Forge.
Roberts, D. 1996. "Georg Simmel's Philosophy of Money: Reflections on the Relation between Philosophy and History." *Thesis Eleven,* 44.
Robertson, R. 1991. "Social Theory, Cultural Relativity and the Problem of Globality," in *Culture, Globalization and the World System: Contemporary Conditions for the Representation of Identity,* edited by A. King. London: Macmillan.
Robertson, R. 1992. *Globalization: Social Theory and Global Culture.* London: Sage Publications.
Robertson, R., and F. Lechner. 1985. "Modernization, Globalization and the Problem of Culture in World-System Theory." *Theory, Culture and Society,* 2.
Robins, A. H. 1991. *Biological Perspectives on Human Pigmentation.* Cambridge: Cambridge University Press.
Robock, S., and K. Simmonds. 1989. *International Business and Multinational Enterprises.* Homewood: Irwin.
Rostow, W. 1960. *The Stages of Economic Growth: A Non-Communist Manifesto.* Cambridge: Cambridge University Press.
Sabbah, F. 1985. "The New Media," in *High Technology, Space and Society,* edited by M. Castells. Beverley Hills: Sage Publications.
Sahlins, M. 1976. *Culture and Practical Reason.* Chicago: Chicago University Press.
Sahlins, M. 1985. *Islands of History.* Chicago: University of Chicago Press.
Sahlins, M. 1993. "Goodbye to Tristes Trapes: Ethnography and the Context of Modern World History," in *Assessing Anthropology,* edited by R. Borofsky. New York: Macmillan Press.
Said, E. 1980. *The Question of Palestine.* New York: Vintage Books.
Said, E. 1993. *Culture and Imperialism.* London: Vintage Books.
Said, E. 1995. *Orientalism: Western Conceptions of the Orient.* London: Penguin Books.
Sandberg, D. 1994. "The Pirate Privateers." *New Internationalist,* September.
Santos, B. 1995. *Toward a New Common Sense.* New York: Routledge.
Sassen, S. 1991. *The Global City.* Princeton: Princeton University Press.

References

Sassen, S. 1995. *Cities in a World Economy.* Thousand Oaks: Sage Publications.
Schmidt, G. 1998. "On the Future of Industrial Relations in European Advanced Industrial Societies at the End of the 20th Century," in *Globalisation: Restructuring Capital-Labour Relations.* URCOT, Melbourne.
Schmidt, G., and R. Trinczek. 1997. "DFG Schwerpunkt: Regulierung und Restrukturierung der Arbeit in den Spannungsfeldern von Globalisierung und Dezentralisierung." University of Nürnberg-Erlangen, Erlangen.
Schmitter, P. 1994. "Democratic Dangers and Dilemmas." *Journal of Democracy,* 5.
Schoenberger, E. 1992. "From Fordism to Flexible Accumulation: Technology, Competition and the Internationalization of Production," in *Human Societies: An Introductory Reader in Sociology,* edited by A. Giddens. Cambridge: Polity Press.
Schrecker, T. 1994. "The Borderless World and the Walled City." XVI World Congress of IPSA. Berlin.
Schultz, M. 1995. *On Studying Organizational Cultures: Diagnosis and Understanding.* Berlin: Walter de Gruyter.
Science. 1987. October 2.
Scott, A., and M. Storpor, eds. 1988. *Production, Work, Territory: The Geographical Anatomy of Industrial Capitalism.* Winchester: Unwin Hyman.
Seabrook, J. 1985. *Landscapes of Poverty.* Oxford: Basil Blackwell.
Seabrook, J. 1990. *The Myth of the Market: Promises and Illusions.* Devon: Green Books.
SEF, ed. 1995. *Globale Trends 1996: Fakten, Analysen, Prognosen.* Bonn: Fischer Tagebuch Verlag.
Senge, P. M., C. Roberts, R. B. Ross, B. J. Smith, and A. Kleiner. 1994. *The Fifth Discipline Fieldbook: Strategies and Tools for Building a Learning Organization.* London: Nicholas Brealey Publishing.
Senghor, L., ed. 1948. *Anthologie de la Nouvelle Poesie Negre et Malgache de Langue Francoise.* Paris: Presse Universitaires de France.
Serequeberhan, T. 1994. *The Hermeneutics of African Philosophy: Horizon and Discourse.* New York: Routledge.
Shaw, M. 1994. *Global Society and International Relations: Sociological Concepts and Political Perspectives.* Cambridge: Polity Press.
Silverman, D. 1970. *The Theory of Organizations.* London: Heinemann.
Silverman, D. 1985. *Qualitative Methodology in Sociology.* Hampshire: Gower.
Silverman, M., ed. 1991. *Race, Discourse and Power in France.* Aldershot: Avebury.
Simai, M., ed. 1995. *Global Employment: An International Investigation into the Future of Work.* London: Zed Books.
Simmel, G. 1990. *The Philosophy of Money.* London: Routledge.
Sklair, L. 1991. *Sociology of the Global System.* New York: Harvester

Wheatsheaf.
Sklair, L. 1995. "Social Movements and Global Capitalism." *Sociology*, 29.
Sklair, L. 1996. "Globalization and Society," in *International Encyclopedia of Business and Management*, edited by M. Warner. London: Routledge.
Skocpol, T. 1977. "Wallerstein's World Capitalist System: A Theoretical and Historical Critique." *American Journal of Sociology*, 82.
Smart, B. 1994. "Sociology, Globalisation and Postmodernity: Comments on the 'Sociology for One World' Thesis." *International Sociology*, 9.
Smith, T. 1981. *The Patterns of Imperialism: The United States, Great Britain, and the Late Industrializing World since 1815*. Cambridge: Cambridge University Press.
Smith, A. 1984. "National Identity and Myths of Ethnic Descent." *Research in Social Movements, Conflicts and Change*, 7.
Smith, A. 1986. *The Ethnic Origins of Nations*. Oxford: Blackwell.
Smith, A. 1988. "The Myth of the 'Modern Nation' and the Myth of Nations." *Ethnic and Racial Studies*, 11.
Smith, A. 1989. "The Origins of Nations." *Ethnic and Racial Studies*, 12.
Smith, A. 1990. "Toward a Global Culture?" in *Global Culture, Nationalism, Globalization and Modernity*, edited by M. Featherstone. London: Sage.
Smith, A. 1991. *National Identity*. London: Penguin Books.
Smith, P., and M. Peterson. 1988. *Leadership, Organizations and Culture*. London: Sage Publications.
Soeters, J. 1986. "Excellent Companies as Social Movements." *Journal of Management Studies*, 23.
Soros, G. 1998. *The Crises of Global Capitalism*. London: Penguin Books.
Speth, J. 1992. "A Post-Rio Compact." *Foreign Policy*, Fall.
Spiegel. 1996. No.12.
Spinoza, B. 1910. *Ethics*. London: J. M. Dent & Sons.
Stallings, B. 1994. *The New International Context of Development: Obstacles or Opportunities?* Madison: University of Wisconsin Press.
The Star and SA Times. 1997. January 8.
Steidlmeier, P. 1992. *People and Profits: The Ethics of Capitalism*. Englewood Cliffs: Prentice-Hall.
Steinmetz, G., and M. Marshall. 1997. "Hoechst is Shedding its German Accent." *The Asian Wall Street Journal*. February 21.
Stillwell, F. 1993. *Economic Inequality: Who Gets What in Australia*. Leichhardt: Pluto Press.
Stopford, J., and S. Strange. 1991. *Rival States, Rival Firms: Competition for World Market Shares*. Cambridge: Cambridge University Press.
Storper, M. 1992. "The Limits to Globalisation: Technology Districts and International Trade." *Economic Geography*, No. 68.
Storper, M., and B. Harrison. 1990. "Flexibility, Hierarchy and Regional Development." Discussion Paper. School of Architecture and Urban Planning UCLA, Los Angeles.

References

Strange, S. 1986. *Casino Capitalism*. Oxford: Blackwell.
Strange, S. 1994. *States and Markets: An Introduction to International Political Economy*. London: Frances Pinter.
Strathern, M. 1992. "Parts and Wholes: Refiguring Relationships in a Post-Plural World," in *Conceptualising Society*, edited by A. Kuper. London: Routledge.
Strathern, M. 1994. "Foreword: The Mirror of Technology," in *Consuming Technologies: Media and Information in Domestic Spaces*, edited by R. Silverstone and E. Hirsch. London: Routledge.
Struthers, J., and H. Speight. 1986. *Money: Institutions, Theory and Policy*. London: Longman.
Sugihara, K. 1988. *Taisho, Osaka, and the Slum: Another Modern History of Japan*. Tokyo: Shinhyoron.
Sugimoto, Y. 1997. *An Introduction to Japanese Society*. New York: Cambridge University Press.
Swatuk, L., and T. Shaw. 1994. *The South at the End of the Twentieth Century: Rethinking the Political Economy of Foreign Policy in Africa, Asia, the Caribbean and Latin America*. New York: St. Martin's Press.
Sztompka, P. 1991. *Society in Action: The Theory of Social Becoming*. Cambridge: Polity Press.
Sztompka, P. 1993. *The Sociology of Social Change*. Oxford: Blackwell.
Tagg, J. 1991. "Globalization, Totalization and the Discursive Field," in *Culture, Globalization and the World System: Contemporary Conditions for the Representation of Identity*, edited by A. King. London: Macmillan.
Tayeb, M. 1988. *Organization and National Culture: A Comparative Analysis*. London: Sage Publications.
Taylor, F. 1964. *Scientific Management*. New York: Harper.
Terpstra, V., and K. David. 1991. *The Cultural Environment of International Business*. Cincinnati: South-Western Publishing Company.
Teweles, R., and E. Bradley. 1998. *The Stock Market*. New York: John Wiley & Sons.
Thirwall, A. 1994. *Growth and Development: With Special Reference to Developing Economies*. Hampshire: Macmillan.
Thompson, J. 1988. *The Media and Modernity: A Social Theory of the Media*. Cambridge: Polity Press.
Thompson, J. 1990. *Ideology and the Modern Culture: Critical Social Theory in the Era of Mass Communication*. Cambridge: Polity.
Thompson, J. 1994. "Social Theory, Mass Communication and Public Life," in *The Polity Reader in Cultural Theory*, edited by Polity Press. Cambridge: Polity Press.
Thompson, J. 1995. *The Media and Modernity*. Cambridge: Polity Press.
Thornton, A. P. 1965. *Doctrines of Imperialism*. New York: John Wiley.
Thrift, N. 1994. "Globalisation, Regulation, Urbanisation: The Case of the Netherlands." *Urban Studies*, 31.

Thurow, L. 1996. *The Future of Capitalism: How Today's Economic Forces will Shape Tomorrow's World.* New York: Allen & Unwin.
Tilly, C. 1984. *Big Structures, Large Processes, Huge Comparisons.* New York: Russell Sage Foundation.
Tilly, C. 1990. *Coercion, Capital and European States.* Oxford: Blackwell.
Tilly, C. 1993. "Changing States, Changing Struggles." *South African Sociological Review,* 5.
Time. 1997. July 7.
Touraine, A., M. Wieviorka, and F. Dubet. 1987. *The Workers' Movement.* Cambridge: Cambridge University Press.
Toussaint, E. 1999. *Your Money or Your Life.* London: Pluto Press.
Trent, J. 1994. "Democracy in Danger." XVI World Congress of IPSA. Berlin.
Turner, B. 1986. *Equality.* London: Tavistock Publications.
Turner, B. 1990a. "The Two Faces of Sociology: Global or National?" in *Global Culture, Nationalism, Globalization and Modernity,* edited by M. Featherstone. London: Sage.
Turner, B., ed. 1990b. *Theories of Modernity and Postmodernity.* London: Sage.
Turner, B. 1991. "Politics and Culture in Islamic Globalism," in *Religion and Global Order,* edited by R. Robertson and W. Garrett. New York: Paragon.
Turner, B. 1994. *Orientalism, Postmodernism and Globalism.* London: Routledge.
UNCTAD. 1981. "Trade and Development Report." New York: The United Nations.
UNCTAD. 1990. "World Development Report." New York: The United Nations.
UNCTAD. 1992. "World Investment Report." New York: The United Nations.
UNCTAD. 1993. "World Investment Report: Transnational Corporations and Integrated International Production." New York: The United Nations.
UNCTAD. 1994. "World Investment Report: Transnational Corporations, Employment and the Workplace." New York: The United Nations.
UNCTAD. 1995. "World Investment Report." New York: The United Nations.
UNCTAD. 1997. "World Investment Report." New York: The United Nations.
UNCTC. 1986. "Transnational Corporations in South Africa and Namibia: United Nations Public Hearings." New York: (United Nations Centre on Transnational Corporations) The United Nations.
UNCTC. 1992a. "World Investment Directory: Asia and the Pacific." New York: (United Nations Centre on Transnational Corporations) The United Nations.
UNCTC. 1992b. "The Deteminants of Foreign Direct Investment: A Survey of the Evidence." New York: (United Nations Centre on Transnational Corporations) The United Nations.
UNCTC. 1993. "Debt-Equity Swaps and Development." New York: (United Nations Centre on Transnational Corporations) The United Nations.

References

UNHDR. 1992. "The United Nations Human Development Report." New York: The United Nations.

UNHDR. 1996. "The United Nations Human Development Report." New York: The United Nations.

UNHDR. 1998. "The United Nations Human Development Report." New York: The United Nations.

UNHDR. 1999. "The United Nations Human Development Report." New York: The United Nations.

Vahlne, J., and K. Nordström. 1992. *Is the Globe Shrinking: Psychic Distance and the Establishment of Swedish Sales Subsidiaries during the last 100 Years.* Stockholm: Mimeo.

Van Horne, W., ed. 1997. *Global Convulsions: Race, Ethnicity, and Nationalism at the End of the Twentieth Century.* New York: State University New York.

Veblen, T. 1967. *The Theory of the Leisure Class.* New York: Penguin Books.

Vigilant, L. 1997. "Race and Biology," in *Global Convulsions: Race, Ethnicity, and Nationalism at the End of the Twentieth Century,* edited by W. Van Horne. New York: State University of New York Press.

Vilanilam, J. 1989. "Television Advertising and the Indian Poor." *Media, Culture and Society,* 11.

Von Pierer, H. 1999. "Managing a Global Player in the Age of Information." *Management International Review.* Volume 39.

Wacker, C. 1994. "Sustainable Development Through Women's Groups: A Cultural Approach to Sustainable Development," in *Feminist Perspectives on Sustainable Development,* edited by W. Hardcourt. London: Zed Books.

Wagstyl, S., and G. Bowley. 1998. "A Strategist who has Everything to Play for." *Financial Times.* April 20.

Walker, R. 1988. "The Geographical Organization of Production-systems." *Environment and Planning: Society and Space,* 6.

Wallerstein, I. 1974. *The Modern World System.* New York: Academic Press.

Wallerstein, I. 1984. *The Politics of the World Economy.* Cambridge: Cambridge University Press.

Wallerstein, I. 1993. "World System versus World-Systems," in *The World System: Five Hundred Years or Five Thousand?,* edited by A. Frank and B. Gills. London: Routledge.

Wall Street Journal. 1993. March 16.

Walters, R., and D. Blake. 1992. *The Politics of Global Economic Relations.* Englewood Cliffs: Prentice-Hall.

Waltz, K. 1979. *Theory of International Politics.* Reading: Addison-Wesley.

Warde, A. 1992. "Notes on the Relationship between Production and Consumption," in *Consumption and Class: Divisions and Change,* edited by R. Burrows and C. Marsh. London: Macmillan.

Warner, M., ed. 1996. *International Encyclopedia of Business and Management.* London: Routledge.

Wasserman, H. 1983. *America Born and Reborn.* New York: Collier Books.
Waters, M. 1994. *Modern Sociological Theory.* London: Sage.
Waters, M. 1995. *Globalization.* London: Routledge.
Weber, M. 1978. *Economy and Society.* Berkeley: University of California Press.
Weinstein, D., and M. Weinstein. 1993. *Postmodern(ized) Simmel.* London: Routledge.
White, T., G. Suwa, and B. Asfaw. 1994. "Australopithecus Ramidus, a New Species of Early Hominid from Aramis, Ethiopia." *Nature.* No. 371.
Wilkinson, D. 1993. "Civilizations, Cores, World Economies, and Oikumenes," in *The World System: Five Hundred Years or Five Thousand?,* edited by A. Frank and B. Gills. London: Routledge.
Willets, P., ed. 1995. *We the People: The Influence of Non-Governmental Organizations at the United Nations.* London: Christopher Hurst.
Williams, E. 1944. *Capitalism and Slavery.* Chapel Hill: University of North Carolina Press.
Williams, R. 1974. *Television: Technology and Cultural Form.* New York: Schocken Books.
Willis, E. 1996. *The Sociological Quest: An Introduction to the Study of Social Life.* New Brunswick: Rutgers University Press.
Wilson, W. 1987. *The Truly Disadvantaged: The Inner City, the Underclass and Public Policy.* Chicago: University of Chicago Press.
Wiseman, J. 1997. "Yes, Mrs Thather there are Alternatives." *Arena.* No. 28.
Die Woche. 1995. November 3.
Wolf, E. 1982. *Europe and the People without History.* Berkeley: University of California Press.
Wolff, J. 1991. "The Global and the Specific: Reconciling Conflicting Theories of Culture," in *Culture, Globalization and the World System: Contemporary Conditions for the Representation of Identity,* edited by A. King. London: Macmillan.
Woodall, P. 1994. "War of the Worlds: A Survey of the Global Economy." *The Economist.* October 1.
The World Bank. 1990. "World Development Report." Washington, D.C.: The World Bank.
The World Bank. 1992. "Annual Report." Washington, D.C.: The World Bank.
The World Bank. 1994a. "World Development Report." Washington, D.C.: The World Bank.
The World Bank. 1994b. "Global Economic Prospects and the Developing Countries." Washington, D.C.: The World Bank.
The World Bank. 1996. "World Development Report." Washington, D.C.: The World Bank.
Worsley, P. 1964. *The Third World.* London: Weidenfeld and Nicolson.
Worsley, P. 1990. "Models of the Modern World-System," in *Global Culture, Nationalism, Globalization and Modernity,* edited by M. Featherstone.

References

London: Sage Publications.
Wouters, C. 1989. "The Sociology of Emotions and Flight Attendants: Hochschild's Managed Heart." *Theory, Culture and Society*, 6.
Wright, O. 1985. *Classes*. London: Verso.
Yahaya, S. 1993. "State versus Market: The Privatization Programme of the Nigerian State," in *The Politics of Structural Adjustment in Nigeria*, edited by A. Olukoshi. London: James Currey.
Die Zeit. 1999. September 30, November 25.
Zuboff, S. 1988. *In the Age of the Smart Machine: The Future of Work and Power*. New York: Basic Books.